Why
Our Schools
Need the Arts

Why
Our Schools
Need the Arts

JESSICA HOFFMANN DAVIS

Teachers College, Columbia University
New York and London

Published by Teachers College Press, 1234 Amsterdam Avenue, New York, NY
10027

Library of Congress Cataloging-in-Publication Data

Davis, Jessica Hoffmann, 1943–
    Why our schools need the arts / Jessica Hoffmann Davis.
        p. cm.
    Includes bibliographical references and index.
    ISBN 978-0-8077-4834-3 (pbk. : alk. paper)
    1. Art—Study and teaching—United States. 2. Art and society—United States.
        I. Title.
    LB1591.5.U57D38   2008
    700.71—dc22   2007028597

ISBN 978-0-8077-4834-3 (paper)

Printed on acid-free paper
Manufactured in the United States of America

15 14 13 12 11 10 09 08   8 7 6 5 4 3 2

FOR MY STUDENTS:
THANK YOU

Contents

Acknowledgments

I am ever grateful to my editor, Carole Saltz, for her generous vision and unfailing dedication to the arts in education. Thanks also at Teachers College Press to Judy Berman, Susan Liddicoat, and Karl Nyberg, who helped direct and shape this text, and to Tamar Elster and Leah Wonski, who helped bring it to light.

Special thanks to John Collins for inviting me to organize a group of graduate students around arts in education terms for his co-edited dictionary of education. I thank that sensational group.

I am proud of and grateful to my colleagues at Project Zero for their groundbreaking research into cognition and art and for their invaluable contributions to the field. Their good work informs and enriches this effort.

Endless thanks to Patricia Bauman and John Landrum Bryant for their leadership in the creation of an enduring safe haven for the arts at the Harvard Graduate School of Education. I applaud the members of the Arts in Education Program's Advisory Council, who helped secure and staunchly guard that haven. Thank you for challenging me on the topic of advocacy.

Thanks dear Carlotta, Dari, Fay, Sara, and Trudy. And thank you my sweet grandchildren—Emerson, 12, Malcolm, 8, and William, 2—for creativity, hilarity, and your delightful artwork. I am grateful to my children for playfulness and ballast, and to my dearest Will for making possible my writing dream and so much more. I dedicate this book to the inspirational students with whom I have been privileged to work, from child artists to adult artist educators. I thank all of you for all that you have taught me and hope you hear your voices resounding in this work.

Introduction

"Of course we need to teach art in school, but not *instead* of something
else. The arts may be fun, but we've got real work to do in the school
day."

"The arts, like athletics, are great extracurricular activities, but they don't
belong in the required curriculum."

"The arts should be taught to kids who have talent. For the rest of us,
they're simply a waste of time."

"With all the time spent preparing our children for so many important
tests, there are no hours or minutes left to squander on the arts."

Sound familiar? The arts have struggled for a secure place in the
curriculum of American schools for as long as those who care can
remember. Census polls and other investigative tools reveal that
parents and teachers value the arts in society and see them as important to a student's education. But when it comes to making hard
decisions about what gets featured in or eliminated from daily
learning, the arts are the first thing to crash to the cutting room
floor. The disjuncture between appreciation and need ("We care
about arts learning, but our kids *need* to do well on the tests") too
often shortchanges our children. It steals from them the opportunities for engagement, sense-making, and the integration of subject-
based learning that the arts uniquely provide.

Consider the following version of a popular arts advocacy legend. At a recent high school parent–teacher conference, an industri-
ous parent dedicated to his son's success in school and hopeful that
his child will be accepted at a fine college, complains to the math
teacher. "Look, I can see that what you're teaching Bobby will help
him get better scores on the SAT and advanced placement tests,

but I can't see anything in your teaching of math that will improve the line quality of Bobby's charcoal drawings. Will it increase his comfort onstage in theater or the expressivity of his musical performance? What good is math if it can't make Bobby better in areas that really matter?"

Sound absurd? Arts advocates have been facing such absurdity throughout the last century. School board members, administrators, principals, and parents have asked of arts learning, "What else can it do?" Besides entitling our children to participation in art's timeless cross-cultural conversation, do the arts help students do better in "areas that really matter"? And advocates have scrambled to the call, urging researchers to demonstrate what many educators have reported anecdotally: that arts education advances student performance in several non-arts arenas.

On this account, arts learning has been credited with improvements in math, reading, and writing performance, and with the elevation of student scores on IQ and SAT tests.[1] But what are we saying? Studying art will make Bobby better at math; we try to prove this through research. But studying math will not make Bobby more proficient in the arts; we don't care enough to explore this issue. Shouldn't Bobby study the arts to "improve the line quality of his charcoal drawings, his comfort on stage in theater, and the expressivity of his musical performance"? And shouldn't Bobby study math to improve his performance on math achievement tests?

It is quite possible that the elegant structures Bobby learns in geometry may give him ideas for his latest sculpture in art class. Similarly, the consideration of multiple points of view in interpreting a work of art may introduce new ways for Bobby to think about an algebraic equation. But if he is not studying both math and art with equal attention, his understanding across disciplines will be limited or lopsided. And while we have considered what it is math teaches and how, we have not spent enough time asking what it is the arts teach and how. We have been too busy justifying them.

Like other academic disciplines, the arts represent the heights of human achievement. But unlike other subjects, the arts have struggled to find a secure place within—not alongside of—our schools and universities. Have our efforts to fit arts learning into the changing aspirations of mainstream education slowed us down in our quest to find out what is unique and important about learning in the arts? Might we get further if we assumed that we share a desire for quality education with those who are suspicious or unaware of the potential of arts learning? What do advocates of the arts in education need to know to address questions like these and to represent the power and promise of the arts to doubters, change agents, and temporarily uninformed players on the great stage of American education?

What new possibilities might be open to all of us if the math teacher, business school professor, science educator, and historian were more loudly to proclaim what so many of them quietly assert: that what they do has more to do with the kind of sense-making in which artists are engaged than with the scoring of right-and-wrong answers that currently preoccupies so much of our teachers' time? The arts need to be front and center in education—taught in their own right to enable students to experience the range and nuance of meaning making across artistic disciplines. This is an essential priority even as we realize that arts learning may enrich and expand students' experience, growth, and productivity across the curricula.

The arts must be featured in our schools so that we can have more artists among us producing works for museums, theaters, concert halls, and the media writ large. But they must also be featured so that we can have more artists among us guiding national policy, running businesses, breaking boundaries in science, medicine, education, and technology. As parents, students, teachers, administrators, community leaders, and policymakers, we need to advocate for the realization of such human potential. We need to open our minds to the possibility that Bobby's father's preoccupation with artistic performance as an objective for his son's education is far from absurd.

NEED FOR THIS MANIFESTO

Research-based reports abound on the value of arts learning from cognitive, developmental, therapeutic, and philosophical perspectives. But these discussions infrequently reach the hands of parents and teachers who seek to expand the time and space devoted to the arts in education. Theoretical tomes on the arts rarely invade the mainstream reading of principals and other administrators. These leaders have much responsibility for what happens in school and little time for ruminations that seem out of touch with their daily realities. Too often arts advocates meet in separate chambers with other like-minded weary warriors at a distance from "them"—the administrators and policymakers whose perspectives on arts learning are assumed to be negative and not explored further.

In what follows, I try to bridge this communication gap and to speak simply and directly to a range of readers whose "take" on it all I may never know, but whose hearts and minds I hope to reach. I think of this text as a manifesto because it contains a set of principles and tools that I hope will be of use to advocates already working hard to make the case and secure the place for the arts in education. Beyond that, however, I wish to reach arts education skeptics and individuals who are deeply concerned about education but have yet to consider carefully what the arts provide. I hope they too will find in this work compelling arguments for insisting on the arts in our children's education.

The time is now for righting the imbalance caused by well-intentioned mandatory testing—the emphasis on standardized performance that obscures the immeasurable and essential flowering of our children as engaged and caring individuals. We need to make sure that our schools are welcoming places where children learn what it is to be human. The time for change is now, and as I hope to convince you, the arts in education can show us the way. But we must travel with deliberate motion, learning from the past as we hold to the light. And we must be wary of pitfalls, especially those that emanate from the very same properties that distinguish the arts. Consider as a key example of such a pitfall, the powerful and promising feature of integration.

THE PERILS OF INTEGRATION

Works of art—like paintings, poems, plays, musical scores, and dance performances—are a priori integrated. That is, works of art incorporate a range of subjects all in one creation. Consider for example, a classical Greek sculpture of a discus thrower. The work of art tells a story in a certain style, as does a literary narrative. We can discuss the presentation of the hero as we do the heroes in books.

There are historical considerations. The throwing of the discus tells us about games and competition at that period in time, the making of sculpture about the wealth and attitude of the society. There are psychological aspects to the work. Is there a view of an ideal body, and how would that view compare to standards for body image of today? And, of course, the materials and methods out of which the sculpture is made introduce issues of chemistry and physics; its size in relation to real life, issues of mathematical scale; the shifting of the figure's weight demonstrating the state of scientific knowledge about gravity.

For this reason, in experiencing works of art, students have the chance to see different school subjects interrelating and making a unified or cohesive statement: "I see these many different aspects of a work, even as I take the work in and react to it all at once." In the same vein, in making their own works of art, students have the opportunity to integrate the learning they are doing in various subjects and to express the interrelationship of ideas and feelings that they are discovering in and out of school. Because of the scope of their integrative nature, the arts open many doors to students and offer unique and important encounters with making sense of learning and putting it to use. But the scope of their integrative nature also makes the arts in education vulnerable—open to exploitation and dilution.

This integrative nature has allowed arts education advocates to defend the arts as able to do everything, or anything that general educators seem to care about at any given time—that tradition of "fitting the arts" into the latest needs or priorities of mainstream education:

> "You need students to improve in writing or scientific investigation? The arts can do that."

> "You need students to learn reading or history or psychology or math? The arts can certainly do that."

> "You need students to do better on standardized tests? The arts may even be able to do that."

But looking at that Greek sculpture, even while considering the play of subjects that are addressed or contained within, is not the same as or sufficient for learning subjects such as history, literature, or psychology. Neither are the lenses into understanding the work that those subjects provide—historical, literary, psychological—sufficient for learning about art. The arts need to be taught in their own right as deeply and frequently as do other subjects prioritized by schools. Their dissolution is a potential peril of integration.

I am not arguing here that the arts in education cannot serve various educational ends. They necessarily do. Seeing narrative at work in the visual arts expands a student's sense of what storytelling entails, just as a visual or dramatic portrayal of an historic event may make it particularly memorable. What I am suggesting is that when explaining or defending the role of the arts in education, we should resist the temptation to package the arts as inservice to non-arts subjects—as a way to help teach math or chemistry or physics. The history of arts education advocacy teaches us that even as the integrative nature of the arts allows us to wrap and rewrap arts education in many colors, the wrapping and rewrapping has made the field seem soft, undirected, and dispensable rather than strong, focused, and essential. If we are learning a lot about scale in math class and some more about it in art class, who really needs the extra of the arts? It is not by arguing that the arts can do what other subjects already do (or do better) that a secure place will be found for the arts in education. It is through pinpointing what it is that the arts do and teach particularly, and daring to assume that we all care, that advocates can make the case for the essentiality of the arts to education.

What would science be without art's ability to imagine alternatives, or math without art's ability to represent the world? What would history be without art's ability to interpret experience or research without art's ability to pose a question to which we do not have one or any answer? What is culture without art's ability to integrate experience in different realms into personal and shared human understanding? What of any of this would our students know without studying the arts?

The arts enrich and add meaning to many if not all arenas. But it is what they do in and of themselves to which we must attend. As advocates, we must focus on the imagining, the storytelling, the representing; the unique questions that the arts pose and their special ability to give shape to human experience and understanding. These are skills best if not only acquired through the making and appreciation of works of art. And just as works of art reflect changing times, themes, and modes of thought throughout history, the content of arts learning can uniquely expand and address timely ideas and priorities—but the arts do so in specific, constant, and invaluable ways. It is these specific, constant, and invaluable ways that I address in this book.

The value of the arts in education is clear and non-negotiable and must withstand rather than respond to differing tides and winds. We need to include the arts in education not because they serve other kinds of learning (and of course they do), but because they offer students opportunities for learning that other subjects do not. In a recent book, *Framing Education as Art: The Octopus Has a Good Day*,[2] I went so far as to say that, rather than packaging the arts in the same tight wrappings that arguably work for other subjects, non-arts subjects would do well to start packaging themselves in the generous colors of the arts. In this text, my direction turns from the challenge of making all subjects more like art to the identification of constant reasons—beyond serving as a model—that the arts are essential to general education.

ORGANIZATION OF THE MANIFESTO

In Chapter 1, I begin this new direction by providing the advocate— or the reader considering the possibility that the arts are important to education—a view of the lay of the land. That view includes examples of the ways in which the arts traditionally, currently, and intermittently play a role in educational curricula. I follow this overview with a selection of frequent objections to including the arts in our schools. Considering each objection, I offer suggestions for responses based on stories from centers of arts education beyond school walls where a belief in the importance of the arts is fundamental to the field.

Moving on in Chapter 2 to make the case for the arts in education, I introduce unique features of the arts and the invaluable and particular learning that emerges therefrom. These examples of learning

that is particular to the arts inform a set of arguments for the permanent place that the arts deserve in our children's education.[3] In ways
that I hope will be helpful to the cause, I argue for the intrinsic value
of what the arts teach our children, for the essentiality of arts learning, regardless of its effect on non-arts subjects and arenas.

In Chapter 3, "Advocating for the Arts in Education," I address
the subject of advocacy, which motivates this manifesto as it has so
many efforts in arts education research and reform. In that context,
I consider a range of understandings of advocacy, as well as some
practical challenges to and recommendations for its success. With
an eye to the future, in Chapter 4 I conclude my discussions with a
few reflections on my own experience with advocacy, a look back at
the territory covered in these pages, and some words of encourage-
ment for moving on.

At the end of the book, the reader will find a list of national advocacy organizations and a glossary of art education terms that
should be useful in the quest. Throughout the work, I have tried on
the one hand to minimize academic rhetoric and reference, and on
the other to record in the Notes a set of resources for the reader who
wants to know more about selected aspects of the discussion.

I begin each chapter with what I am calling "preludes," advocacy
essays that use a different tone, all written in my past and continuing
voyage of discovery through the arts in education. In my writing, I
draw on the work I have done for nearly half a century as a teacher,
researcher, and administrator in the field of arts in education, and on
recent efforts to develop a course of study for an unusually diverse
and dedicated cohort of graduate students in education. I write this
book as a veteran advocate of the arts in education who knows that
the field is enriched and perpetuated by a coalition of informed
voices, including parents, artists, educators, and school and community leaders. It is also moved forward by the voices and actions
of students who resist the reduction of their learning to quantitative
outcomes and strive for lives filled with the kind of human potential
that lies beyond measure. I have tried to keep the format and content of this work concise and to the point. I do this because I know
these many voices—these powerful agents of change on whom we
all rely—are long on vision and short on time.

The Lay of the Land

"Happy and Sad" by a 5-year-old

Medium: marker on paper

PRELUDE:
WHAT'S THE DIFFERENCE BETWEEN SCIENCE AND ART?

Sunday evening at a local restaurant, I am trying to explain to my two teenage nephews what it is I do as a cognitive developmental psychologist who studies the arts.[1] "Piaget!" the older one calls out, "Didn't Piaget do that stuff with liquids and beakers and how children learn?" Yes! Piaget, the most famous psychologist to study cognition (how we think and know), asserted that there were fixed stages of learning development in which a simpler way of understanding the world was predictably abandoned when more complex or abstract approaches took hold. This idea of dismissing what you used to know when you learn something new (even when the new knowledge disproves your old understanding) has never sat well with me. Referencing an experiment Piaget did with children of different ages to make my point, I tell the boys: "You know how it is that young children who have yet to master an understanding of conservation may tell you that the same amount of liquid is 'more' when it is in a tall, narrow vial than when it is in a short, broad beaker? Piaget has said that when we realize that the amount of liquid stays the same no matter the size of the container into which we pour it, we have reached a new stage in our development."

The boys are nodding with recognition, and I am impressed they know so much about Piaget. I go on thinking that what I am about to say will rock their boats, "Although I, of course, know that the amount is the same," I explain, "I still understand how, when the liquid is in the tall vial, in a very real sense, the amount is more." I had shared this view with students who invariably found it amusing. Eric, the 15-year-old, did not crack a smile. Instead, he jumped in with an explanation. "Jess," he confided, "The way you know that the amounts are the same—that's science. The way you know that they're different—that's art."

Eric was likening the arts perspective to the young child's. And I wondered whether it was possible that the retention of early views—like this uninformed perception of difference—was what preserved in adult artists that much romanticized childlike vision. Arts advocates, who maintain that children are artists, celebrate the blurry lines separating children from their flexible roles in pretend play ("Now let's switch parts.") or from the expressive drawings that they create ("I am what I draw."). They maintain that the blurry boundaries between artist and work, or idea and representation, are as truly symptoms of seamless adult artistic production as they are of an early stage in children's drawing that, with development, will be erased or replaced.

But Eric's insight into art and science goes beyond that developmental perspective. His comment expands an understanding of both the firmness and the malleability of knowing; it crystallizes the interconnection between art and science, the relationship between the known and the seen, the "clearly is" and the "what may also be." It is in the territory of these blurry boundaries that human achievements such as the making of metaphor abound. How can we say, "That athlete is a rock" and think it is a good likeness? Are the boundaries between the stone in the driveway and the person on the basketball court so easy to forget?

This fuzzy boundary-defying territory is often thought to be the province of poetry and art. But I believe it is as surely a part of the landscape of science and technology, in which edges can similarly be less than clear-cut. Computers confuse the lines that distinguish expert from layperson, communication from relationship, and immediacy from distance. We can now study on our own the doctor's diagnosis, share our views with countless unseen others, and visit the Louvre in Paris or a watering hole in Africa without leaving our desk chairs. What lets us know that we remain in our chairs is science. What lets us know that we are transported is art.

MIT Professor Seymour Papert, a famous expert on learning and a former colleague of Piaget, explained that Piaget viewed children's responses as neither entirely correct nor entirely incorrect. Piaget respected the child and the developmental context in which responses are framed. Writing for *Time* magazine when Piaget was chosen as one of *Time*'s 100 most important people of the century, Papert described how Einstein was fascinated with Piaget's observation that 7-year-olds think that going faster can take more time. This technically incorrect answer may be perfectly clear to any adult who is easily winded by running. Einstein saw the 7-year-old's interpretation as challenging common sense in much the same way as did his theories of relativity.

Cognitive developmental psychologists have expanded Piaget's stages into realms such as reading, morality, construction of a sense of self, and aesthetic appreciation. In terms of aesthetic appreciation, researchers say that young children or novices will attend more to the colors and subject in a work of art than to the artist's process of making it.[2] But some paintings are more about color, color as the subject of the work, color as the statement of the artist. Are those paintings best left to be viewed by children? Or, in the context of these colorful images, do early preoccupations serve any viewer well?

In a research study at Harvard's Project Zero, we asked numerous 1st and 4th graders some version of the question, "How do you think the artist who made this painting must have felt?" The number one answer to this question was not, as had been expected, "sad" in the case of a sad painting, or, in the case of a happy painting, "happy." No, the number one response for both groups was, "The artist must have felt terrific to be able to make a beautiful painting like this."

Some researchers argue that young children are not at a sufficiently advanced stage in their thinking to actually understand the presence of a painter creating the canvas or to conceptualize the problems of production that artists face. Our observations suggest that 1st and 4th graders, as active makers of images, feel naturally connected to artists whom they see as trying, as they do, to do a good job. The way in which we create a schema—like Piaget's set of hierarchical stages—to describe developing behaviors and abilities—that's science. The way in which we see beyond the schemas—that's art.

It is important that we as parents, educators, and administrators recognize the interconnectedness of science and art. We may labor to find the mathematics in the rhythm of a piece of music by Bach or Duke Ellington, or to make links between the motion of the planets and a dance by Martha Graham. But these literal quests often overlook the more salient connections between art and science, the essentiality of art to science and of science to art. My nephew Eric associates art with vision (what we can see) and science with what we know (beyond visual clues). Observation serves both processes, seeing and knowing. But if we cannot see beyond reasoned knowledge to irrational possibilities, and if we cannot break the boundary of visual clues and embrace foundations of knowledge, how lackluster is our knowing and how limited our seeing?

Breaking boundaries is as much the stuff of creativity in science as it is in art. Metaphor links disparate objects that exist in separate realms, and through their improbable joining, it comes closer to truth than the literal description of either entity. "That child is a whirlwind!" speaks to the vitality of the individual in a way that can be seen and felt, a way that provides the listener with a familiar image or experience that makes the unfamiliar known. The uniting of the whirlwind with the countenance of the child says so much more than the literal description, "He's a very active child." The blurring of lines between disparate entities invites multiple interpretations even as it achieves clarity of thought.

Blurring the lines involves the creation of symbols that invite, rather than control for, multiple interpretations. This is as surely the stuff of conversations between scientists and the wider community as it is between artists and their audience. In a world in which diversity is more common than sameness, we need to remember that science like art is all about multiplicity and rarely about a single tack. We learn from open questions that generate new and better questions, not just from facts that admit no variation and suggest a one-dimensional truth.

We need always to be wary of those who pretend to have answers, just as we need always to keep those who challenge answers at the heart of our thoughts. Why should we mislead our students into thinking this world is made strong by pieces of information, when it is what we do with information that makes us strong? Why should we be so focused on the counting and scoring of right and wrong answers when what matters is how our students see beyond the numbers? In the life beyond school, it is the thinking "out of the box" not "in the box," the breaking of boundaries not the coloring within the lines, that carve our individual and collective futures. What false information and expectation do we endorse by valuing in school those measurable, discrete responses as if they were the ends in view?

The arts in our schools are essential. They shed light on and give direction to the foundations that science provides. The things we think we know, and on which we build, and from which we imagine—that's science. The imagining, the building, the seeing beyond the given—that's art.

EXAMPLES OF THE ARTS IN EDUCATION

Educators frequently use the singular term "art education" to mean "visual arts education;" that is, teaching and learning in and about art that you can see in two- and three-dimensional media such as painting, sculpture, or photography. The singular term "art education" does not usually include, and is in fact differentiated from, learning in other arts disciplines, such as dance education, music education, or drama education. The plural term "arts education," on the other hand, encompasses arts learning in all these different disciplines.

The term "arts in education" represents a still broader perspective—that is, the different art disciplines in a variety of roles within the greater scene of education, including non-arts classrooms and subjects. With this in mind, here are nine examples of the arts in education[3] with which advocates should be familiar. None of the scenarios for the arts that I describe here precludes another, and in an idealized setting all would hold sway. The titles that I give these examples are for the most part standard in the field even as they change and are redefined by the increasing range of arts applications that creative educators continue to design.

Arts Based

When curricula, classrooms, or schools (most often charter, pilot, or private) are arts based, teaching and learning are quite simply based on the arts.[4] The arts supply the content for what is learned, serve as a model for teaching, learning, and assessment, and provide a window through which non-arts subjects are explored. In arts-based schools, the arts are taught seriously in their own right—that is, children have intense and sequential instruction in the different art forms. This is important because students' facility with the arts increases the effectiveness of arts-based learning across the curriculum.

As an example of arts-based learning, think of a high school in which the same classic narrative painting—for example, *George Washington Crossing the Delaware*, painted by Emmanuel Gottlieb Leutze in 1851 (see Figure 1.1)—is studied in several different classes. In history class, using art-historical techniques for aesthetic scanning of art, students attend to the details of the historical moment that the painting depicts. In science class, experimenting with painting in and out of doors, students analyze the state of knowledge behind the painter's use of light. In English class, students are asked to use aesthetic standards and critique the painting or to consider its theme or structure as inspiration for writing a poem. In dance class, students are asked to choreograph a dance sequence that captures the motion displayed in the image. In music class, the work of art is used as a touchstone for learning music from the time period or as a visual depiction of abstract musical concepts like balance, rhythm, and symmetry.[5] The work of art in an arts-based setting—and it might as easily be an opera or play as a classical

FIGURE 1.1. *Washington Crossing the Delaware* **by Emanuel Gottlieb Leutze (1851)**

Oil on canvas, 149" x 255". Gift of John Stewart Kennedy, 1897, 97.34.
The Metropolitan Museum of Art, New York, NY.
Image copyright © The Metropolitan Museum of Art/Art Resource, NY

painting—is the source of and gateway to learning across the disciplines. Arts activities, the informed making and interpretation of works of art, provide the impetus and tools for learning.

Arts Integrated

In an arts-integrated situation ("integrated arts education"), the arts are intertwined with non-arts subjects, included as equal partners with the objective of improving teaching and learning within subjects and across the general curriculum. In an arts-integrated high school setting, for example, the concept of heroism might be explored through the equal strands of (1) art: an analysis of the details of Leutze's portrayal of Washington as the hero in the painting (see Figure 1.1); and (2) social studies: an examination of *Time* magazine's selection of Piaget as a person of the century as discussed in the first prelude. A series of arts-integrated considerations such as these might lead to a discussion of the broader question of what it takes to be a hero respectively in the arts, science, literature, and math.

At the elementary school level, dance and writing might be integrated, with children representing prepositions such as "over" and "under" (grammar) with active physical movement (dance). African drumming might be integrated with math in a mutually informative exchange of understanding of both rhythm and ratios.[6] Dramatics and history are intertwined when students are asked to take on the parts of historical figures (learning about assuming a role in acting) and recreate a scene based on the factual details of a particular event (history).

Arts integration has been cited recently as a most promising curricular vehicle that honors arts education in the reform and improvement of schools in need.[7] But doubters fear that the integration of arts instruction with teaching in other subjects will obscure a view of the arts as unique disciplines. In arts-based venues, the arts are showcased as lead players in the drama of education. In arts integrated, the arts are cast with non-arts subjects in equal ensemble roles. As a consequence of such intertwining, educators in arts-integrated settings must define new outcomes for learning that are hybrids of performance in arts and academics.

Arts Infused

When educators "infuse" the arts into the curriculum, artists or works of art are brought from outside in to enrich whatever is going on in arts and non-arts classes or activities. A recording of music from a particular period is played in history class to infuse an understanding of the past. Found-object sculpture pieces are brought in from a local gallery to inform students' perspectives on preserving the environment. A contemporary poet or rap artist is invited to an English class to share his or her love of language and/or individual creative process. A professional theater group is scheduled to put up a well-known play for the whole school.

Arts infusion finds its roots in the reduction or removal of formal school arts programs, notably in the early 1970s when parent and nonprofit community initiatives were organized to fill the void, infusing the arts into schools by supporting and scheduling visiting artists and arts performances. Thanks to this work, which continues to the present, there are many tried and true strategies for making the most of artist visits to schools. From collaborative planning between teachers and artists to pre- and post-visit classroom activities, methods have been developed that help infuse artists' contributions into the objectives of the curriculum rather than letting them stand as disconnected events or intrusions.[8]

Arts Included

In the arts-included example, the arts are situated among students' required courses and are taught, respected, and allotted time with the same regard as non-arts courses. In elementary schools in which the arts are included, all of the children from kindergarten through 6th grade may study some or all of visual arts, music, theater, and dance. And they do so on as regular a basis as what are more traditionally regarded as core subjects. In an arts-included high school, there are serious graduation requirements for the number, level, and even variety of arts courses taken. Success in arts courses—progress from beginner to intermediate to advanced levels—is valued as much as in other courses. When the arts are seriously included, parents meet with teachers of the arts to discuss student progress as they do with non-arts teachers. Further, students are as encouraged to develop their preprofessional or post-secondary artistic educational intentions as they are non-arts pursuits. Many advocates hold as a simple goal the inclusion of the arts in students' daily learning. While "arts included" is a prerequisite for an arts-based scenario, it may or may not persist in any of the other examples mentioned here.

Arts Expanded

In the arts-expanded model, education in the arts takes students outside of school into the larger community. For example, student learning may include regular trips to the art museum, scheduled activities at the local community art center, or attendance at musical performances in a live concert hall. Within schools, classroom teachers or arts specialists may arrange for these outings, often with the help of parent volunteers. Education departments in museums, like educational collaborations between schools and symphony orchestras or theater companies, have well-developed programs for making the most of student learning in cultural institutions.

Children are introduced through arts expansion to a range of locales for the arts beyond school walls, and they not incidentally learn how people are expected to act in such settings. For example, they may learn when to clap in a theater, dance, or musical performance; how much or how little (and how softly) to speak in any audience; or to look carefully and not touch the objects in an art museum. It is thought that the introduction to these out-of-school settings prepares students for lifelong participation as audiences to artistic performances and as visitors to cultural institutions. Indeed, a study of adults who frequent art museums revealed that most of them were introduced to that activity by school field trips (arts expansion) when they were young.[9]

Arts Professional

Media representations of student life in high schools like the Fiorello H. LaGuardia High School of Music and Art in New York City (on which the movie and television series "Fame" were based) may give the impression that preprofessional arts educational opportunities abound; in reality, they are few and far between. Holding high standards for admission, arts professional high schools offer rigorous artistic training that not only affords students advanced knowledge of different art forms, but also helps them prepare for careers in the arts. Most often students with either or both recognized talent and unwavering dedication find their way into arts-professional settings. They graduate from high school with portfolios of work to show to visual art schools, visual and audio recordings of dance or music performances for conservatories, and audition skills that will help in assuring a role in theater or a musical "gig."

The idea that a career in the arts is as valuable an educational outcome as a career in a non-arts profession is not widespread. This may have to do with the fact that society generally regards artists as outsiders from the norm—passionate individuals who will never make a decent living. But as the entertainment business sweeps the scene with cable television and the Internet providing expanded opportunities for artistic performance, attitudes will no doubt change. When arts-media-related skills, from screenwriting to handling a camera to digital editing, become more valued, pre-professional arts education will more frequently find its way into schools. While such sea changes promise to have a positive effect on the profile of the arts in education, some advocates worry that a focus on the acquisition of technical skills will obscure a view of the arts as philosophic and at the height of human creativity.

Arts Extras

Probably the most typical view of the arts in education today is as nonacademic extras reserved for in-school spaces and time outside of the daily curriculum. Whether it is editing the school poetry journal, acting in the school play, or participating in the school jazz ensemble, participation in the arts is usually thought to be "extracurricular" or nonessential to a student's education. This lack of prioritization can present a challenge for students who are dedicated to the arts and who self-select for these after-school opportunities. With publication deadlines or late rehearsals 5 nights a week, the academic performance of young after-school artists may suffer.

Furthermore, when the arts are set aside from the academic curriculum, arts specialists rarely oversee their administration. A willing English teacher with no dramatic training may take on the school play after hours. Generous individuals from the community may offer their time to help with students' early evening arts efforts. While such participation may forge connections between school and neighborhood, there may be little if any attention paid by school personnel to the amount or quality of teaching and learning in the arts-extras setting.

When schools do not provide arts extras opportunities, parents can find and often must pay for them on their own. But the cost of private piano lessons or membership in the city's children's theater is prohibitive for many families. While dedicated parents may seek out affordable alternatives, adults who have themselves had little if any education in the arts may not see the need to encourage their children to participate after school. Without concern, they may see their children miss out entirely on an education in the arts. Even when the cost of publishing the poetry journal is paid for by its sales, or the school play is the social event of the season, or the jazz ensemble opens to a packed auditorium, an arts-extras scenario reflects and perpetuates a prevalent view: "The arts are nice but not essential to education or to life."

Aesthetic Education

In contrast to arts extras, aesthetic education regards the arts as special curricular arenas for making and appreciating meaning that enriches all aspects of students' thinking and living. From this particularly philosophic perspective, students acquire from their consideration of works of arts unique skills of analytic thinking and familiarity with a wealth of aesthetic texts (books, poems, films, musical compositions) that adroitly illuminate human experience. Coming to light in the 1960s and 1970s,[10] the aesthetic education approach prioritizes the activities of perception (close attention to detail) and interpretation (making sense in one or many ways) that the arts invite and that may be useful to students in any class or activity.

Philosopher Maxine Greene, a distinguished professor at Columbia University's Teachers College and a luminary in the field of aesthetic education, helped to develop the Lincoln Center Institute (LCI)[11] at the Lincoln Center for the Performing Arts in New York City. Through programs at LCI, classroom teachers work with artists to discover first hand (and ultimately employ in their classrooms) the ways in which encounters with works of art enrich experiences in learning and life. Professor Greene uses the word "awakening" to describe the impact that the arts have on our imagination, our ability to notice and care about what is happening in the world, and ultimately even on our sense of urgency and power to effect positive change.

Some arts champions challenge the notion of aesthetic education, seeing it as a way to avoid the "A" word (Art) and to slip the arts into education as another way of thinking without attending to what makes them special: the hands-on experiential opportunities that they provide. But even though the central activity in aesthetic education is the perception of a work of art, many proponents of the approach (this is true of LCI) see the student's creation of a work of art as an important step in learning to make sense out of another artist's work. If a viewer has made her own work, she can identify with the artist who has made the work she is studying and consider the questions and challenges the artist has confronted. In the 1980s, research psychologists who studied the development of aesthetic awareness (the ability to make sense from a work of art) regarded the ability to identify with the artist's process as the highest stage of development.[12]

Arts Cultura

Arts cultura is my own term for the ways in which the arts give form to and connect the many different definitions of culture that pervade our thought and language. From the sense in which there is a culture or worldview that is unique to and differentiated by each individual to the all-encompassing notion of a shared human culture, various forms of the word *culture* address the separate and shared ways in which human beings make sense of experience. The arts give tangible shape to this sense-making which is imprinted on representations of culture from a timely pop jingle to a timeless classical symphony. In arts cultura, arts educators recognize and frame curriculum around the role of making art in the expression of a continuum of views of culture. Briefly, you might imagine that continuum in the shape of a wheel connecting each of the following understandings of the word *culture* through the works of visual art with which, by way of example, I align them here:

1. *The individual's culture (lower case singular use of the word).* The necessarily unique worldview or set of understandings that each of us has no matter what outward similarities align us. Each child in school is developing her own culture and expressing it in her early drawings (so often representations of self).
2. *The cultures (lower case plural use) of communities.* The worldviews of groups of individuals that most closely interact with the individual: the cultures of families and schools. These views are represented for example in the art of the neighborhood (perhaps in murals on building walls) or in whatever visual images (representational art or paper collages) the child encounters on the walls of home and school.
3. *The larger Cultures (upper case plural) of nationalities and ethnicities:* worldviews held in regions or through tradition as defined by geographical, political, or religious frameworks. These views are reflected in the works of art that are cherished by different nations (for example, minimalist Chinese watercolor or literalist American portraiture).
4. *The largest Culture (upper case singular) of humankind.* That profound connection among human beings that can be seen in the expressive portrayals of self and story in the drawings of young children (taking us back to where we began) and in the paintings of artists from all around the world.

The arts provide ways for children to create and communicate their own individual cultures, to experience the differences and similarities among the cultures of family or nationality that are imprinted on different forms of art, and to discover the common features of expression that attest to a human connection contained in and beyond difference. In this last configuration of the arts in education, realized to different extents and in varying contexts by teachers around the country, educators use the arts to introduce students to various understandings of culture and invite them to discover and represent their connections with and distinction from others. In a collection of essays by educators and students from schools immediately surrounding the tragic destruction of the World Trade Center towers on September 11, 2001,[13] we see the arts used in just this way. Group murals and individual drawings depict student reactions to an experience that defies words. Oral narratives connect students' attempts to make sense of the unthinkable event with elders in a nursing home who responsively share their recollections of the Holocaust. Muslim youth raised in this country express in drawings their newly redefined cultural and intercultural reality post 9/11. Brave teachers put aside the usual curriculum to provide their students with the opportunity and tools to frame those poignant understandings that the arts uniquely allow.

These teachers took their students to the theater and to dance studios, and invited artists into the classroom. They encouraged students to write poetry and narrative, to draw, to build with blocks, and to play. Whether or not they called it "the healing power of art," they knew instinctively that when teaching and learning are stripped to the core, school is about helping children build and express understanding as only the arts allow. When their daily routines were hopelessly shaken, through the dust and horror of the crumbling towers, these educators saw clearly that at the root of their responsibility as teachers was the mandate to keep their children safe and whole.

In helping children connect their views as young individuals (culture) in different but equally threatened communities (cultures) populated with different national and religious sectors (Cultures) to a battered but essential view of our universally shared humanity (Culture), these teachers turned to the arts. In their writing 5 years after the event, the educators' accounts are threaded with students' drawings, poems, and narratives, demonstrating clearly that teachers, like students, need the arts to tell the full story. The full story goes beyond the acquisition of information and school-based skills to the relationships and alternative expressions that clarify difference even as they join us together as human beings who strive to make sense of the world. This is what arts cultura is all about.

RESPONDING TO OBJECTIONS TO THE ARTS IN EDUCATION: LESSONS FROM OUT OF SCHOOL

Here are seven familiar objections to featuring the arts in education (and the last one listed may be surprising):

1. VALUE: The arts are nice but not necessary.
2. TALENT: Arts learning really is only useful to students who have the gifts to make a career in the arts.
3. TIME: There isn't time within the school day for including the arts. We barely have time to teach the subjects that matter more.
4. MEASUREMENT: Achievement in the arts cannot be measured. In this age of rampant standardized testing, we need to be able to rate student progress with objective measures.
5. EXPERTISE: To be taught well, the arts require specialists— individuals who are artists themselves or have experience and skill in art disciplines.
6. MONEY: The arts require special supplies, specialist and visiting artist salaries, and administrative time for field trips, performances, and shows. The arts are expensive.
7. AUTONOMY: The arts will survive in the community even if schools eliminate them.

These various objections hold sway in school settings where the arts are always facing marginalization. But we have much to learn about what would be possible within schools from the world of arts learning outside of schools, where for example, in the community initiatives alluded to in the last objection, the arts are taught without apology. In the broader community, where educators begin with a belief in the importance of the arts, supporters do not need to devote time and effort to proving the worth of the arts in terms of curricular objectives. In this relatively unfettered environment, we can glimpse the vital outcomes for arts learning that can be achieved in schools. These glimpses provide fodder for the advocate's responses to school-based objections.

Let's revisit each objection, expanding on its content through the hypothetical language of lead voices in school settings, and consider responses derived from the alternative stage of community arts education. It is important to note that community arts educational centers face their own set of challenges for growth and survival. Striking a balance between changing community needs and a shortage of available funding, many educational centers open, flourish, and close within a few years. The following observations are based on those centers that have survived[14] and through decades of exemplary practice, offer poignant examples of what can happen when the arts in education flourish.

Objection 1: VALUE
The Arts Are Nice But Not Necessary

> Our students have so many demands on them from staying out of trouble to gaining the skills to be successful in the adult world. The important subjects in preparing students for such responsibility are reading, science, and math. No frills. The basics. (*School committee member*)

There are thousands of community art centers dedicated to education around the country. These centers are safe havens in many respects, serving artists, students, and the broader communities in which they reside. At the core, they provide a secure place for arts learning that has been marginalized elsewhere. In community art centers scattered throughout the states but especially clustered on either coast in bustling urban centers, artists and other dedicated community members provide arts training that enriches or exceeds what is offered in schools. These centers have served as alternative options when schools would not offer the arts. Unfettered by the demands and constraints of school administrations, these self-designed centers of learning have been of considerable interest to arts education researchers over the last 20 years.[15]

Often founded by individuals who have personally experienced the power of the arts to "save lives," these centers are not striving to prove the impact of the arts on SAT or IQ scores, they are demonstrating the power of the arts to make positive life-altering differences to youth who have been placed at risk. Bill Strickland, founder of the Manchester Craftsman's Guild in Pittsburgh, Pennsylvania,[16] and a national leader in community development through the arts, designed the educational focus of his center around his personal experience. As Bill was on the verge of dropping out of high school, his ceramics teacher took an interest in him, encouraged him to work in ceramics, and ultimately redirected Bill towards a previously unconsidered place called college. With impressive results, Bill works to recreate that turn in the road for every at-risk student in after school classes at Manchester Craftsman's Guild. The late legendary alto saxophonist Jackie McLean experienced first hand the power of his music making in helping him break the drug habit that had threatened his life and career. McLean founded the Artists Collective in Hartford, Connecticut,[17] as a place where young people could stop getting high on street drugs and start experiencing the highs of intense training and performance in the arts.

A typical story from centers like these involves the student who is or has not been doing well or has dropped out of school. At the center, that student has earned a position of authority—perhaps directing a musical production or collecting and recording monetary contributions at the opening of an exhibit of young people's art. A teacher from the youth's school happens by and is shocked to see the troubled and often troublesome student in a role of such responsibility. At school, the teacher confides to the center director, "this student is failing academically and acting out in class." "Here," directors like McLean's wife Dollie respond, "this child is hardworking and successful. Oh, and have you seen him dance?" Youth at these centers have a chance to find new arenas for learning and growth, and they take charge of their own learning. Working collaboratively on a theatrical or dance production, students find ways to support each other and to put out an artistic product that speaks for them all. Dollie McLean describes the power of performance:

> That's how our kids need to get high—off that adrenaline that's so natural and . . . when you're getting ready to do something and all of your parents are sitting outside and your friends and the boys from the "hood"—they've all come. I heard a few of them [in the audience]. I was sitting behind some of them. They said, "I can do that." I leaned over and said, "Yes, yes you could."[18]

Over and over again, with an acceptance of difference and a belief in potential, these havens for the arts provide opportunities for youth to discover in themselves the ability to paint or to sing or to organize and lead. Young people who have not found confidence or success in the traditional "basics" at school find at these centers alternative languages for self-expression and creative activities in which to encounter their own value. From struggling with the hard work of preparing for a dance performance, to understanding that choice of color, direction of movement, or tone of voice all effect an artistic outcome, students of the arts learn singular and invaluable lessons.

Youth with low test scores and grade averages as well as young people who are successful in school self-select the arts and seek out community-based arts education when schools omit arts learning. While advocates and administrators argue for value and consider the ways in which the arts might be important to non-arts subjects, these students seek out learning that only the arts provide. In non-school hours, they create poetry to read on air at a radio station; work as commissioned artists on a mural in a prominent space in the community; create documentaries about issues of concern to them; and take photographs that literally put aesthetic frames around the individuals and situations that challenge or inspire their well-being.[19]

Researchers studying these sites have found that the arts in these settings offer younger children and teens authentic entrepreneurial encounters, opportunities for work that they see having an impact, and the chance to meet high expectations and experience deep engagement. From the production of works of art to their display and marketing, these centers involve students in activities that as adults they may continue to pursue. From the artistic direction of a video to the organization of a youth film festival, these young people assume responsibilities that predispose them for leadership. Students feel ownership of these centers; they have a voice. When it comes to what's offered and who is teaching, they get to vote with their feet. They show up for classes and take charge of the self-improvement that they know is available to them at these havens for the arts. Students want to succeed. It is our responsibility as parents, educators, advocates, and friends to give them a chance.

Many successful artists remember community art centers in their neighborhoods as places where someone believed in them and where they learned to believe in themselves. As responsible social action, these artists give back to the community by founding or supporting arts education initiatives. But adults in non-arts careers also frequently credit their music or art lessons or their time spent in visual arts programs with giving them the courage or teaching them the self-discipline they needed to succeed. A number of community arts centers call what they teach "life skills." As much as they encourage children to do their homework in school (they never say that reading, math, or science is unimportant), they are mining the arts as resources for children to find and become responsible for themselves and to see in their artistic activities their personal potential.

Advocates responding to the devaluation of the arts might point to this out-of-school playing field in which the arts are valued and where it is demonstrated that the "important" lessons that children need to learn "to be successful in the adult world" are not fully or perhaps even specifically contained in the non-arts subjects that are considered the basics in school. With an eye to what matters, along with and not instead of the teaching of subjects like science and math, arts advocates must argue for the lessons of engagement, authenticity, collaboration, mattering, and personal potential. These lessons must be available in schools. The arts help children to realize the place and need for the basics even as they give them the vision and strength to make use of that learning. Many advocates make the simple point that when you are talking the "basics" in education, the arts are number one. Let's carry that thought along moving forward.

Objection 2: TALENT
Arts Learning Is Really Only Useful to Gifted Students

> Very few of us will grow up to be artists. Sure, those kids who are talented in the arts tend not to be very good at traditional subjects—so arts education gives them chances to excel. But we can't waste precious time in the general curriculum for learning that will serve the minority of students. (*Parent*)

There is an easy response to the objection contained in the idea that some of us are talented in the arts and deserve or need to seek out instruction to develop our abilities while others need not bother learning the arts because they will never grow up to be artists. Here's that response: "Well, not many of us will grow up to be mathematicians or professional writers, but we all need to study math and learn how to write. What's the difference?"

Just as the talented among us or those persistently interested in any subject will go on to advanced study of their field, all students need to be introduced to the arts in school not only so they have the chance to decide whether these are areas in which they desire further training, but also because the arts, as mentioned in the last section, are truly basic to us all. The three "R"s are the basics of school-based education, but the arts are basic to human beings before, hopefully during, and after their lives in school. They are basic in the sense that all children come to school dancing, drawing, and singing—exercising their inborn attraction to and facility with the arts. And they are basic in the sense that the arts will surround or be available to all children throughout their lifespan. Whether an adult will go to a play or concert or take advantage of free Thursday night tickets to an art museum has much to do with whether that adult has encountered the arts in school, been introduced as a child to a cultural institution, or had training in making and doing art so that he or she has the knowledge and experience to truly attend and appreciate.

The noted educational philosopher Israel Scheffler, a favorite teacher of mine, once shared that as a child he studied violin faithfully and thought he was "pretty good" at it. Might he grow up to be a violinist in a symphony orchestra? At age 11 it seemed possible to him. But at age 12 he had the chance to hear on the radio a performance by the world famous violinist, Jascha Heifetz. As he was swept away by the power and beauty of the sounds he heard he understood, of course, that there was a long distance between his success as a violin student and the genius of a virtuoso. Nonetheless, Professor Scheffler explained to me with a light that consumed him even as he told the story 50 years later, "I realized at that moment that the reason I had studied violin so hard was so that I could really hear Jascha Heifetz."

On account of the intensive training offered at the community art centers studied in our research, I often asked students at the centers, "Are you planning to grow up to be a professional artist?"

While many of them hoped so, the more frequent response, so eloquently voiced by a student who took piano, dance, and drumming
lessons and excelled in her classes at school, was: "I hope that what
I learn here will help me to help other kids the way this center has
helped me."

"So would you like to teach here when you grow up?" I asked.

"Or in another center anywhere I live no matter what I grow up
to do," she replied.

Arts education provides students with opportunities to become
professional artists (perhaps most but not exclusively possible for
the talented), engaged audiences (like listeners to the violin), and
agents of change (like the young woman who hoped to help others
by growing up to teach in a community art center). Furthermore,
these options are there for all children. Some people say that artists
do well in art but in no other area, but many practicing artists read
voraciously, write gracefully, and demonstrate in their work complex understandings of non-arts disciplines. One of the most famous
artists of all time, Leonardo da Vinci, was equally interested and
proficient in science and art. There are numerous schools around the
country that call themselves "Da Vinci," and they are based alternatively on the arts, science and technology, or both science and art.[20]

The arts have been shown to provide opportunities for alternative types of success to children with disabilities of all kinds. And it
is true that many creative individuals demonstrate different ways
of making sense of the world that are problematic within, and perhaps only within, the standardized context of school. Nonetheless,
there is no rule that says that students who do well in academic
subjects have no interest in, need for, or proclivity for the arts. The
population of students who seek opportunities for learning the arts
at community centers reflects the diversity of needs for arts training
that young people recognize for themselves. Some of the students
have a passion or talent for the arts and attend to receive advanced
training. Others go or are taken by their parents to add discipline
and rigor to their lives. Many seek the socialization of collaborative
arts experiences; and others are there for self-selected self-improvement or because their teachers have suggested that they attend.

Most students go simply because the community art center is
where the arts are seriously taught. Both the arts and the skilled

professionals who demonstrate and teach them are "draws." Some advocates argue that the attraction that the arts provide works against them, making them seem like arenas for fun rather than for serious learning. Shouldn't serious learning be fun? The move toward marginalizing the arts by reserving them for children with demonstrated artistic talent, or for children with demonstrated risk of failure in other areas, overlooks the basic need of all of our children to gain facility with making and finding meaning in the heights of human expression.

Objection 3: Time
There Isn't Time Within the School Day for Including the Arts

> Our students' reading scores are way below average. We need to use time we would otherwise use for art on additional reading instruction so our children do better on the tests. (*Beleaguered teacher*)

The frequent "not enough time" objection most certainly reflects value: "We barely have time to teach the subjects that matter more." That is, learning to read is more important than learning the arts. But it also reflects missed opportunity for advocates and misguided reasoning on the part of decision-makers. Missed opportunity lies in the notion of the fixed length of a school day. Arts in education advocates, scurrying for place, have dedicated time in their separate endeavors to finding ways that the arts can be sandwiched into a curriculum that is contained in a fixed amount of hours. This sandwich approach inspires instrumental and integrative advocacy. In instrumental advocacy, proponents argue that the arts enhance learning in valued subjects and therefore need to be fit in somewhere. In integrative advocacy, the argument is that the arts taught within the same spaces and places as non-arts learning produce some new result that is better than could be produced in either an arts or non-arts classroom. Most frequently, the notion of fixed length sets the stage for an extracurricular approach to the arts, scheduling them outside of school hours as described earlier in the extra-arts model.

Defensive arguments and approaches overlook the obvious opportunity for arts advocates to join with advocates and administrators across the curriculum and argue for a longer school day. Many advocates in recent years have cited the finding that students who study the arts do better on the SATs.[21] In fact, it seems that the longer they have studied the arts, the higher their scores. But we are unable to prove that the arts are the causal factor for the higher scores. Students with lots of training in the arts may attend better schools, which perhaps unsurprisingly tend to include the arts. But better schools may not only be more likely to include the arts in their curriculum, they are also more likely to offer better instruction in all subjects. Better instruction across the curriculum may be what accounts for the higher scores. In terms of the time factor, however, we may also note that independent schools, frequently included in the larger category of "better schools," have longer school days than public schools. It seems obvious that where there is more time in the school day, there is more time to teach more things. In the face of the time objection, advocates must acknowledge the significance of better instruction even as they seize the opportunity to argue for a longer school day.

Quality of instruction provides another talking point for arts advocates facing the time objection. And it is here where misguided reasoning needs to be addressed. If the reading instruction that is being provided is not working—is not giving students enough of what they need to perform well—we need to critique how we are teaching reading and do it better. Nobody ever improved by getting more of what is not working in school. While an increase in time in quality instruction certainly improves performance in a subject area, more time spent on methods that are not working holds little promise for improvement. You cannot explain a mathematical concept to a child over and over again in the same way and trust that repetition alone will allow the child to hear what he or she needs to make sense of the explanation. The idea of teaching to the test may restrict teachers' pedagogical autonomy, or freedom to approach a subject from many different directions, but effective educators know that when one approach is not working, they must try another way.

Cheryl Smith, a dance instructor at the Artists Collective in Hartford, Connecticut, teaching tap to a group of 5-year-olds, demonstrated this principle in action. A little girl at the far left of the line kept moving from heel to toe when she was meant, as all the other children were doing, to move in the "toe flat" step from elevated toe to heel flat on the floor. Cheryl repeated the verbal direction a few times clearly and to no avail, "Toe Flat, Sandra." With no irritation or distress, Cheryl then raised the "at rest" sign to the larger group of dancers and gently pulled the little girl aside. Demonstrating up close, Cheryl offered the physical hint of bending the knee, "Lean into it and your heel will come up and then down." Beaming, Sandra got it immediately. A moment's aside, a different way in, and the child was tapping in time with the rest.

There are many entry points into a work of art, and there are many entry points into the learning of any discipline. If the particular doorway opened into reading is not showing the way, we need to try another point of entry, but not to eliminate the light that the arts will shed on it all. Stories from community arts settings suggest that a child who has the opportunity to participate in the arts may acquire the very sense of "can do" that she needs to learn to read. On account of the basic life skills that arts learning afford, we must find time for the arts and we must be unwilling to relinquish that time on any account. Whether by extending the school day or assessing the quality and variety of instruction that is being provided in all subjects, educators need to assign and protect time for the arts. We don't cut out math to make room for more reading or vice versa. It wouldn't make sense. Nor does it make sense for the arts. The arts must be included on equal footing with other subjects so that they can serve all children as reliable constants in their lives at school.

Objection 4: MEASUREMENT
Achievement in the Arts Cannot Be Measured

> Performance in the arts cannot be measured. One child can receive high grades for a painting that is wildly expressive and another for work that is realistic. Judgments on student learning or on the quality of arts instruction are at best arbitrary and at worst subjective. In this competitive age, objective measurement is what we need to estimate how our schools are doing. (*School superintendent*)

The notion that progress in arts learning cannot be measured—that there are no right or wrong answers available for counting—is incorrect. Similarly, the idea that students' artistic productions cannot be measured objectively (i.e., a teacher just likes one student's work of art and not another's) is naive. Community art centers offer sustained—intense and over time—arts instruction that is sequential—students move from beginner to intermediate to advanced classes. The beginning tap students in Cheryl Smith's class are learning the moves, the intermediate students study combinations and begin to memorize and perform sequences of steps, and the advanced students move into a choreography class where they create dances that they will skillfully perform.

In Molly Olga's Neighborhood Classes in Buffalo, New York,[22] the youngest children use a clear pallet and consider colors individually before they learn to combine them and make their own shades. They are required to master basic painting skills in tempera paint before moving to acrylics and oils. Students and teachers in both settings know what it takes to advance. Above and beyond teacher preference—arguably a challenge in any classroom—progress in all areas of the arts can be measured; but more in terms of an individual's own developing skill set than in terms of a quantitative or numerical scale.

Some advocates have argued that there are many aspects of the arts that involve the sort of right or wrong answers that can be measured. What is an arabesque in dance, verisimilitude in drama, or chiaroscuro in the visual arts? A student can answer these questions on a multiple-choice test with correct or incorrect answers, and the information acquired is an important part of the student's learning in an art discipline. But what will we know about a student's understanding of the expression of ideas and feelings through movement on account of her correct definition of arabesque? And will the student who knows the meaning of the word *verisimilitude* be the same student who makes her rendering of a part believable? Perhaps yes. But we do an injustice to learning in the arts to reduce it to right and wrong answers, just as we do an injustice to non-arts subjects by only measuring a student's knowledge in those units that we can count.

Presenting ideas such as these before an audience of educators at a regional education conference a few years ago, an administrator and arts advocate challenged my questioning of the rights and wrongs of arts learning. "That we demonstrate that we can test arts learning is a huge step forward, " he asserted vehemently, suggesting that my plea to look beyond right and wrong in every subject was typical of the murky thinking that has left the arts behind other subjects throughout time. "I'm not saying there aren't right or wrong answers associated with the arts," I responded, "I'm just saying they might not be the most interesting aspects of arts learning." Mockingly, the angry inquisitor put his hands on his hips and offered an exaggerated exasperated sigh to the audience. At that indignity (it was pretty exciting actually), the head of the math department in the district in which we were meeting rose to her feet. "And it's the same for math!" She declared with loud passion. "What's interesting about math goes beyond those right or wrong answers as well."

Numerical scoring as a summary of students' overall performance in the arts is conspicuously wrong headed; dare we advocates suggest that this is true for non-arts subjects as well? It may make sense to keep the arts from being thrown from the ring of subjects in which aspects of student progress can be measured quantitatively. But let's not forget that the examples of holistic assessment of student performance that the arts provide have given rise to alterative models that can be applied in any subject. The widely used model of performance-based assessment—involving student activities as demonstrations of learning—evokes the notion of an artistic performance in which the integration of knowledge and skill is put on display.

The specific example of portfolio assessment, based on the ongoing process of the visual artist, has been implemented with interest and relative success in schools throughout the country. In this mode, examples of student work in various subjects are stored for ongoing review, as if they were pieces of visual art, in some kind of portfolio. Rather than the closed process of deciding that an answer is right or wrong on a particular test, the student's work is openly considered over time (how has the work changed from the student's early to late efforts?) and in context (what was the student trying to accomplish in this particular piece of work and how did she make those decisions?).[23] Portfolio assessment sets the stage for project-based work because projects, like works of art in progress, can be revisited and revised. While the time and effort required for effective portfolio assessment seems staggering in comparison to the scoring of a standardized test, the process enriches classroom curriculum and invites an open rapport between student and teacher that is informed by ongoing reflection.

Ongoing reflection, the kind that marks an artist's or actor's or dancer's process of developing work, guides our understanding and ability to assure students that mistakes are generative—we learn and move forward from them; they do not define or diminish us. The advocate may answer the measurement objection by stating, "Wait a minute, there are aspects of arts learning that can be measured on tests." But we must not forget that the unwillingness of arts educators to put a numerical grade on a student's overall artistic effort is not a shortcoming. The alternative methods for responding to and assessing student work in the arts are worthy of emulating in non-arts subjects. Even as they are "beyond measure," a term reserved for the things we value most in life, the arts have much to teach us about assessing learning writ large, at best a messy and complicated process—one that indefatigably challenges the sharp edges of standardized testing.

Objection 5: EXPERTISE
To Be Taught Well, the Arts Require Specialists

> You need experts to teach the arts. Classroom teachers cannot comfortably teach dance and talk about visual arts the way they can teach, for example, both reading and math. (*Teacher supervisor*)

It is curious that our expectation for expertise applies not to every subject that is taught in school, but to the arts, which must be taught by individuals who are artists themselves or have experience and skill in an art form. Teachers of young children are expected to have sufficient knowledge of reading, science, and math to teach all three. But we do not expect a teacher who cannot dance to teach dance to elementary school children, and she wouldn't dare. Dance, as a case in point, is the art form that is least frequently taught in our schools. For drama, we will ask a teacher with no theater experience to step in and direct a show. With regard to visual arts, teachers who have never had an art lesson will feel confident to let their children explore the controllable media of crayons or markers on the confined spaces of desktops. But dance requires comfort with one's body and knowledge of the kind of gesture that separates artistry from everyday motion. The teacher's "I don't dance" will put an end to that activity in her classroom.

Singing in the classroom will meet a similar response. "Oh, I don't sing," a classroom teacher will explain, protesting that her voice is untrained or inadequate. In contrast, no child is exempt from a sing along (in the early grades) on account of an untrained or inadequate voice. And no elementary school teacher will be forgiven the excuse, "Oh, I don't do math." We expect children to enjoy the arts without affording them arts training; we expect teachers who have no arts training to avoid the arts; and we value the arts so little that this self-perpetuating situation does not seem troublesome.

All of the objections to the arts in education that we have addressed are intertwined. Certainly if arts learning were valued more, required of every child and not put aside for the particularly talented or needy, more time would be allotted for the arts in the school day. When it came to issues of measurement, the ongoing process-oriented attitudes of an artist developing a work in progress would be the most celebrated model. That model would not exclude the many factors—and, again, this is important to allow—that can be tallied in numerical skills. It would serve in the quest for measuring learning as a whole. After all, that opus of educational experience that a child is developing is not unlike a work of art. Were we to address it from an artist's perspective, numerical scores would be worthy of a child's attention but more consideration would be given to what she is learning about learning—about what to do with mistakes, how to ask good questions that advance learning, and how to make sense of the world with the many skills acquired in school.

In a scenario that favors the arts, the view of expertise that we associate with arts learning—that special quality that makes us think there is required knowledge and training or even magic that only artists possess—would be extended across subjects. Instead of just inviting artists into the classroom because only they have the expertise and magic, we would be inviting scientists and mathematicians because they have expertise and magic too. All teachers would be required to have some expertise with the arts—enough so that they feel comfortable moving to music or expressing emotion as they dance with their children. Enough so that they feel confident asking their children to step away from their desks and help cover the blackboards with brown paper so that teacher and students can draw images on the walls. Enough so that a song, beyond "Happy Birthday," can be led by a teacher with enthusiasm rather than embarrassment. These arts-friendly teachers would not replace arts specialists. Rather, they would have sufficient expertise to open their classrooms to the arts and sufficient comfort to communicate across disciplines with the arts teacher.

Teachers reflect and model our attitudes towards the arts. If the arts are valued, the teacher will care and be involved and share her positive and enthusiastic interest towards students' artistic creations and the creations of artists in all domains. The teacher will not say "beautiful" to every scratch of crayon that a child lays on a paper. She will have respect for the child's work as worthy of close attention and the confidence and knowledge to look carefully and to model the sort of questions we ask of works of art. "Look where your line goes, how it moves here up and around on your paper. I feel myself moving with that line. And look, now I bump into this enormous patch of bright green that you, powerful artist child, have chosen to place here on this paper, and I, powerful artist teacher, have had the good fortune to see."

Relegating the teaching of art to experts is like relegating the learning of art to the talented. For advanced or preprofessional training, as is true in any subject, students interested in the arts will need to find specialized schooling. But the expert teacher is an artist, a dancer, an actress, and a musician just as she is a reader, a writer, a mathematician, a philosopher, and a scientist. When our teachers have the courage and the caring to explore the arts as active learners alongside their students, no child will feel comfortable—as most do by age 12—saying, "Oh, I don't do art."

Objection 6: MONEY
The Arts Are Too Expensive

From the additional salaries of specialists to the supplies and space they require, the arts are expensive luxuries that we need to trim along with

other fat (like athletics) from the meat and bones of daily learning.
(*Department of Education finance officer*)

Well, money is always the rub, and the arts are seen as requiring special supplies, specialist and visiting artist salaries, and adminsitration time for field trips and performances and shows. The need for restrained delegation of funds ties the hands and clouds the dreams of administrators who truly wish there were time, space, and the necessary financial support to facilitate all aspects of the education of the whole child. As advocates argue for the essentiality of arts learning, they must remember that, along with the players who hold the financial reigns in schools, anyone who pays taxes must be persuaded that there is significant return to be had on an investment in the arts in education.

The graying of the audiences in cultural institutions in New York City, a multibillion-dollar industry, surely provided the financial push needed to get the arts back in city schools. The discovery that arts education was a strong predictor of attendance at art museums, concerts, theater, and dance performances provided the impetus for reinstatement. Educating children in art does more than enrich their spirits and souls—arguably all it would need to do to demonstrate its worth. It also creates a population of caring individuals who contribute to the well-being of the cultural economy. It may seem strange that on the one hand we are advocating for the arts because of what they do for our children and society that cannot be quantified. And on the other hand we are suggesting that there are monetary gains to be earned by investments in the arts—here in the education of our children as "arts consumers" in future society. But these are important and not mutually exclusive realities as are the coexistence of the stereotypes of the "starving artist" who works without recognition or compensation and the "artistic mogul" who has earned both fame and wealth.

There are some arts education advocates who decry monetary associations with the outcomes for arts education or their content. For example, they disavow associations with arts learning and the world of entertainment, understood as light, commercial, and amusing art as opposed to challenging, educational, artistic expression. They spurn as "edutainment" teaching with and through modes of entertainment like television shows or video games, and consider popular media as both the "dumbing down" of the fine arts and a challenge to the nobler purposes of arts learning. Other advocates value opportunities for student learning through the threshold of the media in which students are engaged outside of school. They see as most relevant those discussions of art and its role in society that have to do with monetary gain. Some educators tackle as content the notion of media exploitation through artistic symbols. Others explore as viable issues questions such as how much a museum paid for a particular painting or what accounts for relative monetary worth among works of art.

Resituating the money issue in the day-to-day realities of school finances, it is perhaps ironic that the worrisome cost of arts education has been the source of positive connections forged between schools and the broader community. Schools' dramatic productions are often self-sustaining through ticket sales. Local businesses and national foundations contribute specifically to particular arts initiatives even as federal sources allot funds for schools looking to develop innovative arts curricula. The connections forged on account of a need to support the arts within schools—with the local museum that provides buses for school trips; the National Endowment for the Arts that funds the Shakespeare project; the PTA that raises money at a bake sale to pay for visiting artists—draw attention to and affection for a local school and have a positive impact on the school's sense of and attachment to the broader community.

Beyond the unexpected perks that come from need, the overall allotment of funds from the district budget for arts in the schools is a source of constant distress. The budget goes down; something needs to be cut; arts first and then athletics are the "extras" that need to go. We have begun to see a rise in obesity among children that necessarily is associated with a lack of organized physical activity within schools. The elimination of the arts may be associated with lower levels of attendance to and satisfaction with schools, but there is no visible measure that can be equated to weight gain. The dimming of spirit and energy and the reduction of joyful sense making that results from a cut in arts learning happens deep and out of sight and will always cost more than the most extravagant increase in funds allotted for the arts in education.

Objection 7: AUTONOMY
The Arts Will Survive in the Community Without School Support

> If we were to drop math from the curriculum, it's unlikely that community math centers would pop up around the neighborhood where local mathematicians would teach our kids. But the arts have always been rallied for by community artists who will fill the void that schools' neglect of the arts creates. (Educational researcher)

In light of the activity of responding to in-school objections with examples from beyond school walls, the autonomy objection takes an ironic twist. It is absolutely true that out-of-school centers do provide arts education when schools will not. Indeed, in the 1960s there was a surge in the creation of these centers in response to cutbacks in arts education in the schools. Originally started in the states at the turn of the century as part of the service of settlement houses, the first community art centers offered art classes to help deliver marketable skills to a generation of new immigrants.

Over the years, the tradition continued and grew with arts centers expanding their arts offerings in urban settings, while maintaining their dedication to public service and social responsibility. The sixties saw the aforementioned Artists Collective founded in Hartford with the idea of offering the arts to urban youth as an alternative to drugs; and the Manchester Craftsmen's Center in Pittsburgh with the idea of introducing at-risk youth to the possibility of college. Similarly, Plaza de la Raza in Los Angeles introduced Latino and Chicano youth to the expression of their own culture through art and the telling of their own stories through something called "first voice." The Boulevard Center for the Arts in Chicago started with a vision of neighborhood students from various backgrounds gaining intercultural understanding through art.

In the 1970s in New York City, community centers were working to help mend the fabric of schools damaged by the removal of arts education. The Children's Art Carnival in Harlem placed visiting artists in the schools. The Harlem School for the Arts, like other centers across the country, brought school children in buses to the center to attain quality arts education. New York's Studio in a School, like Chicago's Urban Gateways, and the national organization of

Young Audiences, stepped up to the challenge of providing schools with high-quality artist residencies and performances.

At the time, these alternatives, excellent as they were, were seen as threatening by school arts specialists. With cause in many cases, these specialists worried that if the community offered alternatives to in-school arts education, the few arts teachers and hours for arts learning that persisted would be eliminated from the scene. In communities where arts learning is valued, these community-based offerings are considered as enriching and expanding, not replacing, the arts in schools. But the quality of the educational programs these centers offer, and more recently of those offered by civic-minded art museums, has made way for the shortsighted objection, "If there are so many viable alternatives or even preferable options in the community, why should we waste time and money on arts education within the schools?"

The answer to this objection, fellow advocates, is clear. While arts education in the community is there for self-selection by aware individuals, those who know least of the arts and need most to be exposed to them will only encounter them if they are part of the school curriculum. The statement that schools make by including the arts in the curriculum is clear: "The arts matter. They matter to education; they matter to society; and they will matter to you." There is no equivalent for a school's endorsement of the arts—a school's endorsement of the need for students to gain the vocabularies and to make and tell their own stories through the language of the arts. School is a microcosm of society; it reflects, but it also affects. Let our schools speak to and through our students of the importance of art to life.

The Case for
the Arts in Education

5-year-old's animal image

Medium: "scratch out" (crayon, tempera, and scratch tool)

PRELUDE: WHY MUST WE JUSTIFY
THE ARTS IN TERMS OF NON-ARTS LEARNING?

At a gathering of arts education practitioners and researchers organized by one of the nation's arts advocacy groups in Washington,
D.C., the usual arts-in-school challenges filled the air: assessment
(how we measure the impact of the arts on student learning), transfer (how what we learn in the arts crosses into other subjects), and
research (what we've learned about it all).[1] These issues were all
evoked in the passionate remarks of the director of an arts-based
high school in D.C.:

> We train our students in and through the arts. As a result, they come
> to school and do not drop out. Their lives get better, they stay off the
> streets, they consider the possibility of having a future, but do their test
> scores increase? We've yet to be able to demonstrate that with our
> students. These kids are just beginning to experience sustained time in
> school. We arts advocates care about the positive changes in a child's life
> that come from the arts, but they only want things that can be measured.
> What foundations and school officials care about is whether test scores
> increase. What about those studies that say that arts education makes
> SAT scores go up? Are they for real?

The group began to address the latest findings about the arts
raising SAT scores and especially the fact that arts learning seemed
to have a positive effect on test scores regardless of whether the kids
taking the tests were rich or poor or placed at risk in a number of
ways.[2] What did it mean that in spite of this evidence, researchers
couldn't say that arts learning caused the increase?[3] A researcher
in the group explained that cause is hard to prove in any study but
that what it meant here was that a number of other factors were so
mixed in to a student's life that it was hard to identify the arts as the
single or even the main reason for the finding. Students who have
more arts education may go to better schools, or they may come
from families that prioritize arts learning: Parents who encourage
academic performance may also respect arts learning in and out of
school. "Why did they challenge this study?" the school director
asked. "What kind of researchers try to disprove a finding that can
be helpful to those of us in the trenches who are fighting for the

arts?" Folks at the table looked at each other with distress. Now researchers were being placed in the category of "them"—those who intrude on the progress of the arts in our schools. Was it research's responsibility only to give us good news?

Years ago there was an interesting arts-enrichment program in which classroom teachers were urged to identify artistic talent in their classrooms and to reward that talent with increased arts learning or artistic challenges. Rather than coping with what would otherwise be perceived as negative classroom behaviors, teachers were asked to consider those behaviors as possible indicators of artistic talent. Using this "arts promise" lens for interpreting behavior, the child who was jumping around disruptively in class was seen as having a hidden talent for dancing; the child who was mugging or imitating was thought to have potential in acting. Dance or drama training was offered to these children instead of reprisal, and what was discovered? The child, so distracted in class, was able to concentrate on dance or drama, for which he or she gained approval and ultimately a shot at that elusive but precious entity, self-esteem, which appeared even to transfer to his or her performance in other classes.

But was it the dancing or dramatics that worked the wonder and affected the performance of the child? Or was it the close observation on the part of the teacher—that search for and recognition of talent that told the child he or she was being noticed, and from a positive perspective? Or was it the approval of the dance or drama teacher? Might the recognition of an individual as an individual have been the real change agent here? And might the search for recognition of talent in unexpected activities and the promise of reward and approval be as easily enacted in the arenas of science or mathematics?

An urban school in the South Bronx decided to have The Bronx Dance Theater's education director come in to teach ballet twice a week to a 4th-grade class that had the lowest reading scores in the city. After a year of ballet lessons, the children's reading scores went up. This seemed to those involved certain proof that learning dance had a positive effect on the students' reading scores. But maybe not. When the principal of the school approved the visits from the Bronx Dance Theater, she had one requirement: that the

visiting artist come on Mondays and Fridays—the two most frequently skipped days of the week. The principal knew that the artist would be a draw, and she was right. With the dancer visiting,
attendance on Mondays and Fridays was increased.

Why did the reading scores go up? Was it the 2 extra days of
school a week? Was it the flexibility or increased energy of a teacher
whose classroom was enlivened by a visiting artist? Or was it, as
some arts advocates might like us to think, because the eye–hand
coordination, or perhaps the skill of deliberation, acquired through
studying ballet was transferring to the children's ability to read?
The notion of transfer looms heavy as a desperate and perhaps viable justification for arts learning. Don't worry if the children look
like they're just learning how to make and appreciate art; those
abilities will transfer to the more important skills of reading words
and counting numbers or thinking critically in any academic situation they may ever encounter.

Why must we justify arts learning in terms of other disciplines? A
young teacher in Worcester, Massachusetts,[4] observed that elementary school children who looked at works of art for long periods
of time, considering the details of paintings and discussing their
significance, attended more thoroughly to science experiments and
wrote them up with more detail and illustration than children who
had not looked at art. What if we evaluated the effectiveness of science education on children's ability to study carefully and discuss
works of art? How different, if at all, is that suggestion from the
idea of judging the usefulness of arts learning by an increase in
students' SAT scores?

You are not asked to transfer something that has sufficient value
in itself. And therein lies the rub. The arts are not valued in their
own right in our schools. That is why the champions of arts learning
look to research to demonstrate—to prove—the value of arts learning. And the question of "What do children learn through art?" is
changed to "Why is whatever it is that children learn through art
important?" Instead of challenging a value system that excludes the
arts, we scramble to demonstrate worth in terms of a faulty system
of values. On the one hand, art is a language that cannot be translated. We cannot say exactly what we dance; we cannot sing what
we draw. Each symbol system of art constructs meaning uniquely.

Yet we rush to make art experience "valuable" by encouraging students to talk or write about what they dance or draw.

In another school in Massachusetts, an art teacher worked with university researchers to test further the learning tools that had served the teacher in Worcester so well. When asked how the class had enjoyed looking at an art print and responding to a set of questions about its meaning and presentation, the art teacher shared what students value most about a subject to which schools dedicate painfully little time. She politely replied, "Well, they thought it was interesting, but . . . they really count on that one period a week to use their hands to make something." Students turn to the arts for opportunities that other subjects do not provide—to make something out of paint or pencil and paper or clay or to structure a performance of music or drama; to fill a space in the world with something they have created from their own ideas uniquely implemented by artistic resources.

Artistic activities have aspects that are shared by other academic activities, and it is doubtless that, as it is with any discipline, arts learning will have implications for other kinds of learning. The discipline and hard training that goes into a flawless a cappella tap dance performance by 35 adolescents might be acquired in some other context. But the sound of the students' syncopated collective tapping, the radiance of their energy, the engagement of their audience, and the particular pride they feel—these crucial and most valuable aspects—belong exclusively to the moment of artistic performance.

Artistic activities are most importantly unique, and they satisfy and frustrate uniquely. Children are drawn to the alternativeness of artistic experience, to the otherness of the shaping of something that was not there before, to the joy of making thoughts tangible through the various media of art. Whether the making of art will train students as future arts producers or as arts perceivers, arts learning allows the individual to encounter himself or herself doing what human beings do uniquely: using aesthetic symbols to give experience form.

If experiencing and coming to know one's humanity through art is not as important an exercise as filling in the right blanks on a multiple-choice test, it's time for us to review and revise our values and not to compromise the teaching of art by asking it to be taught to the tests of other domains. We should be careful not to waste the time of teachers and researchers of the arts by applying the wrong questions to their efforts.

Let's once and for all stop asking ourselves how we can teach and evaluate art with the same constraints we apply to other subjects. The time is right for asking ourselves how we can use the exemplary models that the arts provide to improve our teaching and assessment of other subjects. The arts need to be incorporated into every child's learning—not to improve test scores, but to provide individuals with the necessary tools to make and find meaning through aesthetic symbols. The arts need to be incorporated into every child's learning for the more important purpose of enabling future generations to participate across circumstance, culture, and time in the ongoing human conversation that is perpetuated through art. The director of that arts-based high school in D.C. needs the support and vocabulary to stand up to those doubters who ask, "But what about SATs?" and respond, "But what about what's most important?"

INTRODUCING UNIQUE FEATURES OF THE ARTS AND WHAT STUDENTS LEARN

First of all, we must declare that the arts in education uniquely teach the arts. While arts learning finds its way into many non-arts classes and activities in and out of school, it is the visual arts class that is specifically dedicated to teaching the skills and providing the opportunity for students to draw, paint, and sculpt. It is there as well that students gain experience looking at art—the work of great artists, of peers, their own work; making sense (what does it mean?) and critiquing (how effective is it?). This is true for learning the skills of music in music class, dance in dance class, and so forth for all art forms. It is in arts classes that we acquire "knowledge how," that is, how to make or perform and understand the art form, and "knowledge that," facts and information about the art form. All of this is undeniably important. From a pure "art for art's sake" perspective, advocates will argue that the arts are important, like math, science, or history in their own right. Therefore, education in the arts is essential because it is only on its account that you learn one or several of the arts.

In the arguments that follow, I take that claim as a given and extend the conversation to a broader view of what is unique about the arts (any or all art forms) and what is therefore unique about what we learn from them (any or all of them) in education. In the preceding prelude and elsewhere throughout this text, I decry the well-worn but still popular arguments for the value of arts learning as beneficial to learning in non-arts disciplines. At this juncture, I take the challenge of addressing what it is arts learning provides without regard for what we may think we need to prove it does. I focus on what we learn as we produce and make sense from a work of our own making or when we study and gain understanding from a work that someone else has made.

In Chapter 1 in responding to objections to the arts in education, I necessarily assumed a defensive posture, identifying aspects of arts learning that challenge or refute explanations for overlooking its worth. Here I take an unfettered look at the unique features of the arts and at what, on account of these features, the arts uniquely teach. It is from this nondefensive perspective that advocates can rally for what the arts specifically do in and for education. I hope these features of arts learning will serve advocates as talking points or reasons for including the arts in education—reasons that go beyond apology and justification to essentiality and value.

I identify aspects of the arts that I believe apply equally to music-making and listening, creative writing and reading, dancing and viewing, and drawing and looking. While I hope this approach will be of broad use, I know it overlooks the many interesting and important differences that persist among art disciplines. There are salient differences, for example, between dance and drawing, and between learning to dance and learning to draw. Learning how to leap across a stage for a single moment in time in dance class is very different from learning how to draw with perspective on a paper that has permanence and can be returned to and changed. And different students will be attracted to different arts arenas and for different reasons. But in an effort to serve arts education advocacy writ large, I focus on common denominators and save the investigation and discussion of these compelling and most interesting differences for later or others' work.[5]

I assert that the arts are unique among school subjects because works of art feature the following: a tangible product, a focus on emotion, ambiguity, a process orientation, and a sense of connection. Linked to these features are 10 specific and invaluable results of arts learning:

1. Tangible product
   - Imagination
   - Agency

2. Focus on emotion
   - Expression
   - Empathy

3. Ambiguity
   - Interpretation
   - Respect

4. Process orientation
   - Inquiry
   - Reflection

5. Connection
   - Engagement
   - Responsibility

In the discussion that follows, I focus on these links; for example, that the arts' unique feature of having a tangible product sets the stage for the learning outcomes of imagination and agency. A focus on emotion is especially linked to expression and empathy, and so forth. However, while the aspects of arts learning appear to emerge from the different features quite neatly in pairs, in another conversation they might be rearranged. For example, the lessons of engagement and interpretation might be considered in terms of the process orientation that is featured in the arts.

In short, I present the unique features of the arts and of arts learning as I do for reasons of clarity. But I hope the sorting that I've done does not obscure the seamlessness of the various features of the arts and the range of their influence on arts learning. Just as the five identified features of the arts exist together and inform one another, so does each of them inform differently the arts learning they provide. As reasons for keeping the arts in our schools, these features inform a manifesto for defending the arts as essential to the education of compassionate, thoughtful, and responsible human beings. Let's look in more detail at each feature and its associated learning.

Unique Feature 1.
Tangible Product—Imagination and Agency

Art involves a tangible product, whether it is a painting that is being made by one child, a play that is being put up by a group of children, a dance duet, or a chorus performance—there is a something that we can see or touch or hear that we call art. This is an important and unique feature of the arts and therefore of their role in education. It is as true with art as it is with math or science that students gain skills for figuring out problems and discovering new information. And it is as true with art as it is with history or social studies that there is much knowledge to be gained about the subject when it is studied—factual information about which students' answers on a test are either right or wrong. But unlike other subjects, the arts allow children to create something new of their own invention that was not there before it was created. And that something new and tangible—the product (even as it is a work in progress)—can be changed or completed at the child's discretion.

Furthermore, the child's developing product, whether it is a painting, a dance performance, or an original song, is never right or wrong. Dates erroneously assigned to particular events in history or incorrect definitions of words are wrong. But paintings, plays, or melodies can never be. Even when we disagree with what we think the works are "saying," or don't like the way in which the work has been created, the work is not wrong. Children can look at the tangible work of art that they are making or have made, or at a video or audiotape of a performance, and reflect on how they might change it at the moment. Perhaps they will add more yellow to the drawing of a tree or jump higher at the start of their original bunny dance, if and when they do it again. And one change may seem to the child more right than another. But unlike an answer on a quiz that a teacher can see is definitively right or wrong, there is no definitive right or wrong regarding a child's original artistic product. A decision about original work need only be right for the child.

When we say there are no right or wrong answers in the arts in education, then, we are not referring to those aspects of the arts that are laden with factual information—like the rich information about artists and performers and periods of art throughout history—we are referring to the artistic product through which an artist has made some sense of the world and through which an audience makes its own new sense. And, as will be discussed later, we are referring to the sense of the world that artist and audience make from creation and consideration of the tangible product that is a work of art.

Speaking recently to landscape artist Allen Whiting, I told him what I saw in his painting of a horse and barn (see Figure 2.1). I

FIGURE 2.1. *Horse and Barn* by Allen Whiting (1999)

Oil on canvas. Photo by Dari Michele

FIGURE 2.2. Poster paint on newsprint with shellac, by author at age 6

Photo by Dari Michele

explained how the light that changed as I walked around the work made me think of hope and possibility; how the horse with its bowed head eating grass in front of the stable reminded me of the nourishment that I find at home. What did he think? "Well," he said, "it all sounds possible to me. For my part, that's the way my horse bows his head when he grazes in front of the barn, and the light is just that way at the time in the afternoon when I made this painting." Perhaps Allen now saw home and possibility in the work because of what I had shared. Perhaps I now understood more clearly his clear-cut intention to record a particular horse in a particular place. Whatever our individual insights, we both had an object—his work of art—to return to repeatedly with new and different discoveries.

Recently, I found in the bottom of a straw trunk in the basement, a painting that I had made at age 6 (see Figure 2.2 and cover). After more than half a century, the painting was remarkably well

preserved even though it had been done on newsprint. I noted
the drip of shellac still visible on the right side of the sun and remembered how thrilling it was in art class in the 1940s and 1950s
to apply the sweet smelling shellac when you were certain that
your painting was "really really" done. It darkened the coloration
a bit, but thrillingly, it made the painting shine. Perhaps it was the
shellac that had preserved the image over so much time. As far
as I could tell, it had kept the colors true to what they had been
when I first made it. I recognized the work immediately. Indeed,
my eye went directly to what I remembered, with a small chill in
my back, I had regretted in the work. The thing that had seemed
wrong to me.

The entire image was made of objects that I knew how to draw,
that is, objects that I could render with schemas or learned techniques. We learn from images and other children's drawing that,
for example, a round circle with straight lines sticking out all
around will serve well to represent the sun; a rectangle with a tri-
angle on top will make a house. I knew for sure how to use hori-
zontal curved lines for hills and verticals with downward angled
lines for trees. The half circles I usually used for igloos could stand
as well for tepees, and an exaggeration of the curly hair I used for
profile drawings of girls could be exaggerated into feathered head-
dresses for Native Americans in canoes. Although it was an image
of a rural lakeside scene, I knew how to draw a traffic light and an
airplane. The composition seemed to need something more, so I
added them too.

Like lots of children that age, I hadn't planned ahead much in
my drawing and I hadn't mastered the technique of overlap, drawing nearer objects in front of those that are farther away. For this
reason, when I added the traffic light, I had to put it at an angle to
avoid the big cloud that I had already painted. But I wanted someone swimming in the lake, and I had no pattern for such a drawing. I took a risk, and from deep within created a little pink swimmer, arms reaching overhead, white splashes from the kicking of
her feet. I remembered when I drew her more than 50 years ago
how disappointed I was with the rendering. How everything else
seemed neat and "right," but that wild little swimmer ruined it all.
Now, I look at the image and what I love best is that swimmer. She

embodies joyful action and risk-taking. The whole image seems to me now a background for that franticly moving person who is the heroine of the work.

My understanding and appreciation of the work changed over time, and the process of its making was only recollected on account of the permanence of the object. The product, that tangible something on which thinking and learning are imprinted, is one of the features of the arts that make them essential to education. The product reveals and records the workings of the child's imagination and tangibly demonstrates her personal impact, her power to make a difference that she can see a week or half a century later. Let's discuss in terms of the artistic product, the first two lessons that arts learning uniquely provides and that stand as reasons for the arts to have a permanent place in our children's education:

IMAGINATION: The arts in education invite students to think beyond the given, to imagine, "What if?"

AGENCY: The arts in education enable students to experience their significance as agents of effectiveness and change, to realize, "I matter."

The first time a blank piece of paper and four fat crayons are presented to a small child, the notion of "what if?" is introduced. What if I drag this blue line across the page? What if I scratch this red back and forth in this space over here? What if I pour a bit of my milk onto the paper and rub it in with my hand, or bang the crayon up and down so it leaves dots on the page like the footprints of a rabbit running by? What if? Hand-in-hand with that realization is the understanding that "I matter." What I do next will make the difference, effect the change, and realize the possibilities that I imagine.

From the first performance in a school play, children experience the possibilities of "what if?" in a different space than that defined by the edges of the white piece of paper. What if I make my voice very loud? How different will the character I am creating be? What if I move quickly and open my eyes wide—how will she seem? Or if I'm slow in my gait and hang my head low or bellow softly—what if? My voice, my imitation, my movement and sound—they make a difference. I matter.

What if I outline my drawing in dark crayon lines? How much more vibrant will it seem? What if I write a story about a girl like me but instead of living in an apartment like I do, she lives in a tree, and what if instead of having to go to sleep at night, she stays up singing in the forest? What if I change the ending of my story—make it surprising or sad? What if I paint the background green? When I close my eyes before I play the piano and imagine myself playing the piece, what do I imagine? What if? What if I raise my knees high when I dance across the stage instead of keeping my steps low? My drawing, my writing, my painting, and my performance in dance or music—they make a difference. I make the change happen or not. I matter.

What if there were no war or poverty or prejudice or disregard for people's rights and needs? If I can imagine other realities and differences that I can bring about on paper, piano, or stage, how different can I make the "product" that is the world around me? How far will the imagining and the agency that I realize in the arts take me? If I can imagine and change the world I create in paint and in performance, am I not a person who can see beyond the given to alternate possibilities in the greater world? Because I have the ability to make change, can I not make a difference in it all?

The arts enable students to see the impact of change on a product, to experience their own ability to invent and carry out change. The imagination cultivated through the arts in education may serve students well in non-arts subjects, for example, in imagining alternative approaches to a science challenge. But it is because of the creation of an artistic product, a core experience in arts learning, that students have tangible evidence of the importance of their own imagining beyond the given; imagining possibilities ("What if?") determined and realized by the child ("I matter.").

Unique Feature 2.
Focus on Emotion—Expression and Empathy

Although it is certain that the arts engage—both in the making of art and in the viewing or appreciating of art—a certain kind of thinking, the arts are uniquely associated with the world of emotion. We understand that math asks us to think in numbers or in more complex sets of symbols; that science requires methods in which we are trained; and that the stories of history are told and remembered through words. When we liken the arts to other subjects, we talk of the different symbols of the arts. There are the lines and brushstrokes in visual arts, the movements and gestures in dance, and the notes and sounds of music. And we say these symbols can be decoded like math, systematically explored like science, or read like history. But even as we can argue that all the disciplines, like the arts, are approaches to making sense of and advancing our knowledge of the world around us, only the arts are specifically directed toward expressing and sharing human emotion.

We ask young people to read Shakespeare's timeless sixteenth century tragedy *Romeo and Juliet* so that they can experience through the artistry of the poetic language the passion and sorrow of two ill-starred young lovers. It is an emotional experience to read or see the play, or the movies made of that gracefully crafted story, but it is the beauty of the language chosen to express and elicit feeling that brings us to tears. Similarly, it is Leonard Bernstein's stirring music in *West Side Story* (a 1957 version of the same sorry tale) that makes us weep.

We expect works of art to make us feel one way or another and often evaluate them on that basis. "I didn't care about any of the characters," we will say with regret about a movie, "so I didn't feel badly when this or that happened to them." "The painting is dark and gloomy, but doesn't really seem sad to me." And although we speak of the technical acumen of dancers or painters, it is their ability to display and evoke feelings that we value as art or artistry. "He didn't miss a note," we will say of a pianist, "but his playing was cold and without feeling." "Her dancing was flawless in presentation but devoid of expression." Although contemporary artists have explored new forms and objectives for art, our traditional view of the arts as giving form to human emotion persists and is particularly relevant in our consideration of what makes the arts unique and powerful parts of our children's education.

The fact that the arts, unlike other subjects, address, embody, convey, and evoke emotion sets the stage for two more reasons for featuring the arts in education:

EXPRESSION: The arts in education give students the opportunity to
recognize and express their feelings, to acknowledge, "This is how
I feel."

EMPATHY: The arts in education help students to be aware of and
attentive to the emotions of others, to appreciate, "This is how
you feel."

In a research study that I conducted almost 20 years ago, I asked
children of different ages, adults, and professional artists to draw
emotions. "Draw happy," "Draw sad," and "Draw angry." I asked
with no further explication. Expressing a universal understanding
of the connection between lines and feelings, drawings from all
the different participant groups displayed droopy down curved
lines in the drawings that expressed sadness, rounded up-turned
lines in the drawings that were happy, and jagged heavy lines in
the drawings that were angry.[6] Furthermore, an awareness of these
connections seemed to increase with age and experience. Adult
artists, for example, consciously bore down heavily on a marker in
pressing out angry lines. Younger children seemed more connected
to their drawings. Without self-consciousness, they scrunched up
their faces angrily and pressed hard on the markers, assuming the
expression of the angry feeling that they portrayed in their scribbling. When I asked 3-year-old Hannah to draw "sad," she threw
down her crayon and turned to leave the room, "I can't cause I'm
not," she barked at me. Perhaps I should have then asked for a
drawing of angry.

Young children are as connected to movement and sound as
they are to line and color in the expression of movement. Ask a
group of 8-year-olds to move across the floor as if they were happy,
sad, or angry and you will see the same range of motion. Cheerful
skipping, rounded arms for happy; drooping, slow movements for
sad; and heavy pounding with tight-fisted, jagged movements for
angry. Before they can actually play the piano, children will reach
for the high keys to the right of the keyboard to twinkle out a happy
sound, and pound heavily in the low range for angry. The 4-year-
old engaged in pretend play in the kindergarten doll corner shakes
a believably angry finger at the child who plays her naughty baby;
the child taking the part of the baby curls up and hangs her head
with authentic shame.

Very young children know how to express emotion through the arts, to communicate feeling through the artistic product—whether it is a painting, dance, or a theatrical performance (see Figure 2.3). We need only provide the crayons and paint to make the lines, the open floor space on which to dance, the props and backdrop for dramatic play, the musical instruments to learn and employ. The arts, like no other subject, give children the media and opportunity to shape and communicate their feelings.

Unfortunately, advocates for the arts have given up on the emotional case for arts education, believing that no one at this juncture in time—in which performance on hard-edged standardized tests is key—has interest in the soft, individualistic promise of the arts. But especially at this juncture, the case for emotion must not be

FIGURE 2.3. An expressive drawing of the emotion "sad" by a 4-year-old

abandoned. While math, science, history, and the tests they generate inspire, excite, frustrate, and discourage our children, the arts
alone provide the opportunity for recognizing these feelings and
for giving them form. In the development of students who have
the courage and engagement to persevere in their studies, the arts
uniquely and indispensably offer venues for the range of emotions
that accompany and fuel hard work.

That group of 1st and 4th graders mentioned in Chapter 1, who
looked at a painting and shared their thoughts on what the artist
might be feeling when he made it, demonstrated their understanding that emotion is expressed and negotiated through art. Most
grown-ups have distanced themselves from paintings in museums and consider the work of great artists as something beyond
their understanding and appropriate only for the consideration of
experts such as curators and other art historians. But these children—no doubt because they were still creating art in their classrooms and at home—identified with the artist as someone who
has the ability to express emotion in a work and as someone who
strives to do good work.

Their comments tell us that children understand many things:

- That works of art express the feelings of the artist who
  makes them: A sad artist might make a sad painting;
- That the artist can use a work of art to address his own
  feelings: to make a happy painting to cheer himself up;
- That the creation of a work of art can be a joyful experience:
  feeling great to have made something so beautiful.

The fact that children know that emotions are contained in and
communicated through works of art enables them to learn about
the feelings of the person who makes them, to think beyond themselves, and to consider the emotions of others.

Building on the notion of "What if?" and "I feel," childred considering a work of art by someone else, whether it is a painting or a
performance, are invited to consider, "What if that were me? How
would I feel?" "I would feel so happy if I could make a painting
like that." Or they might think, "I would make a painting like that
to bring me cheer when I was sad. Maybe that is how the someone

else who made this feels." The identification with and consideration of another person's feelings is what empathy is all about. Through their encounters with works of art, students acquire an empathetic perspective. And this perspective will serve them well in the sense making they are asked to do in other subjects, throughout their experience with the media, and across the broader landscape on which is written the pain and suffering of homeless children, hurricane victims, soldiers, and citizens beset by war.

Students who are encouraged to recognize and express their emotions in the making of art (I feel) and to identify with others' feelings (you feel) are well positioned to imagine (what if?) and to pursue (because they are empathetic to others) positive alternatives for addressing the injustices that surround them.[7] Do we not still care that our students are prepared in school to be active citizens in a democracy, empathetic towards victims of social injustice, and prepared for positive action and change?

With implications for the empathetic study of history or social studies, the arts in education uniquely and essentially provide students with the opportunity to identify and experience the emotions of others. The famous Russian author Leo Tolstoy defined the work of the artist as the use of "line, colors, sounds, images" to convey a feeling that the artist has experienced so that it can be re-experienced, or felt as his own, by the viewer, listener, or reader of the work.[8] The 1st and 4th graders in our 1995 study give ample evidence for Tolstoy's turn of the century claim.

Unique Feature 3.
Ambiguity—Interpretation and Respect

Numbers in math, like letters in the construction of words, are precise symbols. They represent what they represent clearly and accurately. We know for example that the number 5 is a 5, never 7; or that the letter *B* is a *B*, never *A*. Non-negotiable meaning. And numbers and letters stand for particular meanings. We can count the five whatevers to which a particular 5 refers, just as we can make the "Bbbb" sound to which *B* refers. Furthermore, these clear-cut symbols—numbers and letters—can be combined with other symbols that are like them to create other meanings that may be more complex but similarly precise. Five can sit next to another *5*, and represent *55*, or next to a *6* and a *7* and represent *567*. *B* can sit next to two "*A*"s and represent the word humans say as "Baa" at the same time as it represents the sound a sheep makes; just as the number *2* can represent two sheep. "What does the cow say?" we ask the 2-year-old. And if she responds "Baa," she has made a mistake.

The 2-year-old may take the letter *M* and turn it over and call it *W*. And it's hard to say she's wrong. She and the 4-year-old who sees the capital letter *G* as a *6*, demonstrate that young children are drawn to the blur of the boundaries that we as adults have worked to clarify and that artists recapture in their work. The young child's development is aptly described as "differentiation," a separating out of the "me" from the "other." "I am not the same living entity as my mother. No! This is 'hers' and 'she.' This is [that frequent 2-year-old declaration] 'mine' and 'me.'" And in acquiring knowledge of the clearer, grown-up lines that persist between entities and identities, children lose that sense of the blurriness in between. Works of art recapture that blurriness between object and idea and self and other; it is the deliberate crossing of boundaries that accounts for their ambiguity. In a work of art, one viewer's *M* can as surely be another's *W*.

The 4-year-old child who scrunched her face up and held her shoulders tight, "being angry" so that she could draw that emotion, like the child who wouldn't draw sad because she wasn't, was unaware or disregarding of the boundaries between herself and her drawing. The 9-year-old who drew angry as one stick figure raising a fist at another, understood that the drawing was a separate entity apart from himself, a repository for controlled lines like letters or words that someone else would read. Just in case, that 9-year-old is likely to write alongside the image or in a cartoon bubble emerging from a figure's mouth: "Angry" or "I am angry" (see an image of "angry" in Figure 2.4). What a distance development has traveled from the fluid dark scribbles that emerged when the growling younger child clenched her fist and both drew and experienced angry. The professional artist who emulates the young child's angry stance, assuming the pose and deliberately reaching for the experience of what she represents, is expressing a mature understanding of the virtues

Figure 2.4. An 8-year-old child's line drawing of "angry with words"

of a lack of differentiation—between work and emotions expressed and between artist and work. The lack of clear boundaries makes a work ambiguous and opens it up to multiple interpretations.

The greatest intruder on the messy, intertwined artist-like understandings of very young children is that glistening bright doorway to their future as grown-ups: school. It is school that introduces the precise language of numbers and words—although educational media now does a very good job of that even before children go off to school. In the case of school, it is that holder of the light, the teacher, who says the child's drawings are "beautiful" even as she writes the child's name on the image anywhere she likes—demonstrating to the child that the precise symbols of letters formed into the word that is his name are a better, clearer declaration of who the child is than the colorful, messy lines on the paper.

Resisting ambiguity, the teacher will ask of the tangle of lines, "What is this?" Or less intrusively, "Tell me about your drawing."

Either way the child hears clearly that the drawing on its own says nothing, even as it may represent something other than or beyond words. Spoken words are needed to clarify the image. "Oh," the child will think for a minute, realizing the new function of lines on paper. "Well, here's an umbrella" she will say pointing to a curvy line. "And all these lines are the rain . . . and I'm taking a walk through the park with my mother and. . . ." In reference to the drawings of preschool children, researchers have called this response to the adult question, "romancing"—wishing a story into being at the discovery that an object or action is supposed to dwell somewhere in drawn lines. Five-year-old children, aware of representational intention, may still be exploring the media of finger-paint or charcoal with abstract abandon. The adult call for explanation reminds them that the function of art should be more like that of words.

The implicit message is clear: In school you will learn words like the ones that the teacher now writes on your drawing—"Nancy taking a walk in the rainy park with her mother under an umbrella." And those unclear images that your hand explores will no longer be needed. You may pretend in the doll corner, if you're lucky, until you're 5, but after that we have real work to do. You may illustrate your stories until you can write well enough to make your point in words. You will have space for pretend, music, drawing, and story in your classroom until you can read well enough to work with desks and books. While this is a harsh description that overlooks the stunning exceptions in many schools, the generality holds. The messy, undifferentiated exploration of media and understanding that children attend to so carefully in their early drawings is abandoned for the clear-cut study of codes and information on which you can be tested and scored.

The arts in education differ from the general scene in that they uniquely address the blurry boundaries between right and wrong, the exploration of ambiguous representations, and the world of imagination that lies beyond measure and place the impossible within reach. Allen Whiting's painting of his horse and barn is as truly for him the recreation of a familiar scene at a familiar time of day as it is for me an image of hope and possibility. A neighbor looked at the image and told me, "That doesn't look like a horse to me. A horse with three legs! I don't like that painting because it doesn't seem real." Another visitor perused the image and decided, "It's an excellent painting." She felt confident in this statement, she explained, because she has been taking painting lessons for the past few years, and she went on, "It takes me away to a place that doesn't seem real. A simple, clear scene that transports me from the everyday. I love that painting. I could travel with it in my mind to new places every day."

The declarations of other viewers include "It's joyful," "It's profound," "Unexpected." My 2-year-old grandson screams, "Horse!" as he points boisterously, his arms flailing as if to literally embrace what his eyes take in. Even in a realistic painting, far from the tangled lines of the young child's scribbles, there is no right answer to what it represents or means. Whether the spare words of a Mark Strand poem, the dense prose of a Herman Melville novel, or the blocks of color in a Mark Rothko painting, a truly successful work of art is ambiguous. Because they address the ambiguity of works of art, the arts in education introduce children to the idea of multiple interpretations worthy of mutual respect. The next two aspects of learning that the arts particularly provide emerge from this unique feature of ambiguity:

> INTERPRETATION: The arts in education enable students to see that there are many equally viable ways in and out of the same subject, to know that even if their views differ from others', "What I think matters."
>
> RESPECT: The arts in education help students to be aware of, interested in, and respectful of different ways of making sense of the world. They come to know that even if they disagree with peers, "What others think matters."

I am standing with a group of 4th graders in front of the painting *El Jaleo*, by John Singer Sargent (see Figure 2.5), at the Isabella Stewart Gardner Museum in Boston. The central figure in the work of art, a beautiful Spanish dancer assuming a pose that looks impossible to recreate, has captured the attention of the children. One of the children tries to stand like the dancer in the painting and falls over. They all laugh. "I think she's Mrs. Gardner," another of the children declares out loud, reflecting her interest in the story of the eccentric heroine who reconstructed a Venetian courtyard in the center of the home that is now a museum.

FIGURE 2.5. *El Jaleo* **by John Singer Sargent (1882)**

Oil on canvas, 232 x 348 cm. Gift from T. Jefferson Coolidge, Boston
© Isabella Stewart Gardner Museum, Boston. Photo by Thomas Lingner

"Couldn't be," another child throws in. "Did you see that painting of Mrs. Gardner upstairs?" he asks, referring to another painting by Sargent (1888) of the grand dame stiffly poised in a simple black dress with a string of white pearls setting off her very small waist. "She's really uptight. You'd never catch her like this with her hair all mussed up dancing like that."

"I think it's about a murder," a third child muses.

"What makes you say that?" I ask the boy.

"Well, there's a bloody hand on the wall there." He points to a small, red hand-like smudge on the back wall over the shoulder of a guitar player.

"Oh wow," another child jumps in, "I see it, and I think the dancer knows who did it!"

The children carry on taking turns like visual detectives piecing together a story (their story) from the clues that the painting provides. As the discussion begins to wane, I ask them, "What emotions or ideas do you see expressed in this work?" Around the room, the comments fly. "Murder is bad." "Excitement." "Passion." "I think it's about how beautiful women can have bad secrets." "I think it's about how great it is to dance and forget yourself." "Yeah, but it's a scary place. I think it's about fear." "Right, fear. I hadn't thought that. But, it's about how you have to watch yourself and look carefully even when you're having fun."

The chain of comments from child to child expands each child's exploration of the work of art. "I didn't see that hand," one child admits pointing to the smudge on the wall, acknowledging respectfully the close observation of another child and building on it: "I think the dancer knows who did it." "Right, fear." Another child acknowledges an idea that had not occurred to him on his own, "It's a scary place," realizing that different viewers find different things in a work of art. The different perspectives are not only equally valuable ("What I think matters."), but each child can also learn from the other's perspective ("What you think matters.").

While the story the children were piecing together may not have warmed the hearts or coincided with the interpretations of art historians, the learning that was going on served a different purpose. Where the hard edges of right and wrong answers prevail, we succeed if we both have the same answer. Where the messy boundaries of the arts prevail, we can also succeed when we have different answers from which we learn more about or gain deeper access to whatever art object we are observing. We learn more about each other and ourselves as we reflect on our separate and co-constructed answers, more about collaborative inquiry, and especially we learn to respect each other's different ways of thinking and seeing.

After three quarters of an hour of exciting back and forth about the painting, the children had their own questions, "When was it painted?" "Where is this place in the painting?" "What does the title of this painting mean in English?" These are questions that have factual answers—things to be remembered on which the children could be quizzed after the visit. But the interpretive conversation had begun and these facts were not ends in themselves, things to remember for a test, they were fuel for continuing inquiry.

"1882! Wow, over a hundred years ago and the painting is so now!" One child comments.

"He painted it in Paris? Was that where this was?" another asks.

"No," I respond, "the scene is somewhere in Spain, a place to which Sargent had traveled."

"How did he remember so well?"

"Let's look at sketches he did for the work…" I offer. "Can drawings be like notes made out of words to help you remember the past and plan for work in the future?" I answer their question about *El Jaleo*, "And the name refers either to a dance or to the cheering on of the crowd for a dancer."

"Oh it must be the cheering. Look how they clap and call out and move from side to side. It's cheering."

"Yeah, like in a football game."

In conversations about art, we experience facts in a new context, as breadcrumbs along the path of our journeying into the forest or as catapults into a conversation in which, in our separate interpretations, we may use the facts differently to frame our next idea or question. But your journeying is as valid as mine. As we explore together, we learn how valid and interesting different ways into learning can be and how to celebrate—not tolerate—and benefit from the sorts of differences around which groups and cultures may align.

The product that is a work of art is uniquely marked by ambiguity, a wonderful density of thought that invites multiple interpretations. The act of interpreting that is so tangible in the consideration of a work of art—those created by artists and displayed in an art museum or those made by other children displayed in a school's art room—allows students to risk and enjoy launching their own ideas about a work ("My thinking matters.") and to seek out and enjoy the very different interpretations of others ("Your thinking matters."). The lessons that the arts teach about the skill of interpretation and an attitude of mutual respect may affect the performance of a child in any other discipline or in any other classroom in which student voices are heard and honored. But in ways that cannot be replicated elsewhere, it is the arts in education that introduce these essential aspects of learning and living into the educational repertoire of the child.

Unique Feature 4.
Process Orientation—Inquiry and Reflection

Even as it was the tangible product of my lakeside painting that came to life over half a century later, it was the process involved, specifically my decision to make a swimmer without knowing how, that was the first thing I remembered when I found the work. I had taken a risk. I wasn't pleased with the results, but it was the risk-taking that I remember most. That part of the process of creating the painting, that moment of reflection, "What is missing here?" and of decision, "Should I add this element in this work that I am creating?" was most important to me.

When I look back a lifetime later, after years of studying children's art, I can say that at age 6 when I made the painting, I was deeply immersed in the new world of school, a place where there were "right" ways to say things—like spelling words correctly or making whole sentences—and I took that expectation to the process of making my painting. Where at 3, 4, or even 5, I might be comfortable exploring the "idea" or "feel" of a lake with color and line without attention to the detail of what actually belonged there, at 6, 7, or 8, I was most interested in including the things I knew how to draw correctly: the teepees, the traffic light, the plane. I was no longer fully engaged in expressing my idea of "lake," but not yet limited by conventional constraints of appropriateness in what to include.

It is said that children "draw what they know," implying perhaps what they know of the world. But at a certain age, children draw what they know how to draw. A colleague looking at the drawing as a product exclaimed "Wow, how imaginative you were to include such unexpected elements as the airplane and the traffic light!" But I remembered the process, the comfort zone of doing what I felt I knew how to do and the risky desire to include something new, to reach beyond the edges of what I then saw as the right lines or the agreed-upon parameters for representation. If it is true that to be a good artist you learn the rules and to be a great artist you go on to break them, I was at that moment at a point when I did not have the requisite skills for either.

"Should I add this element here in this work that I am creating?" It was a process-oriented question that had a tangible result imprinted on the product, a result that was neither right nor wrong except insofar as it pleased or met the requirements of the artist, my self-assessment at 6. And those requirements changed over time. At 60, I have no interest in the schematic trees or the formulaic profiles of Native Americans in canoes. Now I value the wild happy strokes of the swimmer, and I study the tiny figures that dot the shoreline or wander through the hills—people that are easily the same height as the homes that I have created for them.

Clearly articulated reflection, a process that is featured in the making of art, develops over time. But from the earliest age, children can attend to the imprint of their process on the product that is their work of art and to the process decisions they are making. At 2, the child will reach for a new piece of paper if it is available when he is ready. Instead of just giving it to him, we can draw his attention to his process. "Done?" we will ask. Instead of just saying "beautiful" to the world of complex lines the 2-year-old has created (see Figure 2.6), we can take our time to reflect on what we see in the work. I trace the lines around the page with my finger,

FIGURE 2.6. Line drawing by 2-year-old child

recreating the movements (process) that the child has used to make the drawing (product). Modeling reflection in this way, I introduce the child to the conversation between maker and viewer that is embodied in a work of art and to the unique features of the arts that we have addressed.

The child's imagination and agency have led to this image that I re-experience by visibly following the lines. My exclamation, "Wow, that is an exciting, big circle!" lets the child know that I feel something from the direction to which his feelings have led him in the work. I interpret the line and the motion behind it as exciting, and he feels the impact of my response. "How did you make these two jagged angles?" I ask, pointing to the angles embedded in the lower right corner of the drawing, while the adult standing next to me is pointing to the same detail and saying, "Hey, there's two Ws." All of us are considering the visible imprint of the child's decision-making (process) on the drawing (product) and the questions we raise do not have right or wrong answers. The two angles are both jagged lines and Ws, no doubt both products of the artist's intention—exploring line and the writing of a letter.

I see the child nodding as we name the colors we find in his painting and know that he knows that we are recreating his process—"Now red, now purple . . ." We let him know that we are interested in what and how he has created through line and color, showing him by attending carefully that we respond to and honor his process. The centrality of process allows children to experience first hand the kind of questions that do not have right or wrong answers (inquiry) and that inform the direction of their thinking on a work in progress (reflection). Let's consider the lessons of inquiry and reflection that emerge from the arts in education's unique emphasis on process:

INQUIRY: The arts in education teach students about questions that make use of information but go beyond right and wrong answers to considerations of, "What do I want to know?"

REFLECTION: The arts in education help students to develop skills of ongoing self-reflection and assessment, moving beyond judgments of good or bad to informed considerations of, "How am I doing and what will I do next?"

The 4th graders considering *El Jaleo* at the Gardner Museum were asked the sort of questions that are associated with and perhaps best accessed by the arts: open-ended questions. If we consider questions that have right or wrong answers as closed, bounded by the known, then we find questions that are open at the opposite pole, unbounded, available to responses that the teacher posing the question may never have considered. Open-ended questions, vividly addressed in the arts, go beyond answers. They use acquired facts as stimulation for new questions, not as benchmarks for learning. In the process of this mode of inquiry that is addressed through the arts, students need constantly to reflect—to assess the shape and determine the direction of their own thinking.

The question I posed about *El Jaleo,* "What ideas or emotions do you see expressed in this work?" is a question that we frequently ask of a poem, a painting, or a play. It is a question that draws on the student's individual experience and analysis of the work. It is an example of inquiry that is open-ended, that goes beyond right or wrong and calls for a reflection on the process of making sense in which the student is involved.

"What do I need to know to begin to respond to this question?" the student considers as she reflects on the nature of the emotion expressed in the work. "I think the painting expresses passion," she responds.

"What makes you think that?" the teacher asks.

Now the student looks for evidence among the visible parts of the image, the powerful colors that are used, the light and shadow, the energy of the figure, the expression on the faces of the figures. They point to passion. But then there is this darkness all about. What else might be going on?

And the teacher goes on: "What would you have called this painting if you had made it yourself?" "What will happen next in this image?" "What questions does this painting ask you?" "What questions do you ask it?" Open-ended questions such as these shed light on the activity of inquiry that is at the heart of making and appreciating art. And we can go on to reflect directly on that activity: "Which of the questions you've posed can you answer with information that you can find in signage in the museum, in books, or on the Internet?" "Which of them can you answer by looking more closely at the work or talking about it with someone else?" "Which of them raise new questions for you, questions about yourself and others that you would not have considered had you not looked carefully at this work?" Questions like these not only invite the student to reflect on her own thinking, but to think directly about the nature of inquiry itself. "What if anything have you learned about yourself and others from looking at this work?"

Open-ended questions demonstrate that both questions and answers are most useful when they generate new questions. This is the basis of inquiry and more broadly of learning. Responding to the open-ended questions raised above, learners move beyond factual information. For example, responding to the question of what the student would have called the painting had he made it, the student realizes, "The painting has a title; this is not about my answering correctly what the name of the painting is. I am being asked to go beyond that fact to identifying with the artist and considering on my own a meaningful title for this work."

In response to the question about what questions the painting asks you and you it, the student realizes that indeed studying the work is not about figuring out the one right answer as to what the painting means. A painting can mean different things to different viewers and in that sense the student is actively making her own meanings out of what the artist has provided. "Does this child remind you of yourself?" the painting might ask the student. "Why is there so much red?" the student might ask of the painting. And from such inquiry-based considerations the student will come to realize, "Yes, the painting does ask questions. I have questions for it. We are in dialogue." In the arts, meaning is made, found, and negotiated out of just such dialogue.

When reflection is prioritized, as it is above, and students are asked about the questions themselves and the ways to go about addressing them, the students are actively involved in a kind of reflection called "metacognition," thinking about thinking. Considering whether available information sufficiently answered their questions, or whether they needed to dialogue with friends or the teacher, students may come to see that, "Some of my questions can be answered quickly with facts; others take longer to explore." Out of such reflection on the process of inquiry students gain a sense of personal autonomy. They come to understand, "My questions have value, draw on the information that I recognize as of interest and importance to me, and open doors to me for more questions that I might never have asked had I not been questioned by this work of art."

We might go so far as to say that as reflective viewers of art, students are as actively engaged in the process of finding meaning in the created work as are thoughtful makers creating works of art. Like artists, they are recreating in their contemplation of a work the process of setting a problem or challenge—posing and addressing questions that matter to them and exploring those questions in the work. In their own art-making, students experience first hand the artist's side of this dialogue, literally setting problems or challenges for themselves (like my unguided creation of a swimmer in my lake) and monitoring (does it meet with my expectations?) and adapting their process. They come to see the importance of revision, of returning to a work in progress and adjusting parts of the whole.

Because of the tangibility of the arts, students see the impact of their thinking (process) on the art object (product), and experience as no other subject will allow the range and importance of their own inquiry and their own ability to assess and direct that process. These are invaluable skills for working in any subject or setting—the ability to ask real questions that lead to further study (inquiry) and the ability to continuously assess, revise, and advance the work (reflection). These essential skills have implications for performance in any arena, but are uniquely acquired through the arts in education.

Unique Feature 5.
Connection—Engagement and Responsibility

The arts are intrinsically human. We know this because as long as there have been tools with which to create, humans have depicted their lives through art—from the walls of caves to objects in graves—in two and three dimensions. We know this because as soon as we give crayon and paper to a child in a remote location of the world who has never used such tools, the child will know what

to do. And she will catch up quickly with the general representational fluidity of children anywhere of comparable age who have
been drawing since preschool.[9] In this age of technology, in the
drawings of their lives that children from around the world share
online, we see cultural influences that differentiate their drawings.
Beyond and within these, however, we find the human connection
poignantly and uniquely expressed through art.

Students feel this human connection through the works they
create in arts classes. This is because those creations—that drawing, that dramatic performance, that found-object construction or
singing of a song—reflect students' imagination, are imprinted
with students' decisions about process and product, and express
in words, gestures, or images feelings and thoughts for others to
experience. Students feel connected to works of art that they study,
like *Romeo and Juliet*, that have survived over time. They are drawn
to the relevance of the universal and timeless themes of great art,
and they feel connected through those works to people who lived
in different times and circumstance.

Similarly, students find connection in contemporary artistic productions, from controversial hip-hop to challenging conceptual art,
because these works reflect the time in which they live and because
students understand that the things they care about are being spoken to and about so that future generations may discover and find
timeless meaning in them. Because of the tangibility of works of art,
students experience connection directly, not just to the work itself
but to the artists who make the work, to the individuals whose stories may be told in the work, and to human beings whom they will
never know who have been touched by the work. When students
look at a painting in a museum, they feel connection to those who
have regarded the work at another time—last week or hundreds
of years ago. Listening to great music on the Internet or car radio,
they feel connection with those across the country experiencing the
same sounds even as they feel connected to dancers who have followed the same choreography that they are learning in dance class.
The arts connect human beings across time and place, and students
feel and are engaged by that connection even as their realizing the
connection across generation and place demands a sense of social
responsibility that the arts awaken.

The social injustices addressed in the artistic expressions of to-day are connected to those addressed throughout history not only because they reflect the continuum of inhumanity that challenges human beings, but because they demonstrate the timeless power of art to embody and convey these human dilemmas. And if art itself does not heal, it inspires healing. The teachers in New York during the 9/11 tragedy knew that the arts held the tools children needed to give shape to their fear and sorrow. They knew that the arts would be the language through which the children could speak to others about the sense they struggled to make out of such violent human destruction. At a time when suspicion was raised about individuals of Muslim origin, those educators knew that through the arts their students would feel connected to children all over the world regardless of their country of origin, religion, or outward appearance. At the same time that the arts illuminate and provide the opportunity to celebrate difference, they also demonstrate and represent the transcendent human connection. We sing, we create objects, we make marks, we dance. We are human beings. Children respond to the humanness of the arts; they care about art-making even when adults suggest it doesn't matter; and their caring connects them to a world of others with whom they become one and of whom they must take care. Let's discuss the two final compelling aspects of arts learning in terms of the clear sense of human connection that the arts uniquely provide:

ENGAGEMENT: The arts in education excite and engage students, awakening attitudes to learning that include passion and joy, and the discovery that "I care."

RESPONSIBILITY: The arts in education connect children to others within and beyond school walls, helping to awaken a sense of social responsibility and action because "I care for others."

The description of artists as dark outsiders who have left the constraints of mainstream life for the freedom of working on their own apart from the responsibilities that tie ordinary people down has been shaken from the trees of stereotype. It has been rewritten by the social responsibility and activism of artists around the world now and throughout history. We see social responsibility in the tireless work of everyday artists collaborating in community arts centers of their own design to educate and help redirect the lives and futures of children and adults—many of whom have been abandoned by the mainstream. We see it in the most visible work of Hollywood celebrities who lend their names or funds or day-to-day efforts to causes ranging from the dearth of arts education in our schools to the need for research into women's cancers and AIDS. Just as works of art frequently address social injustice as a theme, artists frequently address social injustices in their lives beyond the studio.

Children need to study the arts and consider their themes just as they need to meet artists and know the work they do above and beyond, as well as through, the artistic productions they create. Some people say that artists are resented in society because they are so fulfilled by their work. Like teachers, their work should sustain them above and beyond monetary reward. Perhaps this romancing of the hard work that is involved in serious art-making stems from our individual recollections of the deeply engaging process of making art. That engagement—carrying us away from the drudgeries of the day to a place of full involvement and concentration—has been likened to a kind of flow,[10] a mesmerizing involvement. Art teachers over and over describe the atmosphere of their classrooms as "joyful" because the energy and engagement that children radiate, the often noisy level of process-based discussion, and the excitement and passion of making something that was not there before, is quite simply exciting. Children care about what they do and make in the arts, and caring is essential to a child's education.

Ask anyone what they remember from school and you are likely to hear that they remember the time their painting was displayed in a school show, or the time they did or didn't get the lead in the school play, or the time they were asked to sing a solo or, alas, to move their lips and not sing. Some adults can recite the lines or sing the words of a solo performance from grade school. Others remember their mothers sewing costumes or painting sets for the school play, or the trip to the art museum in 1st grade where they felt themselves as tiny beings wandering on marble floors through vast hallways with walls filled with limitless treasures. No matter how the arts are marginalized, children who experience the arts care about and remember them. We need the arts because children's caring and engagement are essential parts of a good education.

Because of the emotion and empathy that the arts allow, because of the heights of imagination and possibilities that children enjoy, because of the respect for multiple perspectives (including their own) that children experience, and because of the thinking skills of questioning and monitoring their own thought processes that the arts invite, children need the arts in education. All these aspects taken together contribute to the caring and engagement that the arts in education instill in our children. Beyond that, the arts connect our children to one another and give them, like artists, the opportunity to express their fears and concerns, and to think beyond to what else might be and what part they might play in turning the tide.

From imagination to social responsibility, the arts teach our children about what it is to be human and enable them to experience their humanity in thought and in action. When doubters say we haven't time or money or space for the arts, we must ask what they think will happen to our schools without the arts. Surely none of us wants to deny our children the opportunity to experience their individual and shared humanity as the arts in education uniquely allow. After years of extraneous arguments, doubters may simply need to be informed or reminded of what the arts actually provide. So that we may all work together, advocates need to communicate more directly with school board members, superintendents, parents, principals, and holders of the strings of possibility for our children's lives in school. I am hoping that the discussions so far and the tools that now follow will serve in that most crucial effort.

Advocating for the Arts in Education

7-year-old's drawing of an archer

Medium: crayon on paper

PRELUDE: MIGHT FAILURE WORK
AS A PLATFORM FOR ARTS IN EDUCATION ADVOCACY?

As a veteran advocate for the arts in education, I am—as is surely clear by now—beyond weary of the unrelenting discussions and debates about whether the arts help children with academics.[1] When was it decided that academic subjects were by definition non-arts courses? When was it decided that over here are academics and way over there are the arts? When in the splitting and sorting of curriculum did we designate some subjects, like math and science, as essential to learning, and others—specifically the arts—as bastions of emotion and play, extraneous to the purposes of school? Certainly the division has weighed heavily on art education's troubled and defensive history. In recent decades, advocates made the decision that they must lift the soft curtain of feeling perpetually associated with arts learning and showcase the arts as "good for thinking."

As we have discussed, this new direction was hospitable to what is called a "cognitive" or thinking approach to the arts. It welcomed questions such as what arts learning may have to do with brain development, whether the arts can make our children read and write with more fluency, and whether music ability goes hand in hand with mathematical skills. Over time, studies were assembled to probe issues such as these and hopefully demonstrate the value of arts learning in terms of outcomes related to any number of hard-edged subjects and skills. But these studies were proved frail, perhaps driven more by advocates' desire for certain outcomes than by reliable scientific inquiry.

As a result, it was decided that we had to have better studies or admit that there were better justifications for the arts than their impact on children's performance in non-arts subjects. We have been so driven to measure the impact of the arts in education that we began to forget that their strength lies beyond the measurable. The arts, like most really significant human behaviors, defy measurement. Can we score character, compassion, empathy, vision, imagination, self-esteem, humanity? But "humanity" was a word like "joy" that seemed to place the arts in extracurricular time slots. So we jumped in with outcomes of arts learning that are valued in academics like "critical thinking," and school smarts like "stick-to-it-iveness." And it seemed it would take forever for arts advocates to embrace a different mantle. And it has.

When will we stop with all the justifications and start facing the fact that if academics were more like the arts, more kids might show up and stay in school? Will we ever get to a place where we bravely assert that the arts may be the most important subjects we can offer our children in school? Will advocates ever point with pride to the different issues that the arts address and to the different ways in which they are taught and assessed, and say, "Oh, non-arts subjects, struggling as you do for the interest and affection of so many of your students, you can be more like us." When do we reconstruct our position as arts advocates from one of weak explanation to one of strong example?

It was there, between weariness, impatience, and the same old same old that I thought: Perhaps the time is now, and perhaps the place to begin is with the ways in which the arts help students deal with what non-arts subjects do less well. The arts have always quietly served that purpose. Behavior problems, children with special needs, potential dropouts—these students are frequently sent to the art room where there is more space and opportunity for difference. Art teachers are experts and unsung heroes in the education of challenged and challenging students. I could begin by singing these teachers' praises and considering what it was they did that made their classrooms more comfortable for a wide range of students. But what was it that they did? How do the arts provide safer places for children at risk of failure? I decided to address the answer to this question straight on. My first new advocacy topic would be "failure."

Imagine me if you will, in my new no-apology mode of advocacy, addressing a room crowded with skeptics who have heard all the usual songs we arts advocates sing but who have graciously made themselves available for a new platform. I approach the podium:

"A frequent rationale for including the arts in education is that they provide opportunities for success to children who do not succeed in other areas. I would like to propose that an equally good reason is that they provide opportunities for failure to children who succeed in other areas. Indeed, the arts provide opportunities for failure to all kinds of children. This may be one of the most important reasons they should be included on a regular basis in general education. Making sense in, through, and of art is demanding work, requiring the use of sensibilities and skills not central to performance in other disciplines. Indeed, the arts pose unique challenges to learners, challenges for which non-arts subjects may not have prepared them well.

The student who has learned not only to think clearly in the medium of mathematics, but even to perform well on a math test, may be overwhelmed by the expectation that his eyes and hands are meant to shape something out of wet clay. The student who has mastered the structure of a five-paragraph essay may be intimidated by the challenge of creating her own dance, just as the student who has demonstrated the ability to write up an experiment in science may be reluctant to invest her voice and emotion in the portrayal of a role on stage.

'All the more reason to exclude the arts,' some may respond. 'Why break the stride of students who are doing well in school?' 'All the more reason to include them,' I argue, 'to provide children who have bought into our preoccupation with unqualified success with the chance to have daring, edgy, generating, and important encounters with failure.'

For artists, mistakes open doors for their work. The painter Jack Levine described the process of coming daily to a work in progress and seeking out what was wrong. It was there, he explained, that he found a place to begin; one had to 'work around' what was right. Artist Robert Motherwell recounted that, in starting a body of new work, 'every painting was a mistake,' and the art he ended up with was 'the process of correcting that mistake.' New York art teacher Charles Taylor, one of my dearest mentors, is remembered for stomping around the art room, bellowing to his students, 'Every mistake is on purpose. Figure it out!'

Arts encounters with mistake making, with facing and building on what's wrong, have tremendous implications for learning in other disciplines. But they are uniquely accessed in the safety of arts classrooms where risk-taking and failure fruitfully abound. Safe from the hard edges of right and wrong answers, safe from agendas that exclude multiple perspectives, safe from assessments that are sure of themselves, arts classrooms provide opportunities for students to explore the messy, uncertain realities that preoccupy their lived lives within and beyond the world of school. Children who are successful in school skills need these safe havens for failure as surely as those who struggle in other areas.

We must ask, who are the children that we describe as having success in art but not in other areas? We expect that they are the artistically talented few who should seek training beyond the limited resources of school. And who are those students who may excel in standardized modes but find discomfort in messy artistic expression? They may be the academically talented few who should find comfort in their mastery of arenas that really matter.

But these distinctions are facetious. I am not seriously interested in such compartmentalization of our children. Regardless of the criteria we use or the arenas we consider, all students need to be able to encounter and make sense of success. But, as importantly, all students need to be able to encounter and make sense of failure.

While we rightly shy away from deficit models through which we 'problematize' our children, we need to find a comfortable way, perhaps even a positive way, to make sense of the things that are hard for them or the areas in which they fail. It is not always success that drives our children's interest. There are as many successful artists, teachers, and CEOs driven by persistence as by success. Are we no longer surprised by the many adults who succeed mightily in life even though they struggled mightily in school? Was their failure somehow a launching pad for what was to come next?

Why this emphasis on success as the optimal and necessary outcome? Do we learn and grow from our successes? Can we ever realistically assess our performance if we fear mistakes and failure? Don't all our children deserve the opportunity to experience failure in a medium that invites revision and growth? The arts offer children positive experiences with failure, invaluable experiences with setting the bar higher than we can reach, with knowing that the passion lies in the attempt, not the realization, that failure can be clarifying and generative, that 'failure' is part of a process in which I am involved, not a product that you can call me.

At a time when standardized testing is supported even in the arenas of artistic expression, we need to equip our children with an understanding of performance as a developing process. A preoccupation with outcome-based testing threatens a student's crucial conception of his or her life as a work in progress. The arts can provide our children with the experience of imprinting themselves in media that challenge measurement.

A celebration of agreed-upon standards may negatively affect a student's incentive to explore personal educational values and goals. The arts provide opportunities for making individual decisions that have immediate consequence. 'I can see what that orange did to my painting.' 'I can hear how the increase in the volume of my own voice changed the meaning of that song.' 'I can feel the difference in the breadth of my movement in this dance.' And these decisions may all seem to me wrong and therefore be the source of future revision—a place to begin."

As I speak these final lines, I hear thunderous applause. I am convinced by this reception, albeit fictitious, that when advocates speak honestly to those they wish to persuade, when they dare to speak about what matters as if their listeners will care, anything will be possible—an argument in favor of failure, and perhaps even a secure place in education for the arts.

WHAT COUNTS AS ADVOCACY

The most obvious understanding of advocacy can be found in the dictionary: "pleading the case for. . . ." Parent advocates plead the case for the arts when they stand before school boards protesting the minimal (if any) attention given to the arts in their children's schools. Educators and researchers plead the case for the arts when they identify and apply for sources of financial support for arts-based programs or investigations. And artist-educator advocates refuel their engines with parental support, the positive results of programs and research studies, and the energy derived from the sense of common cause experienced at professional arts education conferences.

In the preceding prelude, I positioned myself at the podium, speaking before a group of doubters about the importance of the arts in education. I took the approach of "waking them up" with a topic that might surprise them, the virtues of failure, and of speaking to what the arts do that other subjects do not do well. I hope that I succeeded in conveying the risk-taking and alternativeness of sharing these views with individuals who were not members of the choir. If the scene were real, it would seem more likely that I would receive applause from a group of like-minded advocates at an arts education conference than from a group of skeptical superintendents of schools.

One of the reasons that an instrumental position on arts learning—the "helpmate to non-arts" perspective—may flourish among advocates is that it doesn't pit the arts against other subjects. Advocates are wary of alienating the very folks they want to win over by suggesting, "Well, math only does this, but the arts do all that." This concern is not unfounded. Even in schools that focus on the arts in education,[2] where the curriculum is emblematic of a belief that the arts are of equal (or more) importance than other subjects, there is a natural rivalry between the arts and non-arts strands. Because the situation differs from the mainstream—the arts are prioritized and sometimes the academics are given short shrift—the challenge of engaging teachers of different subjects in a dialogue of mutual respect is especially clear.

Similarly, advocates may be reluctant to suggest that non-arts teachers could learn a lot from arts teachers. "Teacher and subject bashing" are dangerous faux pas in the quest to speak across disciplines and consider openly what our students need to learn and grow. When advancing my views that "beautiful" is an inadequate if not dismissive response to children's artwork, I have been approached by early childhood teachers who ask, "But what else should we say?" It was their genuine caring interest that woke me up to the fact that it was not enough to criticize teachers for what they did in good faith; it was important to offer alternatives for them to consider and perhaps add to their repertoire.

Almost every time that I have stepped up to wage the good fight for the arts in education, I have been astonished by the voices of support that come from unexpected regions. Like Don Quixote railing my sword at windmills, I have been unable, except in discourse, to find a real enemy. In arts conferences like the one described in the prelude in Chapter 2, advocates console each other with the fact that "we" know that it matters that on account of the arts, students come to school more faithfully and envision for themselves a viable future, but "they" only care about quantitative outcomes like elevating test scores. I have been looking for "them" for a very long time.

Several years ago, I was invited to give a keynote talk at a summer meeting of New York state superintendents. These school leaders graciously welcomed me to their meeting, and in the introduction to my talk they described my work in the arts in education with open celebration. Nonetheless, tireless advocate that I was, I began my talk with an adversarial air, even as I thanked them for inviting me. I described the dilemma of arts in education advocates meeting behind closed doors and discussing what "they" care about and explained that I was most excited about speaking at a conference of superintendents because they were "they." The room froze. Had they not realized that from the perspective of arts in education advocates, superintendents held the keys to the very schools that locked out the arts? They listened politely to my talk, and at the end I did what I should have done at the start. I asked them what they thought.

At that moment, the room lit up. I had a presentation pad on which I jotted down their comments and I could barely keep up. Did I know how art teachers complained to them that in interdisciplinary educational efforts it was always the art teacher who was asked to go to the mainstream classrooms and find out how to integrate the arts? The art teachers wanted the mainstream teachers to go to the art room to see how they could integrate their subjects. How could a superintendent make that happen? Did I have helpful ideas?

Did I realize that not all art teachers want to have schedules like those of non-art subject teachers? They chose to teach because their jobs were part time and left them plenty of time to work in their studios. Could I help find art teachers who wanted to work the same schedules as non-arts teachers? They noticed that I made fun of the "art cart"—that wheel-in tea cart filled with crayons and paper for table-top art—as an inadequate means of providing arts education. Did I have ideas for raising the funds needed to create artrooms in their schools? Did I know that some children listen for the wheels of that cart with excitement and that some art-cart teachers would quit if they were asked to oversee classrooms and navigate the discipline issues involved in that larger effort?

I was fascinated by all they taught me that I had never heard at arts education conferences. I was embarrassed to say that I had been too busy defending the arts to consider some of these practical issues and that I came to them with theoretical arguments instead of plans. Like many arts advocates, I was more about recommendations for action than actual plans of action. Perhaps plans are what happen after a group of string holders has been convinced of the worth of the arts. Perhaps it is not part of advocacy to plan. Advocates plead the case; others put it into action.

If the lessons from my experience are not then about changing the course of advocacy, they are surely about changing the texture. Advocates need not identify an enemy to gain steam for their efforts. They need to learn what is and isn't happening in the arts, and they need to listen to those who oversee the planning and enactment of curricula. As it is in teaching and learning, listening is key in the advocate's quest. And just as the best teaching happens when we expect the most from our students, the most effective advocacy will happen when we begin with the assumption of mutual caring and proceed with an attitude of respect. If not the planning and actual enactment, what is it that counts as advocacy in this far-reaching and most meaningful conversation about our children's needs for learning in the arts?

Advocacy efforts reach from individual to group to local to national levels and are informed by and support national organizations dedicated to the cause. On the individual level, that parent who meets with the school principal to launch a protest about the lack of arts in the school or to personally thank the administrator for the inclusion of arts learning in the school day (and no doubt to ask for more frequency) is an advocate. That parent who serves at the group level on the city's creative arts committee, raising funds and arranging visits from artists and performance groups throughout the city's schools? She is also an advocate. That intervention, the demonstration of the enrichment of curriculum by a visiting artist or group, is an act of advocacy as surely as the many meetings staged with school administrators to institute the school-wide creative arts committee. Parents or groups of involved parents may be on the phone supporting the election of public officials—school committee members, state senators, governors—who have declared the arts as a priority in their proposed improvements of public schools city and statewide. They are all advocates: both the parents on the phone and the politicians who propose positive change.

The members of the city arts council that picketed in front of school administrative offices when the decision was made to eliminate the arts from middle schools were all arts-in-education advocates. They got the decision reversed and as an honoring gesture started a series of annual principal luncheons at which principals who supported the arts in their schools were honored. After a few years of these luncheons, the names of principals being honored increased threefold. That arts council's creation of the principal's luncheon series was an act of advocacy that reaped impressive results. Each year an expert on the effect of the arts on education is invited to speak at the principals' luncheon. That speaker is an advocate, as are the council members who invited her and the principals who are increasing the amount of time dedicated to the arts in their schools.

State arts councils that fund collaborations between arts institutions and public schools are deep in the workings of arts education advocacy. When our research team began its study of community art centers in economically challenged communities, we called centers around the country to say we were interested in their work. At the end of each preliminary phone call, we asked if the center directors had any questions. I spotted one of my research assistants tearing up as she listened to the response to that simple question. "What did he say?" the rest of us asked. He said he wanted to thank us for studying community art centers. He said that he and others have worked without recognition for decades and the thought that we all wanted to learn from what they did meant more than he could express. Research can be advocacy, even when it doesn't set out to prove claims that will serve advocates.

On the national level, arts advocates have coalesced into groups that seek to influence government policies with regard to the arts in education. Advocates working in and through these groups with the support of government resources and/or dedicated private foundations have issued reports and books that fuel the discourse and offer apparent evidence of the benefits of the arts in education from which to draw in "pleading for" the cause. Beyond recommendations for related research agendas, publications of relevant reports, strategic partnerships, and scheduled meetings of minds, national arts education advocacy groups claim within the purview of their accomplishments the creation of National Standards for the Arts (like the standards established for non-arts subjects) and recognition by federal education acts (such as Goals 2000 and No Child Left Behind) of the arts as essential to schooling or of equal mettle to other subjects in schools. Without a doubt, perpetuation and advancement of these organizations and public policy recommendations supporting the arts in education that ultimately emerge from their efforts are all the work of advocacy. Advocates plead the case for, fight the good fight, and find ways in from the outside place assigned to arts learning.

But a teacher's demonstration of the worth of the arts to any student, parent, or administrator is powerful advocacy in its own right. Furthermore, regardless of the setting, there is no teacher bravely using the arts in her pedagogy who is exempt from having to defend them and to explain to others why she is doing whatever she does. Those of us who incorporate the arts in our teaching; or insist that our children engage in arts activities, go to museums, concerts, or plays; or remind the principal that 30 minutes every other week is not enough time to learn any subject—we are all advocates.

Further, we know our advocacy will work because most of us are the beneficiaries of similar advocacy efforts that allowed us in our youth to have positive experiences in the arts. Our families or schools introduced us to art museums or concerts, or we had the opportunity to participate in school musicals or plays, or we wrote a poem that was noticed by an adult or a peer, or we found that a song or image that we made gave us great satisfaction. Some of us remember a time when an adult or friend told us, "Wow, you're an artist," and we recognized that our pleasurable creative activity was worthy of particular attention. But not all of us have had such experiences.

Years ago as a writing teacher at Wheelock College, a school that trains many fine early childhood educators, I asked the students to write about a teacher who had "done it" for them—who had inspired in them the desire to teach. Expecting laudatory stories of mentorship, I was astonished to see that most of the essays described negative experiences—times when a teacher had abused her power and humiliated a student or had made all the students feel inadequate. These writers wrote about their understanding of the power of teaching and the importance of honoring that position. They vowed on account of these negative examples to grow up to be teachers who would protect children and make learning a joyful experience.

So it is with many arts advocates. Some of us remember the shame of belting out an offbeat note while singing in chorus, or the embarrassment of feeling that our bodies were too big for dance, our hands too unsteady for drawing, our language too limited for poetry, our voices too small for the stage. Even in these burning memories, we acknowledge how much artistic performance meant to us as young people. On their account, we advocate not only for more arts teaching, but also for quality arts education. We want our children to gain the requisite skills for artistic expression, but also the self-esteem that comes from knowing that they have identified an idea or feeling that is uniquely theirs and that has been expressed as only they can do it. "That is my mark on that paper, my careful step in that dance, my decision to make that object that big, my effort that has put before us something that was not there before."

The thoughtless gestures of the educator who overlooks our artistic efforts, doesn't take the time to say more than "fine" about our drawings, or tells us we haven't said the "right" thing about a poem or dance—these responses perpetuate the devaluation of artistic activity as well as the myth that the arts are reserved for the very few. But the teacher, parent, administrator, or community arts educator who takes the time to regard and experience a child's artistic performance and to respond thoughtfully and carefully to what that child is saying through art—these adults are advocates as surely as if they had sat in Washington at any of the meetings of proponents of arts education deciding what the latest recommendations for action should be.

Let us not forget that just as education happens child by child, so does advocacy. Each new occasion of availability to artistic experience provides a moment to be persuaded and to care in ways that will change the scene for others. Persistent and talented teachers of the arts are like that famous pebble tossed in the water making ever-widening rings. They take their caring and knowledge and change the field incrementally, demonstrating in their teaching what the arts can do, representing in their thoughtful discourse what they have learned about arts learning. Obviously, the efforts of coalitions and initiatives that gain the attention of movers and shakers on the highest level of policy-making are invaluable imprints of advocacy writ large. But those behind-the-scenes efforts are no more important than what can happen front and center on the stage of educational reform, where dedicated teachers advocate child by child for the future of the arts in education.

PRACTICAL CHALLENGES

The young actors from the local university's school of fine arts were planning to visit the 4th-grade class at a neighborhood school. It was a distressed school, fraught with multiple challenges ranging from decay of the physical plant to low attendance and test scores. The teacher, Ms. Levine, had heard arts education advocates say that there was evidence that drama—acting out scenes from plays in the classroom—could help students with reading skills.[3] Levine was open to trying it out with her group of students, whose reading skills were well below expectation. Meeting with the actors, the teacher asked if the play to be performed for the class would be one that she and her students could read together before and after the actors' visit.

Funded by a grant entitled "Changing Lives through the Arts," the young actors were not interested in doing scripted scenes. Their work was informed by advocacy efforts that had moved away from selling the arts as helpmates to school-based skills towards a more generalized view of the arts as agents to social reconciliation. Accordingly, the actors were trained in a form of theater in which the children would be the actors and structured improvisation would lead them in the recreation of encounters with difficult decisions that they must actually make in their lives. "For example," one of the young actors explained, "we'll do a scene in which a child is offered drugs. Will she try them or reject them? How will the scene end? We'll let the children play out alternatives and learn that they have choices and can make a difference."

"Wait a minute," the teacher protested, "You'll come in here and bring up these difficult issues and then leave me with all the emotional mess you've stirred up? Who do you think you are, intruding on my classroom? I want my children to experience real theater that lets them know that reading and writing words is very important." Ms. Levine had been willing to have a bunch of actors in her room, even during the precious period that she devoted to language arts, but only if their visit would help her students with academic skills. The actors were interested in helping students to develop life skills through the dramatic recreation, in the safe space of the classroom, of emotionally charged situations. The teacher felt she'd avoided a "pseudo arts" avalanche by refusing to let the actors visit. The actors felt that once again, a stick-in-the-mud classroom teacher had thwarted progress in the arts.

While the actors may have felt themselves on the cutting edge of innovative uses of the arts in schools, the negotiation of decision-making and emotion has a long history with the arts. Way back when, Greek tragedy was about portraying terrible things happening to bigger-than-life heroes with whom the audience could identify and on that account, feel self-respect and relief. "Wow," the Greek philosopher Aristotle told us (in eloquent language), the audience would think, "that hero has problems like mine but much bigger. One small mistake in judgment and the world collapses around him."[4] In what Aristotle called *catharsis*, the audience was meant further to feel relief, experiencing some version of, "I am enlarged by my identification with that bigger-than-life king and deeply relieved that what happened, happened to him and not to me."

Throughout history, from the purging of emotion that is catharsis to notions of personal and physical healing, there have been therapeutic associations with the arts. Now arts therapists ask children to make drawings or to play act scenes to learn what problems they face—problems that are perhaps too awful to put in everyday words. The arts provide alternative languages—drama, drawing, dance, or music—through which experience can be approached.

But many arts advocates have avoided advancing a therapeutic approach to arts learning, assuming it would be associated with the charge of "touchy feely" that has, in actuality if not in discourse, isolated the arts from the core subjects in schools. The thinking vs. feeling dialogue has been a resonant refrain throughout the history of advocacy for the arts in education in this country. It is particularly noticeable from the time of the progressive era, when the arts were relatively secure, to the present, when the oft-tested disciplines of math and reading challenge the security of all subjects, and especially the arts.

In the early part of the twentieth century, during what was called the progressive era of education, influential thinkers were suggesting that we needed to attend to what they called "the whole child."[5] What was education about if not giving children the tools to craft a life beyond school walls, a life made up of rich emotional balance as well as academic success? Arts-hospitable perspectives ranged from a view that claimed that arts learning would help children experience life artfully, making of their ordinary days aesthetic encounters with experience, to the understanding that the arts were uniquely linked to creative energy, essential to the development of the whole child. The visual arts classroom became a place for free expression and untutored explorations of media, an arena for the release of energy and the expression of feeling in powerful and important ways.[6]

But by the 1950s, computers arrived on the scene, as did the Soviet Union's impressive success launching the space rocket, Sputnik. Entering the space race, thinking more technically about the workings of the human mind, the United States demanded that schools become conspicuously concerned with scientific thinking and the relevant skills that would advance the nation to new frontiers. While the arts began to fall into the area of subjects relegated to extracurricular time, arts advocates argued, with little success, that the creativity that children acquired in the arts classroom would serve them well in any arena. The time had come, it was reckoned, for a different sort of advocacy, the reframing of arts activities and performance as serious intellectual science-like endeavors that deserved equal time and attention within the school day.

Arts education movements in the seventies and eighties had titles reflecting this new focus. The Getty-funded Discipline-Based Art Education (DBAE) featured teaching and learning based on the key activities of the discipline of visual art. Specifically, these mutually informative, equally valued activities were aesthetics (philosophic considerations), art history (factual background), art criticism (value-based judgments), and art making (hands-on production). The advocate's claim implicit in this approach was that the arts could be taught in classrooms like other subjects and even, like other subjects, by classroom teachers. But some advocates argued that presenting the arts as like other subjects would compromise what was different and special about arts learning. It might even lead educators to think that the arts could be tested like other subjects, with multiple choice pencil-and-paper tests. That would happen next.

Supported by the Rockefeller Foundation, the Educational Testing Service (ETS) launched an effort with Harvard's Project Zero and the Pittsburgh Public Schools to explore the idea of an arts SAT. Rather than the test they imagined, the initiative resulted in a curriculum called Arts PROPEL,[7] designed for and piloted with visual art, music, and imaginative writing. Out of the notion that you can't test what you're not teaching, PROPEL featured assessment intertwined with curriculum around the cognitive activities of production (making a work of art), perception (attending to, contextualizing the work), and reflection (directing its progress).

These two curricular frameworks incited a debate about the place of making art in the learning process. For DBAE, art making was one of four equally valued activities, for PROPEL it was central. It seems timely to mention that the advocates involved in this process included the Getty and Rockefeller foundations that dedicated funds to the advancement and recognition of the arts in education. The researchers who helped innovate and develop these high profile efforts, Eliot Eisner for DBAE and Howard Gardner and Dennie Wolf for PROPEL, were also advocates. And so were the many schools and museums around the country that stood up to be counted as experimenting with DBAE, as were the Pittsburgh Public Schools that helped develop PROPEL. The players in curricular efforts like this, including the vocal participants in the art-making debate who sided with one approach or neither, were all advocates. Educators, students, and those scholars who, through writing and lecturing critiqued and celebrated the two programs, were also advocates. Their various attentive perspectives let folks in education know that what was happening in the arts was important, in fact, vital to education.

Long after the smoke settled, and the fire was no doubt noticed more by educators and researchers in the arts than by others in schools, the two approaches may seem to be more similar than different. In terms of the feeling and thinking debate, both approaches were cognitive and attended to the call for arts making, appreciating, and learning to be more about thought than emotion. In such soil has been planted the more recent and frequently mentioned inquiries into arts learning literally improving cognitive skills in non-arts areas. The Mozart Effect claimed that listening to Mozart would raise the IQs of babies, and the commercial products that have emerged from that widely challenged claim have influenced a generation of children.[8]

Infants in car seats quiet from their crying at the sound of a Mozart sonata. Toddlers call for "Einstein" instead of Mickey Mouse to be screened on their television. Regardless of commercial intention, it's all arts advocacy from a cognitive approach. The arts make you smarter. Early music participation puts a spot on your brain that you would not otherwise have. Whatever the claim, it excites parents looking for easy ways to make their kids more competitive in schools. Will the children whose parents have tried to make them smarter by introducing them at an early age to Mozart, Beethoven, or Bach (all via DVDs with plastic toys moving to the music) end up doing better in school? Will they as well be particularly or incidentally attached to the emotive power of music? Only time will tell.

Into the twenty-first century, reconsidering traditions of advancing emotional expression and honoring the range of thinking skills accessed by the arts, arts education has entered the postmodern landscape with a view of art as agent to positive social change.

Examples can be found in collaborative efforts like the half-mile long mural known as the Great Wall in Los Angeles, created as an historical tribute to interracial harmony by a diverse group of youth and community members organized by activist artist Judith Baca and her vibrant organization SPARC (Social and Public Art Resource Center). SPARC is dedicated to creating public art that fosters cross-cultural understanding and dialogue.[9]

Among other socially responsible activities, the Youth Insights program at New York's Whitney Museum of American Art brings teen exhibit guides into senior citizen centers.[10] The well-trained young museum emissaries use these visits to prepare elderly people for a trip to the museum, or simply to share reproductions of museum images. Either way, works of art stimulate cross-generational conversations that broaden the horizons of everyone involved.

Working in multiple ways throughout communities, contemporary artists stage performance and conceptual pieces as public art within the community, often accompanying their social commentary with educational materials. Mary Jacob's Culture in Action in Chicago included a number of artists creating as art parades, billboards, a block party, and a permanent youth program.[11] A new view of social action as art speaks to the traditions of social commentary and responsibility that have long been shared by artists in all disciplines, even as it challenges traditional views of works of art as fixed entities to be enjoyed in museums, theaters, and concert halls.

Public art, most frequently associated with statues of heroes, monuments to historical events, or abstract artistic sculptures, is now being redefined by artists who say, "That work I do with the youth in my community, inviting them to confront and comment on the pressing issues of their time—that work is also a work of art." Current conversations about the shape and function of art necessarily inform the new arguments that twenty-first-century advocates will launch.

Advocates need to keep up with the facts that surround the state of arts education in their region, state, and the country. They need to follow current efforts to lay bare the details of how much art is taught and where and how and by whom and to how many students.[12] But equally, they need to keep up with the fascinating debates that fire the energies and intentions of artists and arts educators. The art world is engaged in an ongoing discussion of what counts as art, and the education world is constantly reflecting on the content (Fine art? Child art? Visual culture on a broader scale?) and substance (Making? Viewing? Considering social implications?) of art education. The notion of art as social action may have particular implications for both worlds.

Against this backdrop, actors, like those entering Ms. Levine's classroom,[13] are not involved in a kind of art education that is about the release of emotion involved in a Greek tragedy or the kind of imitative and interpretive thinking associated with the discipline of theater. Rather, it is about theater as a medium for making kids' lives better and thereby perhaps even making better the communities in which they live. Those young artists are seeking to contribute to positive social action through art. And in her effort to improve her student's academic performance through art, so is Ms. Levine.

Ms. Levine expected that by reading and performing the content of a great play, her children would have the opportunity to have hands-on experiences with words, and through the artful activities associated with words, gain new understanding of the importance and possibilities of what they were learning in school. The young actors were eager to step away from the traditions of theater that separated audience from actor, performance from reality, and to put the medium of theater to tangible use as an agent through which students could thoughtfully consider and reconsider the importance of their lived lives. Both parties had the welfare of the children in mind, and both Ms. Levine and the actors had ideas about using art beyond the immediate moment of performance.

Had teacher and actors had more time for dialogue before the visit, they might have developed a plan in which their respective interests could both be served. Planning and follow-up activities are essential to the success of any visiting artist's contribution to the classroom. Structured activities might further the positive discourse around decision making that the artists started without destabilizing the order in Ms. Levine's classroom.

No matter how they worked it out, Ms. Levine's query about the "emotional mess" associated with any rich artistic experience does not reflect the paranoia of a "stick-in-the mud" classroom teacher.

The arts, so visibly associated with feeling *and* thinking, invite a different level of attention, engagement, self-exploration, and risk taking than other subjects do. While artists working in the community seem ready to risk dealing with young people's challenging feelings, teachers in schools, surrounded by pressing academic demands and impossible constraints on time, may be cautious about venturing down such perilous straits. Sometimes, however, as was demonstrated by the teachers confronting 9/11 in New York City and in classrooms all around the country, we may have little choice.

Do we push the arts further and further out of the arena in order to keep schools more apparently tidy and manageable? Or can we place the arts at the center as models and resources for all the teaching and learning that we do? What if the actors knew more of the constraints with which Ms. Levine was dealing in the day-to-day world of her school? Might they not have been able to incorporate *Romeo and Juliet* into a paradigm in which student decision making about issues of vital importance could also be addressed? How do arts advocates, like the young actors whose talents reach so many children, and Ms. Levine, who as a teacher sets the tone for valuing or devaluing the arts, remember that if they cannot speak productively across sympathetic arenas, they will never persuade those whose sympathies are not in line? Time and respect and collaboration are essential for the advancement of the arts in education.

Just as it would be beneficial for the young actors to incorporate the teacher's curricular needs, imagine if Ms. Levine had the time to learn more about the actors' skills and ambitions and to consider the techniques they were eager to introduce. Perhaps she might say, "Ah yes, that sounds great. We're considering decision making across the curriculum, and of course that includes issues of concern in our students' lived lives. Improvisation may be a great tool for me to use in all the subjects that I teach. Let's give it a go."

The urge to label and exclude must be overcome as we move forward to incorporate acceptance with expectation, flexibility with integrity, and the messy lived world of emotion with the structured ambitions of thought. Arts advocates moving further into the twenty-first century need to be mindful of the teachings of the past, respectful of the constraints of the present, and hopeful about the possibilities of the future. Out of these considerations and all that has come before, certain guidelines emerge for advocacy moving forward. These are delineated as Don'ts and Do's in the next section.

ADVOCACY DON'TS AND DO'S

We have seen that arts advocates work in different arenas. There are the immediate territories of small "a" advocacy that include vocal parents, creative teachers, students, researchers, persuasive writers, and local organizers. And there are the far-reaching realms of big "A" advocates who work in Washington or through major foundations and advocacy organizations, influencing policy that may affect education nationwide. Based on the notion that advocates moving forward need to be mindful of the teachings of the past, respectful of the constraints of the present, and hopeful about the possibilities of the future, the following seven pairs of don'ts and do's may help fuel and moderate the range of efforts of twenty-first century arts education agents of change.

1. Polarization vs. Collaboration

The "We/They" Dilemma. **DON'T** play the "we" versus "they" game—assuming that "we" care about the development of attentive, caring, whole human beings, while "they" only care about the advancement of test scores. Don't forget that "they" (individuals with different expectations for teaching and learning) may be our best allies in changing a system that, by wearing blinders and leaving out alternative views, threatens all subjects and students.

The "We/Us" Approach. **DO** assume that we are all on the same side in supporting students. Recognize that we all suffer together (albeit in different ways) administrative constraints that intrude on what we know to be our best teaching and learning practices. Be sure to include constituencies beyond the choir in conferences and other arts education initiatives. If we work together to hear and attend to the challenges that we all face, we will be more likely to develop a collaborative foundation that provides us all with broader support.

2. Overextension vs. Concentration

The "We Can Do That Too" Excuse. **DON'T** say, "Oh sure, the arts can do that too. Arts learning can teach reading, math, or social studies, improve test scores in non-arts subjects, raise IQ, and even be tested like other subjects on standardized tests!" While an inflexible "art for art's sake" attitude may not serve us fully, don't lose sight of what's special about what students learn from the arts as you bargain for a secure place in the curriculum.

The "We Do This" Explanation. **DO** remind doubters that, on account of what makes the arts unique, they teach students uniquely what other subjects do not. You must concede that some skills particularly well accessed through arts learning—like the ability to ask questions, probe deeply, attend closely, admit multiple points of view, and take risks in personal expression—may have positive effects on student learning in other subjects. Of most importance, however, is that these abilities are specifically addressed through the arts in education, as is the knowledge of how to communicate and understand meanings within and across cultures through the languages of art.

3. Isolation vs. Investigation

"Nobody Cares" Funding Blinders. **DON'T** assume that particular foundations, government organizations, administrations, and other sources of funding don't care about the arts. Don't forget that arts learning has found support in Democratic and Republican administrations, from grassroots local arts councils as well as wealthy private large foundations. And arts education has found creative venues in progressive as well as standards-based educational movements. Be sure not to overlook openings for financial support for arts education by stereotyping and rejecting potential resources without searching for opportunities.

"There Must Be a Way" Research. **DO** explore all aspects of requests for proposals to see if there are unexpected invitations for arts-related initiatives or hidden possibilities for bringing the arts

into the fold. If there's funding for teaching Shakespeare in urban schools and you think the support should be for a Latino feminist poet, avoid a "my way or the highway" restrictive approach. Instead, think creatively about ways to integrate your objectives. Don't be put off by "throwaway" lines like the "arts are of course important" that seem only to give lip service to the field. Look beyond your defensive response to unexpected possibilities.

4. Allowance vs. Accountability

"Any Art Education Is Better Than None." **DON'T** accept the half hour every other week that too easily counts as sufficient art education in our schools. In order to gain sufficient backgrounds in the arts, students need intense, sequential, and regular arts instruction by qualified specialists. If advocates are not diligent in observing and assessing the amount and quality of arts instruction that is provided, listening to a CD at snack time will count as music, a slide show of a trip to France will count as visual art, and physical education will count as dance.

"Insist on Quality Art Education." **DO** insist that the school provide the same level of curricular information for arts classes as they do for other courses. Make sure the art teacher reports to parents on what is happening in her classes and that the bar is kept high not only for what counts as arts instruction, but also for how much time is afforded and how well the arts are taught. Inadequate attention to arts instruction not only has a negative impact on students' understanding of the arts, it also reinforces negative stereotypes about the field as ineffective or unimportant.

5. Immeasurable vs. Meaningful

"Quantitative Measurement Is Superficial." **DON'T** polarize "measurement" and "beyond measure" (as tempting as it may be). Don't pit the arts against standardized tests, demeaning the kind of knowledge that enables students to provide right answers. Don't forget that some markers of achievement can be easily counted. But also don't forget that if everything our children were learning could

be measured in terms of right or wrong answers, numerical scoring, and quantitatively determined outcomes, we would be providing them with an oversimplified, imbalanced education. Such oversimplification does not prepare students for the complex real world ahead.

"Education as a Balanced Whole." DO remember that in an era in which standardized tests prevail, the arts are important *not* because they make children perform better on the tests, but because they provide children with arenas beyond the tests, contexts for learning that help them to understand the broader educational landscape of which information is surely an important part. Questions that invite right or wrong answers may set the stage for, rather than stand in contrast to, questions that go beyond facts to investigation, exploration, and reflection. Do explain the role that the arts can play in introducing students to the broader stage of learning, in which right answers are a useful, but not the only, part.

6. Assumption vs. Discovery

"There Must Be Very Little Attention to the Arts Here." DON'T assume a dearth in arts education in every sphere you enter. While the chances are you're likely to be right, it's offensive to those who have been working for whatever piece of the pie they can get to think it's missed your notice. Don't assume a lack of caring in the audience of people you hope to persuade. It is counter productive to have the worst assumed about you by a person who hopes to gain your interest and support. Don't forget that arts learning can persist with little recognition and in unexpected places.

"What Is the State of Arts Education Here?" DO make sure you research the state of the arts in whatever sphere you enter. Does a school system have arts requirements for graduation? How many specialists, classrooms, and students are engaged in arts learning? What are the courses offered and how much time in the school day is devoted to the arts? Join with others to discover this information on the local level so that you can compare your results with what you can discover is happening on the national level. Ask questions.

"Does anyone here participate in the arts?" "How many of you have taken a child to a museum or concert in the last year?" And give folks an opportunity to recognize their caring and to join in your quest from a positive perspective.

7. Exodus vs. Endurance

"Let's Forget About Schools and Look for Quality Arts Education Beyond School Walls." DON'T accept the argument that because there are so many excellent out-of-school community-based opportunities for arts learning, we should give up on our historically failed efforts to advance the arts in our public schools. Too many charter, pilot, and private schools offer clear evidence of what the arts can do when they are given space and time. Don't allow arts learning to be excluded from the school day. That amounts to turning our backs on those students who will not otherwise experience and might benefit most from the arts. Don't forget that better schools include the arts, that the arts make schools better, and that children who have arts education do better in school. Please don't give up on the arts in schools.

"We Will Prevail." DO seize opportunities to discuss the arts in education with folks you expect to be uninterested, attending to the challenges we all face in schools and the dreams we share for our students (collaboration). Focus in your discussion on what is unique about the arts and what they teach that other subjects do not (concentration). Explore opportunities for support for the arts in education in unexpected venues and push open apparently closed doors (investigation). Insist on quality in the arts education that our schools provide, and monitor carefully what is being taught and how (accountability). Work towards integration rather than preoccupation with regard to standardized testing and its emphasis on getting the right answer (meaningful).

Realize that arts education happens in many excellent and alternative venues and find out where they are (discovery). But always keep your eyes on the prize in terms of finding a secure and meaningful place for the arts in the education of children who, without school, would not know the joyfulness of mark-making or of lifting a voice in song or of expressing rhythm and emotion with the turn of one's body or expanding day-to-day reality by playing a dramatic role. Persevere against all obstacles and odds in the quest of improving public education through art (endurance).

With an
Eye to the Future

Three-dimensional figures by an 8-year-old

Medium: polymer clay. Photo by Dari Michele

My advocacy in the arts in education began when at age 16 I was invited to teach art in a summer day camp in New York City. Because I worked hard in that capacity, and in many subsequent years of teaching visual art, to give children a positive experience in the arts, I was an advocate. As I went on to work with children on murals in their community, to help schedule visiting artists in the schools, and to research artistic development and learning, my advocacy gained steam. Ultimately, when I worked to establish a place for educators who cared about the arts at a graduate school that was thought not to care, I was an advocate in full stride. By the way, the faculty members who needed to be persuaded at the place that was assumed not to care? They all cared. And they helped to build a program in the arts in education that could have happened much earlier if anyone had just thought it might.

I realize at this juncture that what I have enjoyed most as an advocate for the arts in education has been writing on the subject, writing to persuade. All of the preludes in this volume came from that writing and have been adapted from their original publication as Commentaries in *Education Week*, a periodical that reaches all educators at all levels in all disciplines. While colleagues suggested that my commentaries would more likely be published in periodicals that were dedicated to the arts, I wanted to reach beyond the choir and so I sent them to *Education Week*. They were published immediately and without editorial change. Please don't assume that general educators and administrators don't care about the arts. They do.

And guess what else? They know the value of stories from the field—the professional experiences that you have had that gave rise to or confirm your belief in the importance of the arts in our schools. They want to hear from that parent whose child had learning disabilities that made school a nightmare but who found inspiration and confidence in music.[1] They want to know how your classroom came alive when you sang for your students or asked them to sing for you. They need to know that acting out the signing of the Declaration of Independence or asking students to keep journals as if they were arriving in this country at the turn of the century, make history come alive. They need to know that the difference between academic and nonacademic may have more to do with the seriousness with which a subject is taught than with the nature of its content.

For me, writing has been the vehicle through which I can express my passion. For others, it is in organizing demonstrations, or leading arts education initiatives that defy expectation and give the lie to weary stereotypes. Still others volunteer for national organizations or bring their professional skills from the corporate to the nonprofit arts education sector. Whether through writing, research, or positive social political action, we must assume that the people we want to reach are listening, reading, watching, and at the ready to be newly convinced or assured again of what they need or used to know and still would like to hold dear.

The following, the last prelude in this little collection of commentaries, is built on an idea that veteran arts advocates have taught me over the years: "If you want to convince someone of the power of the arts, get them involved in making art." Bring that principal or superintendent or policymaker with you to the arts conference but make sure that they have the chance to move with music, put their hands in clay, or collaborate with a group of teenagers on the making of a mural. Ask one of them to speak in gibberish and have another translate what's being said for the audience.

Pull out the finger-paint; they may have forgotten how good it feels. Accompany their entrance to the building with the music of a marching band. They will walk in time with the beat. Ask them to improvise movement to the sound of African drumming. They may have forgotten that they can. Let them paint alongside of a young child and remember the magic of child art and the artistry of education. This last prelude is based on an occasion when my grandson did all that for me.

PRELUDE: ON PAINTING WITH A YOUNG CHILD

Squeezing new tubes of watercolor onto a disposable palette is always a joyful event.[2] The pure white ground of the palette; the individual paint piles of cadmium red, and blue, a bit of cyan, a larger pile of white, and of course black. But under the close and careful watch of an excited 3-year-old, the activity is almost sacred. "Yes, the red." "Oooh, the green. My favorite color." "Lots of white." Approvingly, "black."

We are artists, we two: this small boy and his grandmother. We have been discussing our shared status as we settle into the tiny lakeside cottage and approach our painting. I caution, "This is my studio, and we must take care of our tools." The sacredness is in the ritual of it all. I am reminded of a summer afternoon years before. A 3-year-old girl, the child of a dear friend, came to sit close by as I painted on a Martha's Vineyard beach. Could she, if she was very careful, paint alongside me? Her meticulousness was impressive. She dutifully and repeatedly washed her brush, just as I had instructed, before dipping it into any of the colorful piles of pigment.

My grandson began with such care. As his brush touched fresh paper, each color was clean. A ball of yellow lined steadily with blue, then green. With each stroke, his visible response to the image he was creating mounted. A smile at the appearance of the first color; purposefulness about the application of the next. There was now, without a doubt, a need for red. His brush, with a bit more wantonness than any stroke before, hit the water and then the mound of red, and with emphatic gestural freedom, finally, the paper that was carefully mounted on his easel.

With such a gorgeous stroke, the red spilled from tidily delineated sphere to perpendicular drip. Three-year-olds don't even need the pep talk that "every mistake is on purpose." Without missing a beat, Emerson turned the drip into a powerful down stroke. Interacting with his developing image, he remarked, "I am making a lollipop."

Beyond the colorful center image, another sphere emerged. A muddier circle (the palette was losing its integrity) boasted outbursts of rays embracing a smiling sun. "The sun is out. There is water everywhere." The brush, now without a dip in the water cup, moved with aquatic undulations across the page from left to right, obscuring the clarity of the discrete forms. How many times as an art teacher in the 1960s had I wanted to rip the half-done paintings off the easels of 4-year-olds, before the young artists went on with the undifferentiated athletic stories that ultimately resulted in a muddy painted page?

"And across the water there are fishes," Emerson explained, his pace quickening and the image growing progressively more overall brown. "The fishes are swimming fast," he articulated with enthusiasm growing so great that almost in spite of himself he abandoned his brush and dipped his whole hand into the cup of water that held the brushes. His wet hand now a tool, Emerson swept his fingers across the muddy paper palette and then across his painting. Practically euphoric at the image (which appeared more like a giant smudge than a dense narrative and ballet account), Emerson declared, "My painting is done. Hang it on the ceiling of the cottage."

I had tried to work in parallel motion, tried to share the palette and the space. As Emerson became lost in his story and the medium, I tried to adjust to the progressively more limited choices offered by our shared and muddying palette. With an eye to the mountains and trees out the window, I had tried to balance my need for representation with the gestural freedom of my grandson.

I looked down at the tidy image I had begun to construct. Anyone could see the careful application of blue water edged with small dark trees in one section against a shadowy hill. My planning was evident. It would be easy to return after a break of hours or days to my predictable piece. Emerson's work, however, was done. Complete from start to finish in the process of creation, his muddy brown paper would tell no viewer of the progression from sphere to landscape (perhaps influenced by what was happening on my page?), to unified activity between impressionistic fish strokes and feverish young artist.

Looking at the final smudge, I saw more. The layers of color. The movement and texture. With no eye to this final impression, Emerson had created an image far more interesting than mine. Even in assigning the final work a place on the ceiling (no mention of refrigerator doors), Emerson had broken the rules for art—the predictable expectations for what is made, for what reason, and where.

There is much that Emerson will gain if he keeps painting: techniques, control of tools and media, and differing criteria for when a work is done. But if he is like other children developing in their artwork, he will move from this layered, moving composite of narrative, color, and form to more stereotypical images, self-consciously monitored by cultural constraints. When Picasso said he had painted all his life like Raphael so that one day he could paint like children, he had someone like Emerson in mind. How can we retain the fearlessness of and passion for materials, the confidence and fluidity of creation, the synthetic process of making and finding meaning in marks—the total involvement in it all?

As the two of us drag an old guitar out into the sun to move on to some early morning songs, I am less aware of my losses as an adult than I am enlarged and exhilarated by my association with this child's process. Why do we teach? Are we not as educators just veteran artists hanging out with the very young in hopes of reclaiming early gifts? Or is the sharing of such brilliance, even on occasional moments, not sufficient impetus for it all?

IN SUM

In skeletal summary, I have offered:

- **That the arts appear in education in at least nine configurations:**

  (1) arts based, (2) arts integration, (3) arts infused, (4) arts included, (5) arts expanded, (6) arts professional, (7) arts extra, (8) aesthetic education, and (9) arts cultura.

- **That there are at least seven common objections to securing a place for the arts in education:**

  (1) value, (2) time, (3) measurement, (4) talent, (5) expertise, (6) money, and (7) autonomy. And there are seven good responses to those objections.

- **That the arts are unique in education in terms of at least five different features or emphases:**

  (1) product, (2) emotion, (3) ambiguity, (4) process orientation, and (5) connection.

- **That there are at least ten outcomes of arts learning that amount to compelling reasons for including the arts in education:**

  (1) imagination, (2) agency, (3) expression, (4) empathy, (5) interpretation, (6) respect, (7) inquiry, (8) reflection, (9) engagement, and (10) responsibility.

- **That in advocating for the arts we must be mindful of at least seven pairs of don'ts and do's:**

  (1) polarization/collaboration, (2) overextension/concentration, (3) isolation/investigation, (4) allowance/accountability, (5) immeasurable/meaningful, (6) assumption/discovery, and (7) exodus/endurance.

I hope the 38 items above (please note my quantitative tally!) have been and will be useful to the advocate seeking to persuade others about the value of the arts to education and to the person who is considering the potential value of the arts in education. I also hope that the issues I have identified will be of use to teachers in arts and non-arts classrooms who are considering new and effective ways to approach the arts and to use them in their classroom.

But I especially hope that every reader will see this manifesto as a call for clarity and an invitation into discourse in which we stop apologizing for the arts and stop molding their uniquely moldable features into whatever is the latest greatest need in general education. I hope every reader will agree that it is time instead to start talking about the arts and what they do uniquely that other subjects do not do and about the vital ways in which they serve education that no other subjects provide.

In this light, dear reader, please *do* review the lists I have provided and look for what is missing. Please do step up to add that new scenario for the arts in education, the latest and most vexsome objections that you have faced in the field, the particular ways in which you have observed, in your practice or in your child's life, that the arts have played a unique role in education; and whatever other compelling reasons you have discovered that the arts, on account of themselves and not in service to other subjects, are essential to the education of all our children in grades K–12 and beyond. For if this manifesto has lit a fire under your efforts, provided a structure for clarifying your own beliefs, or helped in any way to direct the continuing efforts that need to be made to ensure the arts a safe place in the curriculum, it will have more than met its objectives.

We as parents, educators, administrators, governing bodies, foundations, students, and community leaders need to hold high expectations for and maintain trust in one another. There is no "they" who believe our children should become test moguls, learning, thinking, and remembering in terms of the penciled-in boxes on standardized tests, and "we" who believe our children should become whole people, learning, thinking, and questioning "outside of the box." All of us who step up for children in school are already on the same platform of caring. And that is a place from which to begin.

Those who advocate for the tests want assurance that our children are learning; those who want our children to have knowledge and experience that defies measurement want assurance that our children are learning. Both sides of the conversation call for respect and communication. We want our children to be educated in both science and art, and we want there to be balance so that our children can know the art in science and the science in art. We want our children to have balance, opportunity, and the tools to carve visions that will better their worlds and the worlds of the people their lives will touch. We need to remember that the tests, the facts, the quantitative measures—that's science. The way education goes beyond the tests, the facts, and the quantitative measures—that's art.

Recommended Resources:
Arts in Education
Advocacy Organizations

The list of organizations at the end of this section either focus on advocacy for the arts in education or address issues of vital importance to advocates working on the national level. It does not include organizations and alliances that exist within the different states, even though a number of them take a national perspective. Advocates can find information about organizations in their different areas by contacting their state's arts council. Indeed, state arts councils are wonderful resources for information about community art centers, arts education partnerships, and other local arts education initiatives.

The websites below, and this list is a sampling, are all excellent resources for advocates. These organizations provide advocates with information on what is happening on the great stage of the arts in education, both the troubles and the triumphs. Beyond that, they either publish or provide gateways to research and other documents that serve advocates' interests and needs. Reports, recommendations, and guidelines—many of which can be downloaded at no cost, and all of which are updated regularly—contain information such as the latest studies demonstrating effects of arts learning on students; positive associations with the arts and the life style of the general population; news on innovative programs and achievements in the field; statistics on the amount and nature of arts learning in our schools; and profiles of policymakers and their attitudes toward the arts.

Beyond that, these organizations offer handbooks and tool kits especially designed to help arts in education advocates. These materials offer practical suggestions for positive action and updates and details on opportunities for funding. An hour or two in cyberspace, traveling from site to site, will amount to that course we all long for: Advocacy for the Arts in Education 101. These organizations can also be reached by phone or mail and eagerly share their materials in hard copy.

This list is not comprehensive, and the active advocate will discover websites and resources of her own. Furthermore, and sadly, advocacy organizations open and close, so some items on the list may be out of date. Nonetheless, and perhaps most important, this list should assure advocates that they are not alone and that there is no need to reinvent the wheel. The reports that these organizations circulate provide inspiration for research on the local level even as they arm the advocate with information and inspiration.

A document prepared for the Education Commission of the States, entitled *Media Paints Arts Education in Fading Light* (Douglas Gold & Co., 2005), provides an overview of the kind and amount of national press coverage dedicated to the arts in education. The message to advocates there is clear: "Find out and tell everyone what you discover. Write letters to the editor, invite the press to your event, get the word out!" I hope that the groups listed below, and others like them, will be of assistance to advocates as they frame new perspectives, gain support for their efforts, and write the new future of the arts in education.

American Alliance for Theater and Education (www.aate.com)
American Arts Alliance (www.americanartsalliance.org)
American Association of Museums (http://www.aam-us.org/)
American Dance Guild (americandanceguild.org)
American Music Conference (www.amc-music.com/)
American String Teachers Association (www.astaweb.com)
Americans for the Arts (www.artsusa.org/issues/artsed/)
Arts Education Partnership (aep-arts.org/)
Educational Theater Association (www.edta.org/)
Getty Education Institute for the Arts (ArtsEdNet) (www.getty.
    edu/education)
International Council of Fine Arts Deans (www.icfad.org)

International Network of Schools for the Advancement of Arts
    Education (www.artsschoolsnetwork.org/)
Keep Art in Our Schools (www.keepartsinschools.org)
The Kennedy Center Alliance for Arts Education Network
    (kennedy-center.org/education/kcaaen)
The Kennedy Center ArtsEdge (artsedge.kennedy-center.org/)
National Art Education Association (www.naea-reston.org)
National Assembly of State Arts Agencies (www.nasaa-arts.org)
National Assessment of Educational Progress: Nation's Arts
    Report Card (www. nces.ed.gov/nationsreportcard/arts)
National Association for Music Education (www.menc.org)
National Dance Association (www.aahperd.org/nda/template.
    cfm)
National Dance Education Organization (www.ndeo.org)
National Endowment for the Arts (www.nea.gov)
National Office for Arts Accreditation (www.arts-accredit.org)
President's Committee on the Arts and the Humanities (www.
    pcah.gov)
Project Zero (www.pz.harvard.edu)
VSA Arts (Very Special Arts) (www.vsarts.org)

A Glossary of
Arts Education Terms

As it is in any discipline, those deeply involved in the arts in education have a cadre of terms that may surprise, baffle, or discourage the advocate who does not have a background in the arts. The terms listed here are not meant to cover the breadth of language used in the different art disciplines that are taught in our schools. Rather, they are selected to scaffold the advocate who is reading research, or writing a proposal, or preparing a talk, or for any reason needs access to the basic vocabulary of terms arts educators and researchers employ.

(A number of these terms, with different definitions, were included in the *Greenwood Dictionary of Education,* Copyright © 2003, edited by John Collins and Nancy O'Brien, Reproduced with permission of Greenwood Publishing Group, Westport, CT. I am grateful to the Greenwood Publishing Group for permission to reproduce revised versions of definitions originally prepared for that volume.)

AESTHETIC DEVELOPMENT: The development over time and with experience of the ability to attend to and discover meaning in artistic creations. Psychologists have observed five stages of such development ranging from the earliest sensual responses to color, form, and personal association to the most advanced understanding of and identification with the artist at work. See the work of Michael Parsons and Abigail Housen.

AESTHETIC EDUCATION: The education of perception, the act of attending to and making sense out of rather than actually making works of art. Focusing as much on literary texts and musical creations as on responses to visual art, aesthetic education helps develop the ability to use the arts as lenses through which to make sense of experience. The Lincoln Center Institute (LCI) in New York, spearheaded by philosopher Maxine Greene, has launched a widely replicated aesthetic education program. See http://www.lcinstitute.org

AESTHETICS: Philosophy that is concerned with issues of beauty and art, such as the nature of art or of the artful aspects of any experience. Scholarship that deals with the arts as special modes of understanding, explores questions regarding the definition of art, the nature of perceiving as a rational or emotional experience, the complexity of relative value in the arts, and the particular connections between artists and those who perceive their work.

ARABESQUE: A ballet position in which the dancer stands on one foot, keeping the torso raised and in place, and stretches the other leg behind, lifting it until it is parallel to the floor.

ART: Creations that express their makers' views of the world, tell the stories of their lives, or describe and question their realities. Some say art is (1) made by recognized artists out of artistic media like paint, clay, or poetic language; and (2) considered by experts to be aesthetic, creative, or beautiful. Others think a work's placement, for example in an art museum or gallery, determines its status as art. However defined, art is a particularly human activity involving thought and feeling and worthy of continued study throughout every child's education.

ART CART: The push cart vehicle stocked with supplies that art specialists wheel into classrooms for arts activities when no space, studio, or room has been designated for art classes. Often referenced as a metaphor for the marginalization of arts in our schools, the art cart holds materials like markers, crayons, papers, and other supplies that allow for limited (not too messy) in-classroom art activities, often restricted to "table top art."

ART CRITICISM: Any writing that judges or critiques a work of art, considering its relative successes and failings. In the art educational movement of the 1980s, Discipline Based Art Education (DBAE), art criticism was featured as a curricular activity in which elementary school students describe, interpret, evaluate, and theorize about works of art.

ART EDUCATION: Teaching and learning in an artistic discipline. While the term *art education* may seem inclusive of all art forms, it most frequently is used within the context of American schools as referring to visual art (e.g., painting, drawing, collage, sculpture, photography), separating it from music education (e.g., learning to play an instrument or to sing), dance education, or drama in education.

ART HISTORY: The history of visual arts, especially painting and sculpture, including the lives and work of particular artists, the invention and dissolution of various stylistic movements, and the philosophy of aesthetics. Included as well are the changing definitions of art. Art history is sometimes taught, especially as an elective, in high schools and was included as a curricular area in the DBAE movement.

ART MUSEUM: A structure in which art objects deemed of great worth to civilization are preserved and displayed across generations. It is thought that art museums are a priori educational because they share their collections and information about them with the public. But some insist it is their carefully designed programs for school children and adults that make them educational. Unlike history, science, or children's museums, replete with interactive educational exhibits, the significance of the art museum to general education is a subject of ongoing consideration.

ART SPECIALIST: A trained and often professionally certified K–12 art educator who works in a designated art room in a particular school or delivers art education to a variety of schools, rotating through grade levels and classrooms. Art specialists have been eliminated from many schools in which budget cuts leave arts learning to classroom teachers and visiting artists. In areas like New York City in which art education is being reinstated, the need for art specialists is growing, as are issues of what counts as appropriate training.

ART THERAPY: A therapeutic application of visual art production as a vehicle of recovery for the patient, and of art perception as a mode of diagnosis for the therapist. The act of making a painting can serve a troubled child as an emotional release and agent to recovery. The child's painting can provide the art therapist with information about the child's concerns, conflicts, personality, and interests. Art therapists are mental health professionals who have studied both art and counseling.

ARTIST: A maker of art, primarily in visual (e.g., painting, sculpture, photography), performing (e.g., dance, music, theater), or literary (e.g., poetry, literature) arenas. Artists in American society are often stereotyped, for example, as always wearing black, envisioning themselves as outsiders, or insanely driven by their talent. They are rarely featured as role models in American schools. Just as the arts are most often offered as alternative subjects, the careers of artists are most frequently seen as alternatives to mainstream professions.

ARTIST-IN-RESIDENCE: A professional artist in any domain brought in to a school or other educational or community site to create a work over time that students can help with or observe. Unlike visiting artists who may visit for an afternoon or a day, artists-in-residence are on site long enough to come to know students, help them with their own arts projects, or lead master classes that introduce students to professional standards and considerations.

ARTISTIC: Behavior of or like an artist (a maker of art). Having to do with the actual making or the ability to make art. While the term might be thought to refer to anybody's art making, it is mostly reserved for art making that is at a professional level. Children who demonstrate recognizable talents in art are said to be "artistic."

ARTISTIC DOMAINS: Different arenas of art delineated according to the various sets of symbols out of which artists craft meaning. Visual arts, drama, poetry, and music are considered different artistic domains because of the different symbols (images, actions, words, and notes, respectively) the artist employs.

ARTISTIC PROCESS: The process through which artists create works of art. The artistic process is characterized by the integration of thought, feeling, skill, and flexibility. Marked by an appreciation of mistakes as generative, and consideration of the perspectives of maker and perceiver. Educators have emulated aspects of the artistic process, such as ongoing reflection, assessment over time, and attention to process over product, in framing pedagogical strategies such as portfolio-based assessment.

ARTS EDUCATION: Education in the various forms of art, for example, music, dance, visual arts, and drama. Has been included in curriculum for almost as long as there have been public schools in the United States. Justifications for including the arts have ranged from the acquisition of technical skills to advance a developing nation in the industrial era, the development of the whole child in the progressive era, the advancement of complex thinking processes in the post Sputnik scientific era, and most recently, the improvement of performance in non-arts subjects in this era of high-risk testing. Arts education is rarely valued for its own sake and remains vulnerable to exclusion or relegation to extracurricular activity.

ARTS INTEGRATION: Arts integration refers to the incorporation of the arts into the non-arts curriculum by combining it with one or more other content area in the consideration of a selected topic or question. As an example, consider a school-wide project exploring democracy that includes as equal partners arts and non-arts subjects; receives equal input from teachers, specialists, and artists; and benefits from learning and assessment methods associated with the arts.

ARTS PROPEL: An arts curricular approach developed at Harvard's Project Zero in the early 1980s that builds on the activities of professional artists in various artistic domains. Features three aspects of the artist's process: production (the making of art, at the center of activity); perception (the attention to details or the response to the work); and reflection (thinking about the work, especially in terms of works that have been made by other artists). PROPEL is often contrasted with DBAE as a cognitive approach that prioritizes making at the center of arts study.

ARTS-BASED CURRICULUM: In which the arts are featured both as core subjects and as entry points into all aspects of the curriculum. In this framework, students study the arts in their own right and learn other subjects through the window of the arts. For examples of arts-based curricula, see the Bernstein Institute and A+ Schools.

ARTS-CULTURA CURRICULUM: A curriculum in which the arts are seen as connecting the individual child's culture or worldview to the cultures of immediate communities (neighborhood, families, and school), to the Cultures of nations and race, and to Culture viewed broadly (the connection to all humankind). Artistic products and processes are selected and studied with an eye to illuminating this interconnected paradigm.

ARTS-EXPANDED CURRICULUM: A curriculum in which the arts are employed as vehicles for extending arts education beyond school walls into the larger community to locations such as the art museum, local community art center, or concert hall. Arts expansion models focus on familiarizing students with the resources of and appropriate behaviors in cultural institutions.

ARTS-EXTRA CURRICULUM: The most frequent scenario for arts learning in our schools in which the arts are viewed as extras, reserved for time and space outside of the daily curriculum. Examples include after-school theatrical productions, musical groups, or the dance, writing, or poetry club.

ARTS-INCLUDED CURRICULUM: In which the arts are taught alongside of and are considered on an equal par with what are more traditionally regarded as important, core, or basic subjects. Examples can be found in arts magnet or pilot schools and in selected independent schools.

ARTS-INFUSED CURRICULUM: In which the arts are infused into the mainstream curriculum, brought in as targeted or general enrichment. Arts-infused curricular activities include visiting artists such as the poet coming into English class, the folk-singer in history, or a troupe of actors performing for the whole school.

ARTS-PROFESSIONAL CURRICULUM: In which the arts are taught with an eye to serious training and preparation for adult careers in the arts. Most often students who seek arts professional curricula have recognized talent, persistent interest, and a willingness to seek out advanced arts training opportunities beyond school walls.

ATELIER: The studio in which a developing artist apprentices with a veteran artist, as did many great artists in nineteenth century France. The Atelier provides a model for education employed, for example, by well-known artist/teacher Tim Rollins and his Art and Knowledge Workshop, KOS (Kids of Survival), in the Bronx.

AUDIENCE: A term that includes listeners, viewers, spectators, and readers—individuals or groups responding to the range of artistic offerings. It was once thought that the audience was a relatively passive group of perceivers, with artists being the active producers of art. Now the attention to and interpretation of meaning in art is also considered an active and demanding process.

CHIAROSCURO: From the Italian for light (*chiaro*) and dark (*oscuro*). The artist's manipulation of light and dark tones (as in shading with pencils) on a two-dimensional surface, creating the effect of physical volume and a range of emotional qualities.

CHILD ART: The art of children has been of interest to adults since before earning praise from the eighteenth-century French philosopher, Jean-Jacques Rousseau. The playful and powerful art of children has been extolled and emulated by modernist artists like Klee and Miro, studied by cognitive psychologists like Gardner and Winner, and celebrated for its inherent embodiment of human expression by scholars such as Arnheim and Kellogg.

COGNITIVE APPROACH TO ART EDUCATION: A view of art education as addressing skills such as critical thinking, interpretation, and the manipulation of symbols to represent ideas. In the 1940s, art education was viewed as a means for children to express emotions. With the advent of the computer in the 1950s and a consequent revolution in our thinking about thought, psychologists, educators, and philosophers revised their understanding of art-making and perceiving. Advocates thought the cognitive approach would advance the status of art education. It spawned movements such as DBAE and Arts PROPEL.

COMMUNITY ART CENTER: A location, often a renovated church, school, or storefront, where arts education is provided by artists beyond the parameters of, though often in conjunction with, school art programs. Featuring adult as well as children's educational programming, urban art centers are thought to be safe havens at which youth who have been placed at risk can find arenas for success and the development of life skills.

COMMUNITY-BASED ART EDUCATION: Any form of art education offered beyond school walls in geographically or more broadly defined communities. Emerged in the United States at the turn of the century in settlement houses when immigrant populations sought the acquisition of marketable arts-based skills. There was a resurgence in the 1960s when art education was diminishing in schools. The field includes any of the many individual or group efforts of artists moving into communities on their own or through galleries and local arts councils, sharing their skills with interested adults and children.

CRAFT: Often distinguished from the more erudite fine arts, craft refers to the down-to-earth making of handmade and often utilitarian goods and the skill involved in that making, for example the work of potters, weavers, and glassblowers. Today, equal regard is frequently given to arts such as painting, sculpting, and drawing, and crafts such as quilting, carving, and printmaking.

CREATIVITY: Originality, innovation, the source of boundary-breaking inventions or ideas. Thought to lie at the core of the artistic process and to involve the identification or invention of problems and the ability to think of numerous and unexpected alternative solutions. While creative adult thinkers have changed our world in many ways, very young children have a natural sense of creativity that is reflected in their work within and across artistic media.

CRITIQUE: The practice in art schools of instructors and peers discussing a student's work critically, focusing on strengths, weaknesses, and relative originality. The "writer's chair" in elementary school classrooms where students discuss each other's work is fashioned after the art school "crit." In the self-critique of youth in community art centers, educators have found examples of students working collaboratively to find ways to support one another even as they reflect critically on what needs to be done to make their work better.

CYBERARTS: Art in any media that is produced with or out of computer hardware or software; all art that is digitally created including visual, dance, music, performance, gaming, and literature (hypertext literature and interactive fiction). Prefix comes from Norbert Weiner who coined "cybernetics" as a term that described related mechanisms, and William Gibson who coined the term "cyberspace" in his novel *Neuromancer*, which led to the science fiction genre known as "cyberpunk." New media is the term given to artworks created out of computer technology and displayed in museums. And as for art made for the web? Experience "web art" aka "net art" at www.turbulence.org. (I am grateful for this definition to George Fitfield, Director of Boston's Ciberarts Festival and Curator of New Media at the DeCordova Museum.)

DALCROZE METHOD: A popular method for teaching music that features three components: (1) Eurhythmics or kinetic movement as students listen to music, (2) Solfege or "do re mi" training of the voice and understanding of music theory, and (3) Improvisation or the spontaneous creation of music primarily on the piano. Along with Kodaly, Suzuki, and Orff, it is one of the four primary methods of teaching music to young children.

DANCE: The performing art in which spontaneous or choreographed movement is the medium of expression. While dance performances are often accompanied by orchestral music or drumming, they are also performed without accompaniment. Dance encompasses a wide range of styles and forms, from classical ballet and folk dance to tap, jazz, and modern dance.

DANCE EDUCATION: As a field, dance education is usually reserved for the training of professional dancers most often beyond school walls in ballet or modern dance companies and community art centers. Historically and currently, dance is taught less frequently than any other art form in our schools. Reasons range from the regard of dance as being nonverbal and therefore not academic, to the shortage of specialists in dance or teachers who can teach dance along with their other academic duties.

DISCIPLINE-BASED ART EDUCATION (DBAE): Pioneered by the Getty Education Institute for the Arts in 1983, Discipline-Based Art Education was the largest and most heavily funded arts educational initiative of the twentieth century. DBAE provides a framework for curriculum design based on the disciplinary foundations of art making, art criticism, art history, and aesthetics. Throughout the 1980s, the Getty Foundation supported implementations of DBAE in numerous American schools. Proponents include Eliot Eisner, Ralph Smith, and Brent Wilson.

DOCENT: Most frequently a lecturer or tour guide in a museum, historic home, art gallery, cathedral, or other cultural or educational institution. Art museum docents are primarily either volunteers or are paid small honoraria, but they receive rigorous training from the museum regarding the collections they will introduce to viewers. Docents often make visits to schools to prepare students for a trip to the art museum by presenting and discussing slides of artworks and preparing students for the museum's "don't touch," "talk softly," environment.

DRAMA-IN-EDUCATION/THEATER-IN-EDUCATION: Both terms include the use of drama in schools to enrich teaching and learning, aid in student counseling, or promote communication among peers. Finer distinctions are emerging. Either term may include drama education as the teaching and learning of acting in designated classes. And while drama-in-education may refer to the use of dramatic techniques like improvisation for numerous purposes, theater-in-education seems always to involve the performance or viewing of a scripted play.

EXPRESSION/EXPRESSIVITY: The manifestation or representation of inner experience or emotion. Expression in the arts—performing, visual, or literary—is achieved through gesture, facial configuration, shape and direction of lines and forms, and the use of metaphors and other descriptive language. Author Leo Tolstoy described the artistic experience as one in which artists pour their emotions into their work to be re-experienced by their audience. Philosopher Nelson Goodman saw expression as an aesthetic achievement mastered by artists and recognized by viewers without any necessary exchange of felt emotion. Young children's artistic performances are thought to be highly expressive apart from any consideration of respective mastery.

FINE ARTS: Fine art is that which has stood the test of time, epitomizes the heights of artistic achievement, and exists for no other reason than to be studied and appreciated. This is in contrast to low art, often regarded as "mass" or "popular" culture that includes art created for commercial, illustrative, or functional purposes. Painting and sculpture are fine arts, as are other art forms associated with aesthetics and beauty such as drawing, printmaking, poetry, and classical music.

FLOW: Named by psychologist Mihaly Csikszentmihalyi, flow is the intense level of engagement experienced by individuals deeply involved in activities such as art making, sports, rituals, pageantry, and children's games. Described as optimal experience in which self-consciousness, worry, and feelings of inadequacy disappear. Exhibited by children engaged in pretend play in their apparent disregard for anything around them outside of their activity.

GRAPHIC SYMBOLIZATION: The activity of drawing: the representation through graphic (drawn) marks on paper of ideas, emotions, themes, objects, and events. Of interest to researchers who consider children's drawings as reflections of their cognitive development with regard, for example, to facilities such as planning, short-term memory, and for some, control of aesthetic features. Arts therapists look to what children draw for insight into that which children will not speak.

IMAGINATION: The ability to envision artistic products, invent stories and worlds in our minds, and conceive of alternatives to perceived realities. Imagination is associated with pretend play, the creative process, and human inspiration. Advocates argue for the importance of education in the arts because the arts provide media through which imagination finds form, and arts education challenges students to think beyond the given to unexpected possibilities.

IMPROVISATION/IMPROV: Spontaneous, unrehearsed performance. In music education (see Kodaly, Orff, and Dalcroze), students' creation of new melodies in response to music they've heard. Jazz musicians improvise in performance by responding to each other extemporaneously, inventing melodic variations or new phrases. In "improv" in dramatic training or in theater games in classrooms, the actors are given a problem to solve, or a set of parameters for characters and a scene, and they carry on as if they'd been scripted, inventing dialogue and action on the spot.

INTERDISCIPLINARY ART EDUCATION: When any art discipline is one of the multiple academic disciplines brought together in curriculum around a single issue or question. An example would be the study of heroes approached from the various and mutually informative subjects of history, folklore, Greek myths, and classical sculpture. Debate centers on whether this approach enriches school curriculum overall or dilutes the effectiveness of learning in each discipline, especially the arts. (See also Integrated Art Education.)

JAZZ: Regarded as the one American contribution to the world of music, jazz is a twentieth-century musical genre invented by African-American musicians (often classically trained who were denied participation in mainstream venues) in New Orleans and throughout the country. Jazz features complex rhythms, a swing beat, blues notes, and artful improvisation by solo or ensemble performers creating harmonic variations. While jazz has for a long time been featured in community arts education, jazz groups and bands have only recently appeared in secondary schools.

KODALY: A method for teaching singing in schools that is used worldwide and was named for Hungarian music educator Zoltan Kodaly. It offers a unified sequential music curriculum that attends to children's developmental stage, uses folksong and dance, a capella singing, and hand signs coordinated with solfege (do-re-mi). Along with Orff, Suzuki, and Dalcroze, it is one of the four primary methods of teaching music to young children.

LITERAL STAGE: A proposed period in middle childhood (8–11) in which children's drawings seem less expressive when compared with the work of younger children. In an effort to make things as they "really look," children at this stage frequently resort to stereotypical representations of individuals and objects. Frustrations with reproduction cause many individuals to cease art-making entirely. Some researchers defend the literal stage as a time of expanding repertoire rather than of the loss of early skills.

MEDIUM/MEDIA (PL.): The materials out of which works of art are made: paint, clay, words, or in combination as in "mixed media." It can also refer to the industry that determines and disseminates newsworthy and commercial information through television, documentaries, magazines, newspapers, etc.

MULTIPLE INTELLIGENCES (MI THEORY): In his theory of Multiple Intelligences, psychologist Howard Gardner redefines intelligence as the ability to find and solve problems, and to fashion valued products in at least seven areas or intelligences: linguistic, spatial, bodily kinesthetic, inter- and intrapersonal, and musical. The theory is frequently misunderstood in two ways: (1) that individuals have one of the seven intelligences and not a profile or admixture; and (2) that there is an artistic intelligence instead of the potential for artistry with any profile of intelligences.

MUSEUM CURATOR: The "keeper of the collection." In an art museum, the curator is a lead player—an art historian/scholar responsible for the content (what works of art are included) and presentation (how they will be displayed) of exhibits in the museum. In ideal settings, the museum curator collaborates with the museum educator in mounting exhibits with an eye to educational priorities.

MUSEUM EDUCATION: The institution and development of educational programming in the context of the museum. Children's and history museums have traditionally focused on educational programming, but art museums only seriously began to do so within the last decades of the twentieth century. A 1992 report by the American Association of Museums, *Excellence and*

Equity: Education and the Public Dimension of Museums, was pivotal in this change, charging art museums to embrace education in their mission statements.

MUSEUM EDUCATOR: Oversees educational activities in the museum, from visits for school-aged children to a variety of adult activities. Links museum resources to educational theory and practice, forges collaborations with schools and community organizations, trains museum docents, plans curriculum with classroom teachers, and assesses overall educational effectiveness. The museum educator helps to develop audiences by considering issues of diversity and access in the production of educational materials.

MUSIC EDUCATION: Teaching and learning in playing musical instruments (as in a school band), developing singing skills (showcased in school choirs), understanding music theory (reading notes, rhythm, pulse, etc.), and less frequently within the context of public schools, acquiring the skills required to compose original music. The National Association for Music Education (MENC) at www.menc.org advocates the benefits of music education.

MUSIC THERAPY: The clinical use of music as an intervention to restore, maintain, or improve emotional, physical, and physiological health. Music therapists are trained professionals who engage with their clients in selected activities such as listening to or improvising music and discussing lyrics. Used in the treatment of problems associated with aging, pain, and substance abuse, it can also be effective with physical and learning disabilities.

MUSICAL INTELLIGENCE: One of psychologist Howard Gardner's original seven intelligences. Musical intelligence is exhibited in the work of composers and performers of music who regularly explore musical problems and fashion musical products. It is the only one of Gardner's intelligences that is clearly attached to a particular field or discipline.

NATIONAL ARTS STANDARDS: Agreed upon and published in 1994, marking the inclusion of the arts in the nine core subjects officially recognized for a complete education for American children. Developed by a consortium of national arts education associations, the Standards outline what every young American should know (both content and process-based knowledge) in visual arts, dance, theater, and music, organized at three levels (grades K–4, 5–8, and 9–12). The Standards are voluntary and offer frameworks—not curriculum content—for individual state design.

NATIONAL ENDOWMENT FOR THE ARTS (NEA): An independent agency of the federal government that for the last 40 years has had as its mission the support of the work of outstanding artists and the dissemination of their work throughout the country, beyond the parameters of urban cultural centers. Beyond that, the NEA has a commitment to fostering leadership and excellence in the arts in education and encourages private foundations to support arts initiatives of reach and promise. http://www.nea.gov/

ORFF METHOD: An approach to teaching music to young children developed by German composer and music educator Carl Orff. Listening to music, playing music, moving to rhythms, and especially improvisation are cultivated in a playful, child-centered, and noncompetitive atmosphere. Percussion instruments like the xylophone and the glockenspiel are famously included. Also known as Orff-Schulwerk. Along with Kodaly, Suzuki, and Dalcroze, one of the four primary methods of teaching music to young children.

PERCEPTION: The act of attending through sight, sound, taste, smell, or touch. Looking at a work of visual art, listening to a musical composition, or taking in the sights and sounds in a play. The act of paying close attention to the features we perceive: the details of color and texture in a painting, the rhythm and cadence of music, the imagery created by the stage set, and the pace of action and modulation of actors' voices.

PERCIPIENCE: The power of perceiving especially keenly and attentively. Associated by art philosophers such as Ralph Smith and Harold Osborne with the perception of objects and experiences in the world of art. Smith sees percipience as the goal of arts education: to imbue students with the heightened capacities of intellect and sensitivity required to find understanding in the products and worlds of art and culture.

PERFORMANCE: An individual or group presenting for a live audience a play, dance, musical composition, or other artistic creation. There is an art to performance, beyond the skills involved in acting, dancing, and singing, that involves the confidence and timing to read and please an audience. The arts in education give students invaluable experiences with performance, helping them to develop a sense of themselves and their impact on others.

PERFORMING ARTS: Art forms like drama, dance, and music that are performed in front of or recorded for a live audience. With writing or the visual arts, the artist rarely meets readers and viewers, but in the performing arts, artists are aware of and can actively relate to their audiences. Viewers and readers have the ability to revisit works of visual art or literature, but live performances occur in limited space and time.

PHOTOGRAPHY: Photography is the manipulation of reflected light, usually through the lens of a camera, onto a sensitive medium like film. The result is an image that seems to be a more accurate reproduction of what we see than what artists achieve with other media. Most generally regarded as an art, photography is alternatively thought to be more of a mechanical process. With cameras, students can place aesthetic frames around their lived worlds and learn about formal artistic properties such as the composition of an image.

PLAY: The spontaneous, challenging, pleasurable activity of young children that develops from parallel (side by side) exploration of objects and movement, to interactive pretend-play scenarios, to the rule-bound game play of older children. A play is a dramatic piece written for and performed in theaters. In the creation of a work of art, artists are said to play, as in experiment with ideas, media, and stylistic options.

POETRY: A piece or the art of writing that has aesthetic or artistic features. A poem both delivers and transcends the meaning of its words. Likened to music because of the rhythm and meter of its lines (even when rhyme is not a feature) and harmonious arrangement of sounds. A compelling medium in the classroom because children enjoy poetic language. See for examples of children's poetry, the work of Richard Lewis and Kenneth Koch.

POPULAR CULTURE: Low (as in class) as opposed to high (as in elitist) culture. Comic books, reality television, hip-hop, rap, and video games are a few examples. High culture is found in classical works of art in museums and concert halls, supposedly reserved for those who have the educational and social backgrounds to appreciate them. Low, or popular, culture is more likely to be disseminated by the media and is accessible to everyone.

PORTFOLIO: A holder (often a folder or flat suitcase) containing samplings of the general work or selections of the best work of an artist. High school students applying to art school compile such portfolios for use in the admissions process. Portfolio assessment in non-arts subjects is based on the practice of professional artists who regularly review and revise works in progress. It allows teachers and students to evaluate progress across a number of qualitative learning objectives.

PORTRAIT: A rendering of a person or group of people—most often a painting or sculpture—usually created as a close visual likeness. Can also be abstract, focusing on a key aspect of the individual's appearance or personality. Portraits are created in many media, including language. The model of portraiture (creating a portrait) frames a research methodology that tries to capture along with social science documentation, aspects of artistic depiction. (See, for example, *The Art and Science of Portraiture* [1997] by Sara Lawrence-Lightfoot and Jessica Hoffmann Davis. San Francisco, CA: Jossey-Bass.)

PRETEND PLAY: In which young children assign to each other and take on parts enacting scenes and stories that they create or select. Sometimes involving props, like stuffed animals or household objects, and costumes of the children's own design. Participants will incorporate symbolic play (for example, a banana representing a telephone) and explore through pretense the roles and responsibilities of the adult world they are preparing to enter.

PROCESS DRAMA: A method of improvisation that uses drama for holistic learning (engaging all aspects of the learner), advanced specifically for use in classrooms by English drama educator Dorothy Heathcote. Imagine a lesson in marine biology with students playing the parts of lobster fishermen, environmentalists, historians, politicians, scientists, all learning through dramatic action what information and which issues are of importance to the topic.

PROCESSFOLIO: An expression coined by the research group Project Zero in their 1980s curriculum and assessment project Arts PROPEL. As opposed to a portfolio, which is traditionally a collection of the best completed products, a student processfolio contains examples of works in progress or sample sketches that reflect the process of a student's learning over time in an arts domain (e.g., visual arts or writing).

PRODIGY: A child with an extraordinary ability equivalent to or surpassing the genius or expertise of a trained professional. Educational researchers have noted that prodigies more often have prodigious ability in one area only, like Bobby Fischer in the game of chess or Mozart in music, rather than "globally" across all areas of performance.

PRODUCTION: The creation, presentation, or performance of a work of art (e.g., visual art, literature, theater, music, opera, dance, or film). From a cognitive perspective, production (the making of a work) is distinguished from perception (the viewing of a work) with both processes requiring active meaning making. There has been debate as to whether production should be featured in art education when perception may be more relevant to our adult lives as consumers rather than makers of art.

PROSCENIUM ARCH: The arch that frames the stage in a traditional theater, marking the separation of the usually elevated performing area from the audience. A way of making theatrical performances like paintings—something to look at within a frame. The proscenium arch defines the distance between actors and audience both physically and dramatically, separating the unreal (action on stage) from the real (lives of the audience).

PSYCHODRAMA: A kind of drama therapy developed by psychiatrist Jacob Levy Moreno. Improvisational role play used in therapeutic situations to help individuals (as opposed to interacting groups as in sociodrama) work through specific crises by enacting and resolving difficult situations. Psychodrama is conducted by therapists, counselors, and other trained professionals.

PUBLIC ART: Works of art that are created for and located in public places. Includes unexpected graffiti, murals with neighborhood themes on the sides of building walls, statues memorializing famous figures, three-dimensional works of abstract art, landscape architecture, and performance pieces intended to provoke awareness and conversation about a controversial issue.

ROLE PLAY: The taking on of a character, playing the part of someone else. Dramatic work done in the classroom frequently involves improvisational role play through which teachers and students explore an issue or topic. Young children role play (note the authentic performances in the kindergarten pretend-play space) to try on the identities and responsibilities of the adult world.

ROMANCING: The invented responses of very young children who are asked to explain what their drawings (apparently drawn without intent) represent. As they begin to understand what adults expect, young children will point to a tangle of lines and say, "That's me and Daddy taking a walk." An hour later, they may point to the same tangle and say, "That's a dog."

SCHOOL ART: Art making that children are taught to do in school. Educational researchers like Brent Wilson have made the distinction between school art and the artwork youth do on their own. For example, unlike school-based assignments, the narrative comic book drawings of American preadolescent artists (and see the Manga drawings of Japanese youth) are deeply personal and self-directed.

SCRIBBLING: Writing or drawing that is done aimlessly without creating recognizable shapes or words. Preschoolers are thought to be scribbling when they draw, but some educational researchers (see Rhoda Kellogg and John Matthews) regard the activity as a purposeful exploration of media and symbolic functioning.

SCULPTURE: A work of visual art that is made in three dimensions. Among numerous techniques, students can choose to create sculptures by carving out of wood or stone, modeling with clay, welding with metals, or assembling structures out of paper and plastic.

SELF-PORTRAIT: When an artist, in any media, creates a descriptive image of him- or herself. Visual artists and writers deliberately make self-portraits, but young children instinctively draw "themselves" whenever they draw a figure. The activity of self-portrayal is a popular and generative one in all areas of the arts in education.

SKETCH: A brief description of an object or idea often used as a preparatory step for a more detailed work. A sketch can be done in words—perhaps as a short piece of writing or a rough draft for something longer, or drawn in a few lines on paper in preparation for a painting or a piece of sculpture. Many sketches are considered complete and valued for their economy of form.

SOCIODRAMA: A form of improvisational role playing (see psychodrama) specifically dedicated to interpersonal situations. Teachers can use sociodrama in the classroom to explore social interactions, improvising scenes in which students change roles and experience each other's perspective. The actors in Ms. Levine's class were students of sociodrama.

SOLFEGE: A method of singing and teaching music, both the performance of music and the reading of notational music. It employs the well-known syllables do, re, mi, fa, so, la, and ti to represent pitches with a single syllable corresponding to a single note (from sol-fa). Taught in schools of music with young children and at the conservatory level.

STYLE: The personal imprint of the individual artist (in any art form) that can be detected within and across a collection of work. Very young children can recognize the artistic style of other children in their classrooms. They will tell you, "Oh, Jason made that one!"

SUZUKI METHOD: Japanese violinist, teacher, and philosopher Shinichi Suzuki invented this world-famous method of teaching music to young children. Features careful listening to selected music, imitation, praise, and scaled to child instruments including violin, viola, flute, and piano. Along with Kodaly, Orff, and Dalcroze, it is one of the four primary methods of teaching music to young children.

TABLE-TOP ART: Visual art made in the non-arts classroom and constrained by the size of desktops and the requirements of classroom tidiness. Frequently associated with precut paper shapes glued and colored at holiday time or "color within the lines" photocopied work sheets. By contrast, artwork done in studios and art classrooms can be large in scale and involve rich and messy media of expression.

TALENT: Notable ability often associated with the arts—having a talent in music or dance. Actors and other performers are even referred to as "the talent." Thought to be inborn and not acquired through training, though training may provide the opportunity for talent to emerge and be demonstrated. While it cannot be measured, children's talent may be easier to recognize in music than in other artistic domains.

TECHNICAL THEATRE: The areas of theatre production that focus on stagecraft: sets, lighting, sound, props, special effects, and stage management. "Techie" is the affectionate name for technicians in these areas. In school productions, invisible to the audience, techies enjoy backstage camaraderie as they gain important knowledge and shoulder great responsibility, often with little public acknowledgment for their work.

THEATER GAMES: Originated by educator and actress Viola Spolin, doyenne of improvisation, to help actors gain presence on stage. Spolin envisioned making a game out of the problems we face and designed short, structured improvisational activities that teachers use in their classrooms to excite students' creativity, spontaneity, and interest in learning. Theater games are useful in many arenas.

U-CURVE IN GRAPHIC SYMBOLIZATION: A U-shaped trajectory proposed by cognitive psychologists (see Jessica Davis and Howard Gardner) to describe the development of drawing. Young children's highly expressive drawings (one peak of the U) are likened to the work of professional artists (at the other peak). But the facility disappears over time, and the apparently less expressive work of children ages 8–11 (in the literal stage) occupy the trough of the U. Some children develop into adolescent and adult artists, but most abandon the activity. More arts education could reverse the downward curve.

Verisimilitude: In acting or literature, that quality of a character or situation of appearing real or seeming believable. The question of achieving verisimilitude can be a provocative one for integrated arts education. How is it achieved in and across art forms? More generally, what do we mean by "true to life"?

Visual Art: The rendering of an artistic statement in visual form (two or three dimensions). Usually associated with traditional arts such as painting, engraving, sculpture, and architecture. The terms art and visual art are often used interchangeably (as in "art education"). In our schools today, art specialists, visiting artists, and classroom teachers most commonly teach visual art.

Visual Culture: The visual images that surround us from museum works of fine art to illustrations in children's books to the animation of television commercials and video games to icons for girlhood (like Barbie) or boyhood (like GI Joe). There is debate over whether the commercial aspects of visual culture should be included in art education. Proponents argue that studying how images reflect the values of an era teaches students to be critical consumers of visual culture.

Visual Learner: An individual who attends most closely to the visual in any experiential realm and therefore is thought to learn best through modes of observation. While visual perception and processing of visual stimuli are part of everyone's repertoire for learning, visual learners favor and find most success in these areas.

Visual Thinking Strategies (VTS): Developed by educational researcher Abigail Housen and museum educator Philip Yenawine, VTS is an inquiry-based interactive approach to looking at art, usually used in a museum. The viewer is asked, "What do you see?" and to defend responses ("Why do you say that?") by referring to particular aspects of the work. For more information see www.vue.org.

VOICE: The sound each of us makes when we speak or sing or make a noise. In the arts, we think of the voice of a violin as its tone or the voice of a writer as his or her particular style. Voice is also associated with the privilege and power to speak for oneself: "To have a voice."

Notes

Introduction

1. For a range of such claims, see a classic book on arts education advocacy: *Strong Arts, Strong Schools* (1996), Fowler, C., New York: Oxford University Press.

2. See Davis, J. (2005), *Framing Education as Art: The Octopus Has a Good Day.* New York: Teachers College Press.

3. See also Eliot Eisner's flyer (available from www.naea-reston.org) entitled *Parents: Ten Lessons the Arts Teach* adapted by the National Arts Education Association from Chapter 4 of his book (2002) *The Arts and the Creation of Mind.* New Haven, CT: Yale University Press, the interview with Derek E. Gordon at: http://artsedge.kennedy-center.org/content/3270/, and note Hetland, L., Winner, E., Veneema, S., & Sheridan, K. (2007). *Studio Thinking: The Real Benefits of Visual Arts Education.* New York: Teachers College Press.

Chapter 1. The Lay of the Land

1. A version of this essay first appeared in *Education Week* (October 2000), Editorial Projects in Education: Washington, D.C.

2. For further discussion, see Parsons, M. J. (1987), *How We Understand Art: A Cognitive Developmental Account of Aesthetic Experience.* Cambridge: Cambridge University Press.

3. See earlier discussions of the "eight ways" the arts enter education in Davis, J. H. (2005), *Framing Education as Art: The Octopus Has a Good Day*, New York: Teachers College Press, and in Davis, J. H. (1999, May–June), Nowhere, Somewhere, Everywhere: The Arts in Education, *Art Education Policy Review*, *100*(5), p. 31.

4. See, for example, the Artful Learning model at the Leonard Bernstein Center for Artful Learning at Gettysburg College: http://www.artfullearning.com

5. See, for an example of visualizing abstract concepts, the Metropolitan Museum of Art's Explore and Learn analysis of this painting: http://www.metmuseum.org/explore/gw/el_gw.htm

6. See the work of Bob Moses' Algebra Project: www.algebra.org

7. See *Putting the Arts in the Picture: Reframing Education in the 21st Century* (2004), Rabkin, N. & Redmond, R. (Eds.), Chicago: Columbia College.

8. Consult the work of Urban Gateways in Chicago (http://www.urban-gateways.org/); or Young Audiences (http://www.youngaudiences.org/); or Studio in a School (http://www.studioinaschool.org) in New York.

9. For greater detail, see Project Zero's national study of museums and learning described in J. Davis (1996), *The MUSE BOOK (Museums Uniting with Schools in Education—Building on Our Knowledge)*. Cambridge, MA: Presidents and Fellows of Harvard College (available through Harvard Project Zero Bookstore).

10. See Madeja, S. (2001), Remembering the aesthetic education program: 1966 to 1976 in Congdon, Blandy, and Bolin (Eds.), *Histories of Community-Based Art Education*. Reston, VA: NAEA, pp. 117–127.

11. See the Lincoln Center Institute at http://www.lcinstitute.org/

12. See Housen, A. (1983), *The Eye of the Beholder: Measuring Aesthetic Development*. Ed.D. Dissertation. Harvard University. Parsons, M. J. (1987). *How We Understand Art: A Cognitive Developmental Account of Aesthetic Experience.* Cambridge UK: Cambridge University Press.

13. Maureen Grolnick (Ed.) (2006), *Forever After: New York City Teachers on 9/11*. New York: Teachers College Press.

14. See our research at Project Zero: J. Davis, E. Soep, S. Maira, N. Remba, D. Putnoi (1994), *Safe Havens: Portraits of Educational Effectiveness in Community Art Centers that Focus on Education in Economically Disadvantaged Communities.* Cambridge, MA: Presidents and Fellows of Harvard College.

15. Ibid and see *Coming Up Taller Reports* (2005 by Elizabeth Murfee; 1998 by Judith H. Weitz) published by and available from the President's Committee on the Arts and Humanities, www.pcah.gov/; and see especially the work of James Catarall and Shirley Bryce Heath in the *Champions of Change* report available from artsedge.kennedy-center.org

16. See www.manchesterguild.org

17. See artistscollective.org

18. p. 42 in J. Davis, E. Soep, S. Maira, N. Remba, D. Putnoi (1994), *Safe Havens: Portraits of Educational Effectiveness in Community Art Centers That Focus on Education in Economically Disadvantaged Communities.* Cambridge, MA: Presidents and Fellows of Harvard College.

19. For a representative list, check out finalists and winners at the Coming Up Taller awards website: http://www.cominguptaller.org/

20. As examples, the DaVinci School in Dallas, Texas, is dedicated to science; the DaVinci Academy of Science and Art in Ogden, Utah, is dedicated to science, technology, and art; and the daVinci Arts in Portland, Oregon, and the Academie Da Vinci in Dunedin, Florida, are arts-based.

21. See results from SAT student self-report questionnaire from 2001–2005, posted by the National Association for Music Education at www.mence.org/information/advocate/sat.html

22. Now called *Locust Street Neighborhood Art Classes*; see locustst@buffnet. net

23. Guidebooks for portfolio assessment in writing, visual arts, and music as well as other publications related to assessment based on understanding can be found at the Project Zero website: http://www.pz.harvard.edu/ ebookstore

Chapter 2. The Case for the Arts in Education

1. A version of this essay first appeared in *Education Week* (October, 1996), Editorial Projects in Education: Washington, D.C.

2. Such findings are included in David Fowler's *Strong Arts, Strong Schools* (1996), New York: Oxford University Press.

3. This study was done by Ellen Winner and Lois Hetland and is described in the monograph *Beyond the Soundbite* (2001, J. Paul Getty Trust).

4. Now principal, Susan O'Neil, who collected materials and wrote *The MUSE Guide* (1996), Cambridge, MA: President and Fellows of Harvard College.

5. Interesting discussions of the function of arts learning broadly and in terms of the different art forms can be found in a document of considerable importance to arts education advocates: Consortium of National Arts Education Associations (1994), *National Standards for Arts Education: What Every Young American Should Know and Be Able to Do in the Arts*. Reston, VA: Music Educators National Conference.

6. For further description, see Davis, J. H. (1991), *Artistry Lost: U-Shaped Development in Graphic Symbolization*. Doctoral dissertation, Harvard Graduate School of Education; Davis, J. H. (1997), Drawing's demise: U-shaped development in graphic symbolization. *Studies in Art Education, 38*(3), 132–157.

7. This point is eloquently emphasized throughout the work of philosopher Maxine Greene. See for example, Greene, M. (1995), *Releasing the Imagination*. San Francisco: Jossey-Bass; and Greene, M. (2001), *Variations on a Blue Guitar*. New York: Teachers College Press.

8. See Tolstoy, L. (1995) [orig. 1898], *What Is Art?* London: Viking Penguin Books.

9. A much-cited study challenging the myth of the universality of early children's drawing was done by Professor Alexander Alland and described in his 1983 book, *Playing with Form: Children Draw in Six Cultures*. New York: Columbia University Press.

10. Csikzentmihalyi, M. (1990), *Flow: The Psychology of Optimal Experience*. New York: Harper & Row.

Chapter 3. Advocating for the Arts in Education

1. A version of this essay first appeared as a commentary in *Education Week* (October, 2003). Editorial Projects in Education: Washington, D.C.

2. See *Passion and Industry: Schools That Focus on the Arts* (2001), with Ackerman, J., Bernard, R., Brody, A., Gatambidés-Fernandez, R. Cambridge, MA: President and Fellows of Harvard College.

3. See E. Winner and L. Hetland (Eds.), The Arts and Academic Achievement: What the Evidence Shows in *The Journal of Aesthetic Education, 34* (3/4), Fall/Winter, 2000.

4. See Aristotle's *Poetics*, e.g. (1951) translated by S. H. Butcher. *Aristotle's Theory of Poetry and Fine Art with a Critical Text and Translation of the Poetics.* New York: Dover Publications.

5. The term "whole child" is attributed to the great American philosopher, John Dewey (1859–1952), who had an unforgettable humanistic and democratic approach to education.

6. As a key thinker of this period, see Viktor Lowenfeld in Lowenfeld, V. and Brittain, W. L. (1970). *Creative and Mental Growth* (5th ed.). New York: Macmillan [First edition 1947].

7. See the Glossary of Terms in this volume for further explanation of Arts Propel.

8. There is much interest in and debate around the effects of listening to classical music on the brain function of babies and preschoolers. It is nicely described in Weinberger, Norman M., "The Mozart Effect: A Small Part of the Big Picture." *MuSICA Research Notes*, Vol VII, Issue 1, Winter 2000. Available online @ http://www.musica.uci.edu/mrn/V7I1W00.html

9. See http://www.sparcmurals.org/

10. See http://www.youth2youth.org/resources/frameset.html

11. See *Culture in Action: A Public Art Program of Sculpture* with essays by Michael Brenson, Eva M. Olson, Mary Jane Jacob (Eds.), Sculpture Chicago (1995). Seattle, WA: Bay Press.

12. See *From Anecdote to Evidence: Assessing the Status and Condition of Arts Education at the State Level,* Ruppert, S. and Nelson, A., an AEP Research and Policy Brief. Washington, D.C.: Arts Education Partnership, November, 2006.

13. See Boal, A. (1992), *Games for Actors and Non-Actors.* New York: Routledge Press.

Chapter 4. With an Eye to the Future

1. See *State Policy Makers' Views on the Arts in Education*, April 2006, Miller, J., published by the Education Commission of the States and available at ecs@ecs.org; also check out the new report from the Governor's Commission on the Arts in Education at www.ecs.org/huckabee

2. A version of this essay first appeared as a commentary in *Education Week* (March, 1999). Editorial Projects in Education: Washington D.C.

Index

About the Author

Jessica Hoffmann Davis is a writer, researcher, and educator with an abiding interest in the role of the arts in education. At Harvard University's Graduate School of Education, Davis was the founding director of the Arts in Education Program, a senior lecturer, and the first appointee to the Bauman and Bryant Chair in the Arts in Education. In national studies at Harvard's Project Zero, Davis explored educational effectiveness in urban community art centers and inquiry-based learning in art museums. This work is described in several monographs: *Safe Havens* (1994), *Another Safe Haven* (1996), *The Wheel in Motion: The Co-Arts Assessment Plan from Theory to Action* (1996), and *The MUSE (Museums Uniting with Schools in Education) Book* (1996). Her study of portraiture as a qualitative research methodology is addressed in her co-authored book, *The Art and Science of Portraiture* (1997) and represented in *Passion and Industry: Schools that Focus on the Arts* (2001). Widely published in academic journals and texts, Davis devoted her most recent book, *Framing Education as Art: The Octopus Has a Good Day* (Teachers College Press, 2005) to the challenge of making non-arts education more connected to and like the arts.

WINDOWS *into the* LIGHT

WINDOWS
into the
LIGHT

A Lenten Journey of Stories and Art

MICHAEL SULLIVAN

MOREHOUSE PUBLISHING
An imprint of Church Publishing Inc.
HARRISBURG—NEW YORK

Morehouse Publishing, 4775 Linglestown Road, Harrisburg, PA 17112

Morehouse Publishing, 445 Fifth Avenue, New York, NY 10016

Morehouse Publishing is an imprint of Church Publishing Incorporated.

Cover art courtesy of istockphoto.com
Cover design by Jennifer Glosser / 2Pug Design
Interior design by Corey Kent
Interior illustrations by Dorothy Thompson Perez

Library of Congress Cataloging-in-Publication Data

Sullivan, Michael, 1966 Nov. 20-
    Windows into the light : a lenten journey of stories and art / Michael Sullivan.
    p. cm.
ISBN 978-0-8192-2322-7 (pbk.)
1. Lent. I. Title.
BV85.S825 2008
242'.34–dc22
2008026995

Printed in the United States of America

08 09 10 11 12 13   10 9 8 7 6 5 4 3 2 1

For Mattie and Jack,

whose love is a constant window to the light

☙❧

CONTENTS

ACKNOWLEDGMENTS

THE PAGES OF THIS BOOK capture the lives of people I've been lucky enough to encounter along my journey. Some I've known very well; others only for a moment in time. But however long we walked the path together, we found God in seeing each other face to face. At times, we knew of God's presence within the event itself. The steps of the path revealed God's faithfulness and mercy as life unfolded before our eyes. At other times, especially stories that reflect upon my childhood, seeing God took years; God came in bits and pieces assembled over weeks, months, and years instead of in one package nicely wrapped. For all that each person shared and for all given to me in our meeting, I give thanks. This book is really about them—each of them a window to God who entrusted me with the darkness and light in their lives.

In some cases, I have used real names with permission. In other cases, especially when I could no longer contact the person, the name has been changed.

I thank the members of St. John's Episcopal Parish in Lynchburg, Virginia, who have honored me by accepting writing as a part of my priesthood. They have been a supportive congregation and have heard some of these stories in various stages of formation. Indeed, they have lived some of them firsthand.

I also thank my editor, Nancy Fitzgerald of Church Publishing, whose expertise and insight is never judgmental, but always professional and encouraging. I am a much better writer because of her tremendous help.

In addition, Ryan Masteller, my copy editor, has pulled the manuscript together, making sure that I remembered all the details that make a book like this one flow and read better.

My secretary, Gayle Rhodes, has juggled many an office task to make my writing possible. Without her ever-patient help, this book would have taken months longer in the manuscript stages.

And above all, I thank my family. My children, to whom I dedicate this book, are nothing short of the clearest windows into the love of God. For mornings when I have been writing, instead of spending time with them, I owe them greatly. They often read my writing and make suggestions; they are incredible. And Page Poston Sullivan, my partner in life and stalwart companion, without whose love, care, grace, and support I would not be complete.

INTRODUCTION

I REMEMBER WHEN I was child, riding with my parents through the countryside for what seemed like an eternity, waiting anxiously to turn onto the gravel drive that wound its way through trees to my grandparents' house. There, on the farm, things seemed simpler, even to a child. Running barefoot in the flower gardens, finding rocks along the streams, wondering from which tree a branch had fallen all became the occupations of a young boy without television or next-door-neighbor-friends. The farm provided memories I revisit almost every day of my life.

In the middle of afternoons there, I took a nap. With a window open beside the bed, the gentle mountain breezes would flow into the room, caressing my body. Old, cranky windows with roped weights in the frame, it took effort to open them. Their years of paint and splintering evident to even the smallest child, the windows seemed heavy as if they were witnesses to life, full of wisdom. As I fell asleep, I sometimes wondered what they had seen. What had happened in the house that they had held in, holding close to the pane, close to the crosses separating the glass? What had they secretly witnessed in their hundred-plus years? Childbirth and death. Health and sickness.

Harvest and famine. Wealth and poverty. Abundance and drought. Happiness and fear.

My grandmother claimed that windows begged to be open. She talked of them as if they had a spirit, a soul or something, as if opening them was a secret commandment Moses received, possibly written on the back of one of the tablets. So no matter how cold the weather, she always cracked at least one window in the house somewhere. Usually, it was in the front room, the guest bedroom that had years earlier served as my mom's room. With the window cracked there in winter, it was freezing when I tried to take a nap. But Granny claimed that a window had to be open so that the good spirits could come in and the bad ones go out. Spring, summer, and fall were easier seasons for napping under the mysterious commandment, "Thou shalt always open a window."

I remember thinking that Granny had to be crazy or something she talked about the windows so much. One summer, after I read the *Lion, the Witch and the Wardrobe*, I wondered if she was right after all. Could there be a window somewhere in her house, a special window to a magical land, a window she didn't want to tell me about? One day while visiting that summer, I decided that the window in her bedroom was the most likely candidate to lead to such a special place. So, into her bedroom I went, opened the window some twelve feet above the ground and jumped into the meticulously trimmed, thick greenery only to discover the hardness of both the ground and my Granny's spanking hand for breaking one of her prized boxwood specimens in the garden. Even though she punished me, I sensed a glimmer of laughter, knowing that I had opened a window, and jumped through it to search for something beyond, something from another world. In retrospect, I know my grandmother was proud of me for jumping out that window. I think she knew that I hadn't found Narnia—she was just glad I was looking through the panes toward a brighter light. I could see it in her eyes.

No wonder windows have always been icons for me. They have framed my life. They watch everything that happens each day, standing silently by as witnesses to the light. But when they remain closed, the pain they hold cannot escape and we cease to look through them toward something brighter, better, and holier. The air within becomes stagnant and the rooms they enlighten become dark, as the drapes of our hearts are pulled together and shut tight. We've all closed such windows. We've all held things in. We've all known this struggle.

Lent lets us open the windows to invite fresh air and sunlight back in. It's the time to crack the window just like my Granny did, let the bad spirits go, and usher in God's redeeming love through light.

This book frames that journey. It provides a way to face whatever holds us back and helps us to let go of all the things claiming our lives, preventing us from living as the people God called into being. It's your opportunity to find wholeness when you throw open the drapes, thrust up the panes from the sill, and embrace your new life with openness.

Our journey follows the Lenten pathway of the Christian year. The trek begins on Ash Wednesday, and in the chapters that follow, the church's readings for the Sundays in Lent continue to guide us. The lesson, printed at the beginning of each chapter along with traditional and contemporary prayers, will help you consider how God invites you to open the window once again, to take that leap into the unknown, seeking new light shining before you. Hopefully, along the way you'll be able, little by little, to face directly into all the unresolved darkness of life and discover a loving and nurturing light from God. We'll make our trek from the hurt, despair, and difficulty of all our Good Fridays toward the hope, grace, and mercy of resurrection.

The chapters unfold according to this ancient rhythm of sacred story, certain that in their words we'll discover a common bond with the characters of scripture who walked before us. But to make the connection even clearer, each sacred narrative of the past is accompanied by a sacred expression from the present followed by an exercise that will help you find the story in your life. By hearing both the ancient story and the way that story is lived out in lives today, we find our common place along the pathway and begin to hear sacred texts anew.

Monastic communities have long known this common bond and have valued it in their lives together. Abbots and nuns have sought to engage each other and all before them in their quest to open windows to the light. Most of us think that monks and nuns are all about personal, introspective relationships with God; it's the communal nature of their experiences that we often forget. The contemplation and meditation, the work and discipline, are all carried out among the fabric of the community's narrative. The individual gets closer to God through the experience of the sacred story in self and in other. In the best of these communities, devotion doesn't enforce belief but engenders life through shared story. Doctrine isn't the focus. Faithfulness to the ground of all being in the daily lives of the community focuses the life of prayer. The personal quest for God and the communal belief that the relationship has already been found in our common bonds are interdependent: there's a constant ebb and flow from the person to the community and vice versa as each learns from the other. The sacred story is lived as each person's narrative intersects with the community's story and the church's experience in scripture. In that intersection, the windows of life open and fresh air and warmth blow in. One person's midnight of the soul is transformed into the noonday brightness of the sun.

The stories of each chapter form a monastic community of sorts, a place for you to abide in safety as you consider how your life intersects with God's story. The Lenten readings are illumined through the story of someone I've known. These people, gracious enough to allow their narratives to become words in a book, now see the struggles of the past as light for a new day. In some cases, I've changed names if I couldn't get in touch with them. Narratives of doubts, fears, and struggles become windows of opportunity as the sill is broken and resurrection light streams in among the pains. By sharing their lives, they become your brothers, your sisters, your fellow pilgrims along the path.

As you set out for discovery, the hardest challenge may be deciding which windows you'll need to open. Sometimes we're intimately aware of the windows in our lives. The sill that separates our darkness from the light is apparent. A disease, estranged relationship, or other event in our lives is so present that we know where God's grace is needed. But at other times, the darkened windows are hard to find. The pain of an experience, the loss of someone or something is so great that we've shut the windows long ago, covered them completely, and abandoned them to the darkness. In some cases, we've abandoned them to our subconscious and we no longer realize that they're there. This book addresses both the windows we know and those we've forgotten in the hope that God's light can come to them all.

As we begin our journey, a few suggestions might help as you begin to hear the stories of sacred scripture and people I've known.

Reading the stories

How you read both the Bible and the stories is critical to your self-discovery. Too many of us read the biblical narrative only to find some external kernel of hope and truth within it, completely dissected from our real life. We're also tempted to read others' stories in the same way, as if we'll find an answer to cut and paste into our own lives. To find the true meaning of scripture in our lives, we must seek both the comfortable and uncomfortable among the texts. We can't read stories of faith as if they were textbooks with things to memorize in order to do well on a test. The Bible isn't about external truth—something isolated from us as if discoverable in a science lab. Likewise, people's personal stories are not merely facts to import into our own experience. How the sacred story is present in other people's lives will often appeal to the rhyme and rhythm of your life, but the melody won't be identical. The real invitation of sacred story is to discern the narrative within our own lives that intersects God's life. That's the window we need to open, the place where our story collides with God's.

An example might help illustrate this process. We could read the story of Joseph and his brothers and draw a simple conclusion about forgiveness. The brothers sold Joseph into slavery. Joseph found favor with the rulers and ended up in a place of authority. During a drought years later, the brothers appeared, and Joseph forgave them. End of story. Lesson learned: forgive and forget. An external truth. A cookie cutter lesson to apply to our lives.

That's not the point at all. The story is about God and God's faithfulness in spite of the horrors of life. Instead of coming up with a pithy statement to apply haphazardly in our lives, we step into Joseph's shoes, lamenting with him the actions of others only to discover God's love in spite of it all. It is in that place, a place that God creates, that estranged relationships hear of God's goodness, and small cracks begin appearing in the windowsills. The story is not about forgiving and forgetting. It's about God moving in us and giving the power of new relationship while acknowledging the hurt and despair that came from estrangement.

So embrace the difficulty of the stories, their very realness, and ask how the metaphor within them is present in your life. The facts may be different, the plot may not be as thick, or the themes may take you in a different direction. But look for the places of similar rhyme and rhythm to explore what happens as your story and God's collide.

Opening our souls to the unknown

Facing the realities of your life is not as easy as it seems. Openness to the journey with God means openness to the unknown. God is, after all, the very definition of unknown. None of us knows the fullness of God. But what we know of God leads us toward a fuller, more complete relationship with God. God as the ground of all being has given us all we need as full human beings created in the image and likeness of God. And as Christians, we have the love and mercy of God present in Jesus Christ, which encourages us to make the trek out into the unknown. Christ and his love for us form a kind of blueprint for our willingness to face the threshold—for in Christ's love for us, we know we go there with him and that in the end, Christ will walk the darkest night with us to find the hope of morning.

The soul and the body

Hearing the stories and using the exercises that follow will help recover the relationship of the soul's movement to that of the body's. This relationship is another trait taken for granted in monastic communities but hardly even acknowledged in modern life. The monk knows the daily cycle of prayer, the constant movement toward relationship with God. The monk, waking to pray, working to pray, walking to pray, resting to pray, is in constant conversation with God. In life outside monastery walls, most people have lost the bodily relationship to prayer. Sitting quietly in a room and listening for God has been replaced with telling God our litany of things wished for, as if our petitions were the most important avenue of prayer. If we can discover something of the monk's bodily experience of prayer, we might be able to expand our spiritual life into mindfulness at all times—not just a few words said before meals or just before sleep.

What to do when you discover an old window

Don't be surprised if following the Lenten journey opens old wounds still in need of healing. Some wounds are so deep that jumping into the narrative of God's love can be traumatic; it reveals the windows we've hidden as we walk the path to the cross. If we're willing to engage the cross of our own life so that Christ can bear it with us, then the deep wounds of life will have a way of being reopened as we engage the Lenten journey. If you uncover windows that are particularly difficult or painful, don't hesitate to talk with a pastoral counselor or therapist. Such professionals can be of enormous assistance as we walk our journey. Seeking a professional's guidance isn't a sign of weakness but of greatest strength.

Sharing with a spiritual friend

You might also consider a spiritual friend to help you along the way. You could read this book with one or two others, or form a small group within your church or community. In some cases, you might also consider a spiritual director. Spiritual directors are not therapists, but trained professionals who ask about the voice of God in your life. They provide accountability and are often skilled in the identification of spiritual disciplines for our lives.

Encourage silence

Finally, don't be surprised if your time with God becomes more silent, meditative, or contemplative. As you engage the narratives of scripture through the experiences of others along the journey, sacred story will begin to live within you. As it does, your soul will crave more silence, God's opportunity to speak. Consider joining a contemplative prayer group, especially one that uses centering prayer, or carving out time to sit in silence each day. You might use that time to reflect upon the soul questions of each chapter or to review your progress through the book. Silence can be key in pulling back the drapes and opening the windows of your soul. After all, the light in the window has no sound.

All these suggestions provide a means for your soul to make its own way down that curving country road toward a welcoming house with open windows. As you go, allow the people of the biblical and contemporary narratives to guide you, their stories intersecting with your own life to reveal God's trusting love in all that you encounter. Trust God's Spirit to reveal the pathway you're intended to take as you embark upon the journey. To guide our way and shape our prayers, the next chapter illumines the methods we'll use to help the soul reflect upon our journey.

WINDOW ONE

The Spiritual Exercises:
Art as the Soul's Expression

THE SPIRITUAL EXERCISES that follow each narrative provide an opportunity to open the windows toward God's light. These exercises use various artistic methods to surprise the soul with new awareness and hope. They create bridges between what you read and your own life, a way to jump from the light in another person's life into your own. These exercises are easy to follow and require no artistic experience or expertise. You don't need expensive supplies or a studio. All you need is an open heart and mind—a willingness to engage God's journey with you as you discover your life.

Art opens our experience to newness in our prayers. Most of us use far too much of our left brain in daily life; the side that processes rational, linear thought drives most of what we do. The creative, metaphorical part of our brain, the right side, begins to slumber. The richness of the sacred story, an art form in itself, is not perceived when we read because we haven't nurtured this creative side of our creation. To get back into the narrative of God's love for us, to jump back into all the possibilities of grace and mercy, we must find a way to awaken this creativity.

Because art relies almost exclusively on this creative, encompassing side of the brain, it's the perfect way to bring our whole being back into the sacred story. By using a right-brain activity such as collage, our senses experience the depth contained within the narrative. It's as if the art gives us permission to enter into the drama of God's redemption anew, just as if we're seeing God on stage with us in the day-to-day experiences of our lives.

As you take this journey, you might remember a few helpful hints as you walk toward God's love. And because many people don't think of themselves as artists, consider first these easy, artistic pointers:

- *You are already the masterpiece, so don't worry about what you create.* The old saying "God don't make no junk" is the first law of our spiritual life. We'll take more time to work with this theme later, but know that you are the masterpiece and that the art you create, while good, is not the focus. You are.

- *Technique is not as important as willingness, for willingness to engage the process is central to the journey.* When I lead art workshops, time and time again one or two participants get stuck. Instead of jumping into the expression of the soul, they get caught up in the red herring of "How do I do this . . . how do I do that?" After years of using the left brain, they are stuck there, going from point a to point b, linear, rational, cerebral the whole way. It's not their fault at all; they are just doing what they've been trained to do.

  In the end, techniques aren't important at all. We're trying to get to an artistic place of openness where we can express our complete selves on the spiritual canvases of life so that we can expose the richness of who we were created to be. Stick with the method and let the creative process take a life of its own. But just in case you need to know more about art, how to uninstall all the linear, left-brain thoughts, and what you can do to bridge the gap to your right brain, here are some simple techniques that usually work.

All you needed to know about art you knew when you were three years old. When we were young, we were uninhibited. Because we didn't know that there was a "right" way or a "beautiful" way, we just colored, drew, and scribbled to our heart's content. In such a place, our inner thoughts and feelings were freely displayed upon the paper and canvases we employed. We didn't have to try—it just happened. Later, when we discovered high art, especially realism, our inhibitions came front and center and expressions of the heart became more difficult. Without the freedom of childhood, we became fearful and anxious.

The exercises in the book build upon each other. The methodology is constructed to take you back to a place of freedom and openness—the same place you had when you were in kindergarten coloring away without a care in the world. If you follow the instructions, inhibitions will slowly fall away and you will find a place to be more honest and open in your expression along the journey.

Working quickly is the fastest way back to childhood. With all the fears of doing it right, we slow down and painstakingly try to mimic the great art forms instilled through galleries and images all around us. We take our time with each line, every curve, and the precise color. But if we take away the time for reflection on the method, the right side of the brain, the more creative, free side, takes over. By working as quickly as possible, we trick our minds into creativity and open our beings to a place of freedom few of us usually tap.

In most of the exercises, you'll note an instruction about working without reflection. It'll probably take time to embrace this concept fully, but with practice, you'll find a place of "unknowing" where you'll gain the freedom to work creatively. Ironically, when you engage this place of freedom, you'll express the clearest picture of who you are and what you need to present to God in your spiritual life. By going to this place of emptiness, where you're mindful only of the task before you, the inhibitions of the brain let go and the soul takes flight.

Collage is the basic method of most meditations. Collage is our basic method because it allows us to work quickly and without reflection. By cutting or tearing images from magazines and other print media, we're able to respond immediately to any image that claims us. We don't need to reflect why—we just tear it from the page. If an image grabs our attention, we take it from the page and know that we can use it later. If part of an image speaks to us, we take only that part and need not worry about the other form left behind. Because we don't need to draw or color the form ourselves, we're able to work quickly and effectively, relying on the images others have created but that speak to us. This technique gets us into the metaphorical life quickly and frees us from lack of artistic experience. Expression comes in the arrangement of the collage, and in later exercises, mixed media is also employed for those who wish to be more expressive or technical in their work.

If you are drawing or doodling as a part of the exercise, try using your nondominant hand. Just as collage fools our brain into creativity, using your nondominant hand for some exercises will as well. If you are right-handed and use your right hand to draw a picture, the same part of your brain that processes information on a daily basis is employed. But when you use your nondominant hand, you force the brain to use the more creative side. By asking your body to employ a part you rarely use, it's as if that part goes back to the three-year-old way of doing things—if for no other reason than it has not caught up to the other side's way of doing something.

When doing a collage, try assembling it upside down. Working quickly and using your nondominant hand are two tricks of the trade often employed to increase creativity. One used less often, but sometimes with amazing results, is working with the paper or canvas upside down. When creating an image upside down, the brain cannot as readily see relationships. Because seeing things right side up is the norm, the brain becomes so accustomed to the orderly arrangement of images that it cannot process them in the same way when inverted. Fear of doing things wrong eases. Because we are not able to process it as readily, a collage or other art form created upside down can reveal deeper creativity, and thus, expose the soul's journey more readily. The mind makes uninhibited, free associations between images as they are pasted together. We'll use this method after working with collage several times, but if you feel you're ready for it early on, try it to see what happens.

Don't purchase expensive supplies. These exercises may produce great art you want to keep for many years. But don't worry about breaking the bank to do so. Most of the exercises will use old magazines easily obtained from neighbors, friends, or even from the recycle bin of your local library, as well as other everyday materials.

You might also look for mixed media supplies such as yarns, old greeting cards, natural objects, and daily items you no longer need. In early chapters, you'll probably stick to the instructions given. But as you gain confidence, you might incorporate other objects to provide depth and a three-dimensional effect. When we use markers or paints, the most inexpensive variety will do. Any local store will be a perfect supplier.

Create a gallery in your home to see your progress along the journey. As you create the collages in the exercises, keep them. If you can, find a place to display them. By creating your own gallery, you will not only see the progress of your journey, you will acknowledge its integrity and authenticity.

Some people enjoy keeping a portfolio of their work, a kind of journal. Although such a process will limit the size of your creations, it does provide a chronicle of your spiritual journey. I like this practice for those who are seasoned with the discipline of daily prayer and are looking for a new way to journal. I usually don't recommend it to those just beginning their journey. Having a smaller space, as required by a portfolio or large sketchbook, can be too limiting for any person just beginning to express the longings of the heart. On the other hand, some beginners desire the privacy such a portfolio provides. I leave it up to you.

If you follow these simple suggestions, you'll be amazed at how quickly you'll find new meaning in the exercises. The artistic method really does open the process quickly and provides the way to move to the sills and thresholds of life. But enough with our process and method; it's time for the journey.

WINDOW TWO

Ash Wednesday

Almighty and everlasting God, you hate nothing you have made and forgive the sins of all who are penitent: Create and make in us new and contrite hearts, that we, worthily lamenting our sins and acknowledging our wretchedness, may obtain of you, the God of all mercy, perfect remission and forgiveness; through Jesus Christ our Lord, who lives and reigns with you and the Holy Spirit, one God, for ever and ever. *Amen.* —*The Book of Common Prayer,* page 217[1]

God who rises from the ashes, go with me into my places of grief and doubt; fill me with love and respect for the life I have been given; and teach me to hear my life speak of your light no matter the darkness that I feel; through Jesus the Christ, who always liberates and loves with abandon. *Amen.*

---

1. Collects at the opening of each chapter are from the 1979 revision of *The Book of Common Prayer* (New York: Oxford University Press).

MATTHEW 6:1–6, 16–21

(Beware of practicing your piety before others)

Jesus said, "Beware of practicing your piety before others in order to be seen by them; for then you have no reward from your Father in heaven. So whenever you give alms, do not sound a trumpet before you, as the hypocrites do in the synagogues and in the streets, so that they may be praised by others. Truly I tell you, they have received their reward. But when you give alms, do not let your left hand know what your right hand is doing, so that your alms may be done in secret; and your Father who sees in secret will reward you. And whenever you pray, do not be like the hypocrites; for they love to stand and pray in the synagogues and at the street corners, so that they may be seen by others. Truly I tell you, they have received their reward. But whenever you pray, go into your room and shut the door and pray to your Father who is in secret; and your Father who sees in secret will reward you. And whenever you fast, do not look dismal, like the hypocrites, for they disfigure their faces so as to show others that they are fasting. Truly I tell you, they have received their reward. But when you fast, put oil on your head and wash your face, so that your fasting may be seen not by others but by your Father who is in secret; and your Father who sees in secret will reward you. Do not store up for yourselves treasures on earth, where moth and rust consume and where thieves break in and steal; but store up for yourselves treasures in heaven, where neither moth nor rust consumes and where thieves do not break in and steal. For where your treasure is, there your heart will be also."

☙❧

Three-year-olds are the best theologians.

When my son Jack was three, he was a regular Paul Tillich, a small active body with eternal truths thrown out at a pace one couldn't fathom. My wife and I would be standing in the kitchen, having our glass of wine and preparing dinner, when Jack would casually stride in and pronounce something like, "God is sad today; people were hungry on TV," referring to a segment on the news, or "Jesus loves that man on the street, Daddy," remembering the homeless man we passed each morning as we drove to pre-school.

And without a doubt, he showed me up. All the post-graduate work at Duke, seminary, and even my law school years had not taught me what he already knew about life. I had known this truth since the day he was born; Jack just had that extra something that so many of us want so badly. But his infinite wisdom came clearly into focus when a young man in the parish I was serving died of cancer. My son, growing up in the house of a priest, had long known that people died in the middle of the night; beepers and telephones at three in the morning wake even the smallest among us. But this death, one that came over months and not in an instant, served as a catalyst for something deep within my son—something at the core of his being and at the core of the Christian journey.

Jack had known about this particular parishioner for a while. Because the man was young and because I talked about him all the time, Jack had known the name William and the idea of his cancer for about two years. Somehow, even at his age, Jack seemed to accept the fact that life was throwing this young man a curve ball early on, and he'd long decided that the inevitable would happen. So when William died, Jack was ready—well, at least at the end of the whole story he was. But nothing had prepared him, or me for that matter, for all that we would learn together over the unfolding days and months surrounding William's death.

William had planned every detail of his funeral. The service was to be held in a gorgeous gothic structure—you know, the kind of heart-pine, country gothic parish that was built all over creation back when Episcopalians had more money than God (well, I suppose some things never change). Stained glass, some of it Tiffany;

dark, oak, much of it hand-carved; slate roof and stone walls from a local quarry; and a gallery organ imported from Europe—they all set the scene for the unexpected—a band of guitars, bass, drums, and even a little brass. You see, in a very non-Episcopal fashion, William had selected some of the best hits of the rock and roll era for his service. No Bach or Beethoven for this young man. No, the cancer had made William more sure of himself at the age of twenty than most people are at eighty, and in the process, he knew how to make a liturgy reflect the spiritual journey of his soul; this wasn't going to be yet another cookie-cutter liturgy from the pages of yesterday. No, William's life was going to make its mark amidst the story of God's amazing grace. His own reflection on twenty years would be the narrative of God's love.

I'd told Jack a band would be playing for the funeral. Now, in addition to being an early theologian, Jack was also an early musical artist. His guitar, which had come in a box from China, probably constructed by another child not much older than my son, had been played so much in his short life that the strings were starting to fray. The type of child that would listen intently to his mom and dad's music and then mimic every syllable, he lived for music in his life. I'm not sure if it started when he fell asleep to Enya night after night or when he heard Van Morrison or U2 for the first time, but whatever the cause, music lived within his little soul. So, the thought of going to hear a live band in church when he had already endured the organ for three long years was just too much for him to pass by. He'd already asked me, in the car one day, as usual, why we didn't hear church music anywhere but church. He had asked, "Is that the only music God can hear?" in another of this theological moments. Knowing that I'd probably messed up the answer once again, I told him we'd go listen to the band rehearse for William's funeral. I wasn't too sure about him attending the service—I figured he wasn't ready for that—so on the morning of the funeral, I took him over to the parish while the band practiced. When we walked in, Jack's face lit up—he loved it. And so for over an hour, he sat there listening to the band rehearse the music of William's soul, hits from the rock and roll greats.

But as we left the church, I made a massive mistake. I took Jack through the tower doorway, crossing the threshold into the columbarium. And there, right at his eye level on the right side of the tower as we walked through was an open niche—a gaping eight-inch square hole in the side of the tower wall. Seeing the open niche, Jack innocently asked what it was, and without thinking, without using my eleven years of college and post-graduate education, I replied, "That's where we'll place William at the end of the service."

Immediately, I could see that this small space was not computing in my son's head. His random access memory was whirling in his mind trying desperately to figure it out, and I was kicking myself again and again in my own mental anguish over having said something so foolish to my three-year-old son.

"How's he fitting in there, Daddy? He was tall."

And again, without using any of my common sense, let alone all that education, I uttered massive mistake number two from my lips. "Well, all that's left of him are his ashes."

"Ashes?" Jack replied. Again, the wheels were turning. "You mean like in the fireplace?"

And again, massive mistake number three came from my lips as I explained how the funeral home helped nature along and heated the body until it became dust, as it had been from the beginning of the time. Ridiculous me; I was actually proud I had said "heated," a more pastoral, priestly, understanding answer this time, I thought.

My son's education once again exceeded my own. He immediately burst into tears. I knelt down by the niche opening, and Jack ran to me in anger, beating me on my chest, screaming, "No, Daddy! No! No! No! No!" And for the next five, maybe ten minutes I held him in my arms as he wept deeply. In his own way, Jack was crying for William, but more importantly, for the loss of something innocent in his own soul. Seeing the small space, realizing that William was really dead, that his body had been reduced to ashes, and that all that was left of this young man would be placed in a wall and closed off forever was just more than Jack could take. It was more than I could take. It was more than anyone would fathom. So we wept together, and even though I tried to talk with him about it later, Jack never really wanted to. The theologian had seen death and the child within began to contemplate life.

So, three months later on a Wednesday in March the wisdom of the three-year-old came screaming into our world. We were back in the country gothic parish, sitting among the oak, stone, and stained glass, reading the service in the Book of Common Prayer. We had finished the collect of the day, the lessons, the psalm, and the sermon. We had invited people to a holy Lent, placed ashes upon everyone's foreheads, and taken Communion. Just another service in the liturgical cycle of the Christian Church. Just another step along the journey of the seasons. Just another year, or so I thought.

But as we ended the service, everyone standing to exit in solemnity, my son issued forth an exclamation to an unsuspecting member of our congregation, a professor from a local college no less. "You've got William on your head," Jack exclaimed. And turning to another, "See, you've got William on your head too." And then to another and another and another. Everyone heard. I remember feeling like I should crawl under a rock or into a hole—the priest's kid is acting up again, I thought. Great. More attention. Exactly what we need.

And then I saw the tear. The professor was crying. The lady next to him was crying. And a tear, one I had not even noticed, was falling down my own cheek. My son the theologian had made the connection I had not. Earth to earth, ashes to ashes, dust to dust. I had merely placed burned palm branches from the prior year's Passion Sunday on people's foreheads while Jack had received the ashes of those who had gone before him. He was making the sacred connection between William and Jesus, between cancer and the cross, between the vessels of the sacred heart of God and the soul's journey upon the earth. My three-year-old son was teaching me, was teaching each of us, what it meant to find new life amidst the darkness. Jack was telling me the old, old story of God's redeeming love.

It very well may have been the first time I understood Ash Wednesday. For you see, the best theologians are three-year-olds.

EXERCISE
PREPARING FOR THE JOURNEY

Throughout this Lenten journey, the spiritual exercises will provide a way to live into the sacred stories. As we embark, the first exercise is a simple one, but one that is foundational to the rest. It's based on an activity many people love from time to time in life: reflecting through pictures.

Materials

- Photographs from your life (baby photos through current day).

Method

Get out the photos! Retrieve all the old photographs of your life that you can find. The old square ones with serrated edges, the ones still sitting in drawers with faded envelopes from the photo shop holding your first 35-mm shots when you were twelve years old. The school pictures. The sports team pictures. The best friend's candid shot that captured that moment you wanted to forget then but treasure now. The recent ones you'll view on your laptop. Get them all.

After assembling all the photographs in one spot, take the time to look through them. Remember what your life has been and treasure the good and the bad. Let the images of your life remind you of all that you have faced, all that you have accomplished, and all that you have done. See the people you have loved and the people you have abandoned in fear or anger. Treasure the images. Let them speak.

Work joyously. Say a prayer before you begin, and if you can, pause to pray again from time to time as a photo brings up a thanksgiving, a lament, or even a confession. Let the photographs open your life so that you can share the fullness of who you are with God. If you like, spend several days on this project. Enjoy it and let it be an outward and visible sign of the graced life that you have lived.

The difficult part of the exercise is the final step. You'll need to select at least a hundred or so images that capture your life as you understand it. You'll use these photographs several times in the spiritual exercises throughout the book. If you select images that remind you of your whole life, all the joys and all the pains, the exercises will be much more fruitful. You will present a more authentic self to yourself and to God as we walk the Lenten journey. You might consider making photocopies of the photos instead of using originals, especially for old photos. You could also scan them and run copy sheets from your computer printer. Black and white or sepia tone is often more dramatic for the exercises than color. You might print both or a combination.

When you've finally narrowed your photos down to the final group, take the time to review them. Use these Soul Questions to reflect on this beginning exercise.

Soul Questions

- How did you react to assembling the photos of your life? Was it a scary exercise or did it immediately energize and excite you? Why?
- Were there themes for various times in your life? Could you see times of happiness? Sadness? Celebration? Defeat?
- Did the pictures say anything about your relationship with God? Did a photo or two remind you of any significant spiritual event in your life? Did you remember a spiritual hero? Have you ever looked at your life as a reflection of the spiritual journey?
- Who was missing from the photographs? Were you surprised not to find various people in the snapshots of your life?
- Do you see your childhood and earlier years differently after viewing the photos? Is the memory of them better or worse

than you recall? How does your current life influence how you remember your past?

- Are the photographs accurate portraits of what was really going on in your life or are they just one dimension of what you were really experiencing?

Thoughts for the Journey

- Photos are about as close as we ever come to seeing ourselves as others see us. How do you think you would look if you could observe yourself one day? What would you see? Would it surprise you? What would you want to keep? What would you want to change?
- Someone once said that history doesn't repeat itself but it sure does rhyme. Having visited all the photos of your life, are there old "scenes" that repeat themselves or rhyme? What do they say about your life?
- Find a photo that captures you. Don't look for the "best" photo but the most "poetic"—the one that says, "This is me." Why does it bring all of you to mind? What about it speaks so clearly?

WINDOW THREE

First Sunday in Lent

Almighty God, whose blessed Son was led by the Spirit to be tempted by Satan: Come quickly to help us who are assaulted by many temptations; and, as you know the weaknesses of each of us, let each one find you mighty to save; through Jesus Christ your Son our Lord, who lives and reigns with you and the Holy Spirit, one God, now and for ever. *Amen.* —*The Book of Common Prayer,* page 218

Loving God, you formed us from the dust of the earth and filled us with your life-giving spirit: let us find beauty in our creation, and trusting in your never-failing love, help us to see all our days as opportunities for the freedom you give; through Jesus the Christ, who stooped so low as to know dust himself, and who with the Holy Spirit, still breathes life into us each moment. *Amen.*

MARK 1:9–13

(Baptism of Jesus and temptation in the wilderness)

In those days Jesus came from Nazareth of Galilee and was baptized by John in the Jordan. And just as he was coming up out of the water, he saw the heavens torn apart and the Spirit descending like a dove on him. And a voice came from heaven, "You are my Son, the Beloved; with you I am well pleased." And the Spirit immediately drove him out into the wilderness. He was in the wilderness forty days, tempted by Satan; and he was with the wild beasts; and the angels waited on him.

CB80

Before that Ash Wednesday, I had wished I'd never crossed the threshold into the tower that cold January day. As a father, I wanted to take the whole thing back—to somehow erase my son's experience of death at such an early age as if his experience were a document on a computer. I wanted to take him back to a place where death wasn't in his dictionary, where I was fully in charge of his life, where Daddy could solve anything, make it better, and restore order amidst threatening chaos. When the calls had come in the middle of the night and the deaths had been unknown characters in Daddy's priestly life, Jack had been protected. But when I took his little hand in mine and walked into that church and through the tower door that fateful day, everything changed. I was no longer the supreme daddy of the universe but just an ordinary human being. And more importantly, my son was no longer a toddler, or even a child on some deep level. He had seen life fully, the whole circle, and the three-year-old had grown up.

All this guilt evaporated in the tears streaming down my face when the three-year-old theologian was revealed on Ash Wednesday. Crossing the threshold, Jack had seen the ashes; he knew death. But miraculously, he had also seen light and life. In the simplicity of his proclamation, he had reminded me and all around him that the key to life lies just beyond the threshold.

Few of us realize we're dust: our lives are far too comfortable for us to be in touch with our earthiness. The modern life, with incessant hand-sanitizing, sparkling marble bathrooms, crisp linen sheets, and thick absorbent towels, is quite like checking into a five-star hotel where our dusty lives pass into the distant past. We buy our packaged meat at the butcher, peering into nice little Styrofoam containers to select the best cuts of prime beef, totally separated from the reality that something died for the food we will consume. Our carrots, something grown in the dirt, in all the dust of life, are even clean. They don't even look like carrots anymore—they're just perfect little orange bullets, a virtual dirtless pill of beta-carotene.

Our ancestors didn't bask in this luxury. Death was a constant companion, always lurking behind every shadow. Children often died during birth, and the odds weren't good for the mother either. Toddlers fell prey to the common cold. A woman in her thirties was getting pretty old. The obstacles of getting enough food to eat, protecting one's family from invasion, figuring out where good water flowed, all took precedence over the comfort of a bed. Survival was key, and being in touch with the dust of the earth wasn't a problem at all. Dust was everywhere.

So, why on earth did early Christians leave the comforts of civilization and venture ever deeper into the dust? Why did they make their way to the deserts of Egypt, the recesses of Spain, the north shore of England? And most certainly, why did a group of people venture off the coast of southwestern Ireland to a rock jutting from the depths of the ocean floor?

Skellig Michael is a mammoth rock, rising some nine hundred feet out of the North Atlantic. On a clear day, you can see it jutting from the ocean, with its companion island, Little Skellig, standing close by as if saluting its neighbor, that marvelous monster of a rock. Sometime early in the fifth century, a monk or two dreamed of sailing to Skellig

Michael to seek a deeper relationship with God. But of course, the diesel-powered boats had not pulled into the bay as of yet, so the dream was just a dream—or so it seemed. With time, these monks told others of their desire, and in either great bravery or great stupidity, they joined forces and began building boats, some from logs and others from leather. After many a test in the strong currents of the bay, a group ventured out toward the Skelligs. The boats were small, holding one, two, or three men at most.

Arriving at the Skellig is not fun in the best of boats. The forces of the ocean, rising up against the large rock in the deep sea, produce dramatic and destructive waves that crash upon the jagged edges like a hammer upon an anvil. Even today, visitors to the sight are dismayed at the landing, a narrow gate some sixty feet wide with a varying swell of a good twenty feet on a calm day. How fifth-century people made their way to the Skellig in such small boats, how they garnered the strength to row through unbelievable seas to arrive to jagged, sharp rocks, is incomprehensible to any modern visitor today. But by the end of the fifth century, many a believer had made the trip and the beginning of a monastic community upon the Skellig was taking place.

Instead of a nice organic grocer, these disciples arrived to one small piece of soil, a field between the two peaks, about two-thirds of the way up the Skellig. They named this plot, about the size of two tennis courts, Christ's Saddle. And there, the community raised all its crops. Going back to the mainland to shop wasn't quite an option. On Christ's very back they grew potatoes and other root vegetables to supplement the fish they caught and dried in the summer and fall months. Eventually, they even brought over several cows for milk and some meat—imagine that boat landing! They chose to come to this wilderness, this great rock of dust, and they did what they had to in order to survive.

But the dust of the rock was harsh. Winters were cruel, with cold winds, upwards of seventy miles per hour, howling sometimes for weeks. The monastic community was built some six hundred to seven hundred feet up the rock, probably for defense purposes when the Vikings came calling. But being so high meant facing winter head on; it wasn't at all like checking in a nice Franciscan retreat center with a fireplace and a cozy chapel for contemplation. No, going to the Skellig, facing the lack of food, staring into the wind, listening to the howling silence of God swirling all around the cracks and crags upon the rock, was hard core dust work. Hearing "remember you are dust and to dust you shall return" was the way of life here, not some liturgical rite for once-a-year observance.

But they found something there that gave them life. There on the rock, in the very incarnation of dust, shallow adherence to doctrine for the sake of doctrine was not the theology of the day. Whether one was in the Church or out, whether one believed correctly or not, whether one had defined God forever and ever amen was not even on the radar. Those matters didn't come up in the dirt of Christ's Saddle. No, in this small place of holy women and men the pursuit of God among the dusty dirt was life itself. Prayer with a howling wind and freezing rain was the mantra; contemplation with the birds of the air—puffins and gannets galore in the summer—were the sacraments of redemption and reconciliation; toiling with Adam in the rocky soil and fishing with Peter, James, and John were the oblations of daily work. Life upon the rock was life amid hardship, life within the dust. But more importantly, to toil upon the metaphor of God's earth was where the believer found salvation. In each molecule of dust there was life, the promise of something that had been before and something that would come after. Every spec of dust was essential to growing the crops. Every splinter of wood meant just enough warmth. Every drop of milk. Every single potato, the beautiful and the one half-rotten. Everything, literally every thing, was dust pointing to God—something beyond the rock, something beyond the shore, something worth pursuing in every moment.

We need to be a little less tidy in our spiritual journey. Lent asks us "to remember that we are dust," not in some holy, ritualistic way, but in reality. Each and every one of us must leave the tidy, clean lives of our antiseptic world behind and reencounter the life the monks sought upon the Skelligs. Underneath all the suburban shopping malls, underneath all the brick houses we build, underneath every shoe we wear is the same dust the monks of the Skellig tilled just a few years ago. If we can see our own dust, and if we can see the dust of those who have gone before, then we do not take life for granted. Instead of merely breathing, we start living when we embrace the dust of life.

That's what the monks believed. It is what our souls long for each day. It is what it means to be sons and daughters of the dust.

EXERCISE
FACING OUR DUST

Having discovered the niche with Jack and having reclaimed the dust of life with the monks, facing our own niche and dust become possible. In the first exercise, we remembered our life and selected copies of photographs. Now, we create a resting place for our life—a place to hold us as we journey deeper and deeper into God's love for us. Seeing the niche in the tower scared Jack; it was the moment he understood dying and death. But ultimately, seeing the niche brought understanding, the same understanding the monks held daily. By seeing the dust of death, one discovers life. We now seek to prepare our niche with Jack and venture into the Skellig's hope.

Materials
- A shoebox or other small cardboard box. If you have time, you might visit a flea market and find a wooden crate or old jewelry box that draws your attention. Wine crates work very well, especially if you can find one with a top.
- Construction paper or a collection of nicer papers, such as rice paper and other handmade papers from an art and crafts store.
- Photographs selected from the previous exercise.
- Glue, preferably rubber cement if working with paper and cardboard boxes; for wooden boxes, a glue gun or stronger epoxy works well.
- Scissors.
- Markers, colored pencils, etc.

Method

We're not just decorating a box in this exercise. Instead, we're creating a vessel to house all the dust of our lives. As the chapters unfold, you'll have the opportunity to place items within this box for your niche: all the darkness and difficulty of your life can be given to this burial place, praying and hoping for God's grace and mercy in the Easter moment. So don't just wrap a box as if for a birthday present. Instead, create your urn, your vessel to hold the dust of your being so that in it you might find new light and life.

As with all our exercises, take several minutes to assemble the materials you need in an area where you will not be interrupted. Turn off the phone, the television, the radio, and other distractions you can control. Create a holy place of intentional silence for your workspace. Then, after you have prepared the area, get a comfortable chair in which to work and just sit down. If you can, close your eyes and let the thoughts flow through and away from you like a stream. Clear your mind and invite God into the time you are giving for this exercise.

Start with a prayer. You can use one of the prayers at the beginning of the chapter if you like, but you really don't have to use such a formal prayer. A prayer as simple as one word, such as "love," "peace," or "ashes" said repeatedly might form a contemplative time for you. Other suggestions might include a phrase like "remember you are dust" or "nothing can separate us from the love of God." Live with a word or phrase for several minutes. Let the prayer center your preparation for the exercise.

When you're ready to begin, decorate your box without much thought. If you've assembled all the materials in one place and put them on a worktable, you'll be able to work freely and without constraints. Just begin to work and try to free yourself of any distractions. If an inner critic emerges, let it go. Just work.

A few practical pointers will probably help as you begin. The first step is likely creating a background. You might wrap your box in paper to create a background color or colors for the photographs you will eventually assemble and glue as a kind of collage on the outside of the box. As you work, remember to wrap the top separately. You'll want to place items inside later and you must be able to remove the top or open the box. If you are using a wooden box or a heavy cardboard one, you might choose to paint instead of applying papers. If so, you can divide your work into a session for painting and then a session for applying the decorations after the paint has dried.

Your next step is applying a collage to the box. Assemble photographs from the first chapter and select an assortment to apply to the box using glue. Creative papers, glued behind each photo, or other items can also be incorporated to provide depth and create more interest. Could you weave a ribbon underneath the pieces of paper as they are glued, a kind of thread running through your life? You might even use a ribbon as a time line when you begin pasting photos or other images. A baby picture could begin your trek and a recent photo to end it. There's really no correct way to assemble the collage on the exterior. You could apply photos in the timeline method or you could arrange them thematically. You can keep the photographs distinct or you could paste them together in a more extravagant collage. Be creative and see where the Holy Spirit takes you as you go.

Continue to pray throughout the exercise, repeating your word or phrase as a kind of mantra. When you start feeling off track, return to the prayer and let it re-center you. Also let the words of the lesson from Ash Wednesday enfold you and Jack's story illumine you. Let God's love surround you as you contemplate your life and its meaning as you face the reality of dying and death for all of us. Get in touch with the dust of the earth, going to your own Skellig within your life.

And when you've finished, take time to sit and reflect upon your work. Use the soul questions to help discern what your work says to you for this journey.

Soul Questions
- What images or drawings did you use for your box? What do they say to you about your life's journey? How might they be asking more of you for the future?
- What emotions do you see among the decorations? Are they mostly sad? Happy? Excited? Do you see common emotional themes among them that indicate what you're feeling as you face the narratives of Ash Wednesday in scripture and in Jack's story?
- What other images came to mind as you began to work? How do they relate to where you are in your journey now?
- What images are missing that you wish you could incorporate? What do they say about the dust of your heart, the things still waiting upon God?
- What word or phrase did you use as your mantra? What's the meaning of your prayer as you understand it for now?

Thoughts for the Journey
- What are you afraid of as we begin our Lenten journey?
- How does Jack's story speak to you about dying and death? Are you afraid of death? Has the death of a loved one caused you much pain? Do you need to think more about what death means to understand more about life?
- How might you begin to see things as a three-year-old theologian?

WINDOW FOUR

Second Sunday in Lent

O God, whose glory it is always to have mercy: Be gracious to all who have gone astray from your ways, and bring them again with penitent hearts and steadfast faith to embrace and hold fast the unchangeable truth of your Word, Jesus Christ your Son; who with you and the Holy Spirit lives and reigns, one God, for ever and ever. *Amen.* —*The Book of Common Prayer,* page 218

God of refuge and comfort: you are always graciously present with me, even in moments of despair and loneliness; show me the presence of your life in all that I say and do, that through times of trouble and challenge, I might find my cross in your hands, and my life in your life. *Amen.*

MARK 8:31–38

(The Son of Man is to suffer; take up your cross and follow me)

Jesus began to teach his disciples that the Son of Man must undergo great suffering, and be rejected by the elders, the chief priests, and the scribes, and be killed, and after three days rise again. He said all this quite openly. And Peter took him aside and began to rebuke him. But turning and looking at his disciples, he rebuked Peter and said, "Get behind me, Satan! For you are setting your mind not on divine things but on human things." He called the crowd with his disciples, and said to them, "If any want to become my followers, let them deny themselves and take up their cross and follow me. For those who want to save their life will lose it, and those who lose their life for my sake, and for the sake of the gospel, will save it. For what will it profit them to gain the whole world and forfeit their life? Indeed, what can they give in return for their life? Those who are ashamed of me and of my words in this adulterous and sinful generation, of them the Son of Man will also be ashamed when he comes in the glory of his Father with the holy angels."

CR℘

How do we move from merely knowing the dust of life to embracing it daily? Most of us find such a task anxiety-producing, a moment of Paxil or Xanax endorsement. But some people know to the depths of their being that they're dust. Unlike most of us, they somehow have a gift of life because they have seen death so very clearly. Instead of being afraid of death, instead of shutting the self off from its reality, these people see it as a natural part of the journey. Because of that fact, they have a meaningful life in almost every moment as they bask in the light of God's newness as it unfolds each day.

A couple of summers ago, I met such a man. He was a wild man, with curly blond hair growing in wild abandon, falling down his back in twists and turns; he looked like a virtual Tristan from the pages of folklore and mythology. When you looked at him, you saw adventure, openness, honesty, and life. He looked like the cross between a laid-back surfer and an intense college philosophy professor. The contradiction was authentic and in it there was incredible beauty.

Michael was about my age, had practiced as a lawyer in the entertainment industry, had a pre-teen daughter, and loved his wife unreservedly. We shared so much in common, including our first name, and yet, were so very different. He was a carefree wanderer of sorts, and I a careful priest, very different on the surface yet fellow journeyers in the soul. In our chance meeting on a pilgrimage to Ireland, I met this man, much like a figure from Chaucer's *The Canterbury Tales*. It was as if he just strolled up to me along the path; and in our journey together over a few days, we became brothers. Intense talks, good pubs, and great surroundings had made for an immediate family reunion between two long-lost Irish souls.

Michael was intensely spiritual. Everything about him yelled of another place, another being, another sacred spot just beyond reach. In talking with him, I got the feeling that he had seen more of life than I had. It wasn't just his stories, full of angst commingled with joy and laughter. It wasn't just his keen observation of other human beings. There was something deep within him that just spoke a true word. At first, I couldn't quite put my finger on it. I thought maybe it was growing up Catholic in all sorts of parochial schools. Maybe the nuns had been able to open his soul and pour lots in at an early age, liturgy and doctrine oozing out of his body involuntarily from time to time. Or maybe it was the love of his life, his wife of many years, that that gave stability, grace, and mercy to a brokenness deep within only he knew.

But the more I talked with him, the more this priest saw, the more I discovered that it really wasn't any of those things in isolation. Instead, it was all of them combined into his vocation—his true calling in life. You see, Michael was a rock climber. Someone, who for some insane reason, liked to climb high above the earth, holding onto each jagged edge. He was a world-class climber, captured by professional photographers and television stations all over the world. But in Michael's case, it wasn't just a job; it was truly his calling, his vocation. For Michael wasn't just an internationally known climber. He was a free soloist, one who climbed without ropes.

He called it climbing naked. And to see him scale a rock was so pure, so natural, that the description fit him rather well. He could read a rock instantly, setting off to climb as if going for an afternoon stroll. Many had doubted his claims over the years—they were so insanely pompous. But film crews had long erased doubts about Michael. He wasn't pompous; he actually could climb like no other. I think he knew himself so completely, it was as if the climbing part of him was before the fall—back to that part of Adam and Eve that could climb and ascend in nakedness, unashamed of their bodies before God their creator.

After our chance meeting, I had emailed him a couple of times. And in the most unlikely of scenarios, this priest and that rock climber became friends. He sent pictures of climbs in Ireland, gorgeous images of Michael dangling from rocks in the Gap of Dunloe outside Killarney. He talked about life and what it meant to him. And he shared with me his excitement about climbing on the coast, something he was doing for a new documentary. I responded with my own climbing, a kind of interior questioning of the rocks before me, and in his wisdom, Michael just knew how to say the right thing, the line that would help me see the crag and stronghold just above where I was temporarily hanging out upon my own rocks. The naked climber was helping me, one ever afraid of heights, reach beyond my stuckness to a place of light and hope ever higher.

So when my phone rang and the caller ID read from Ireland, I thought it might be Michael calling to talk about his upcoming filming. We had discussed a couple of ideas for it and he had said he'd let me know how it went. Instead, it was my other Irish brother Con, a climber in his own right who had introduced me to Michael. Con's voice was still, quiet and somber, as if he had captured the dust of the Skelligs in his very words. He told me Michael was dead. I immediately thought of a fall. My mind wandered into blame so quickly thinking, "If he'd only used ropes, he'd still be here." And then Con's words awakened me from my wanderings and I heard the horrible story of how Michael died. He was not climbing. He had finished the final climb of his month-long Irish journey, and was standing upon a shoreline rock at the base of Valentia Island when a rogue wave of epic proportions came and swept him out to sea. A line was cast and within minutes the Irish Coast Guard was there, as their station was just yards above where Michael had climbed that day. But my curly-blond-haired Irish brother, my newfound soul mate along the journey of life, was never seen again. The raging Irish Sea had claimed him forever.

The pain of his death was no doubt unbearable for his family. He left behind his beloved wife and daughter, and with them a whole host of admirers across the globe grieving his death. As I reflected upon my own grief, I realized many days later that Michael had lived more than I ever had dreamed possible. In his short life of just over forty years, he had accepted his dust, had accepted his death, and because of it, he had been able to live life fully. Considering his own death while dangling upon the rocks many a day had not brought depression and destruction to him. Instead, death and its inevitability had brought the possibility of life for Michael. He had accepted the dust of his life, had seen the possibility of his own true fall from grace, and knowing it fully he had returned to a place of creation few of us ever see. It was that place in the Garden, that place of incredible hope and beauty that had let the wild man climb naked, without anything tying him down, without anything covering him up. I realized that I could learn this secret from Michael, I could open this window to life, or I could just go back to my ever busy, anxious life.

Many months after Michael's death, I was making my way to an island in the Grenadines. My wife and I were heading out to a small island for a few days of true relaxation and rest. On the large ferry, I stood at the rail and watched as the hull pierced the ocean. It was early morning. Deep blue swells and waves were rolling in from the east. The sun was coming up over the water. And there, in the deep, dark ocean, the first hints of sunlight began to reflect upon the waves, the sea foam curling wildly upon itself, a messy palate of twists and turns. At once, I saw Michael, his curls cascading down upon his shoulders, his piercing eyes staring up from the ocean depths. And I knew he was all right, all of his dust now commingled with water, once again at home swimming naked in the place he had known from his mother's womb.

I am no longer afraid of falling.

EXERCISE
ACCEPTING DEATH

Few of us face our death, and hence our life, like Michael did. Because he was able to so fully accept the fact that he would die one day, Michael was able to live freely, uninhibited, taking each day as a gift from God. If we're to find this same life, then accepting our own death is the key to true life. In this exercise, we stare directly into the face of death and then find ourselves freed to live the life God has given.

Materials
- One or more local newspapers.
- Paper or a journal.
- Pen.
- Alternatively, a computer for word processing.

Method

This exercise consists of two parts. In the first, we reflect upon the lives of others, people we may or may not know. By considering what they left behind, we then move to our own life and consider how we want to be remembered.

Begin by preparing your area. This exercise is particularly contemplative, so the quieter the space you can ensure, the better. You might appreciate having a table or desk if that makes writing easier. Say a prayer, using those at the beginning of the chapter or select a word or phrase from the reading that might appeal to you. Repeat the prayer throughout this exercise.

Turn to the obituaries. Select several to read. Obituaries can vary from a simple notice of the death of someone, listing basic family information and services times, to elaborate narratives of every achievement and activity in a person's life. Religious and cultural variations can also influence how they are written. As you read the obituaries, notice what they share in common and how they are different. Notice what kind of language is used in each, whether historical, religious, narrative, or otherwise. Try to figure out which obituaries were written by the family or perhaps even the person who died. Compare those to ones that appear to have been prepared from a template, the funeral home's attempt to plug in all the information that it deemed appropriate. Use the Soul Questions for further reflection.

Now, consider your own obituary. As difficult as it might seem, begin to think about what you would want listed about your life. Don't think about publication costs or other restrictions. Write it as if you could provide an uninhibited statement of what your life had been. Don't dream about what it could be in the future. Write it for today (hoping, of course, no one needs it!). You might make a list of accomplishments, including education, civic and religious involvement, and other activities. You should also consider what family should be listed and how. And is there anything you definitely want to highlight? Is there a particularly meaningful item you should list because it captures something of who you are? When you've gathered all this information, begin to compose the obituary as you would want it to appear in print. Edit and revise freely, and if working on paper, write your revisions in the margins and to the sides of the paper. Let the composition, edits and all, become a living testimony to what you find important in your life.

As a final step, place your own obituary into your niche, the box you created in the first exercise.

Soul Questions
- What was it like to read obituaries in the paper? Did it make a difference not knowing the people listed? How did you react

emotionally to reading about the lives of other people, knowing that they had just died?

- Which obituaries captured your attention? What about them drew you in?
- What cultural or religious influences did you see in the ones you read? Did you discover any new customs or practices you didn't previously know? How did you react to them?
- What relationships were highlighted in the family portions of the obituaries? Did you see any strained relationships? Loving ones?
- Was grief expressed in any of them? If so, how did that make you feel? Was there a death for which you would have expected grief to be expressed, such as the death of a child or young adult, but it was not? How do cultural norms influence decisions about the composition of an obituary?
- What was it like to contemplate your own death?
- Was writing your obituary something that brought deep reflection to your life or did you find it hard to engage in the process? What might your reaction say about your death? Your life?
- If you wrote revisions in the margins as suggested, go back and take a look at the process you went through as your wrote. What do the revisions say about the way you perceived this project? What became clearer as you worked?

Thoughts for the Journey

- Do you see the connection between accepting the fact that you will die and living your life to the fullest?
- What might help you see your life as a gift from God, something to be cherished and lived fully each day?
- Have you ever met someone like Michael who was able to live freely? Do you believe they were able to live fully because they understood the relationships of life and death? Can one live fully without that understanding?

- How honest was your obituary? Did you want to embellish it?
- What was missing from your obituary that you want to be listed there one day? How might you change your life to make sure your obituary reads as you dream it will?
- How could revisiting your obituary from time to time become a way to keep your life grounded?

WINDOW FIVE

Third Sunday in Lent

Almighty God, you know that we have no power in ourselves to help ourselves: Keep us both outwardly in our bodies and inwardly in our souls, that we may be defended from all adversities which may happen to the body, and from all evil thoughts which may assault and hurt the soul; through Jesus Christ our Lord, who lives and reigns with you and the Holy Spirit, one God, for ever and ever. *Amen.* — *The Book of Common Prayer,* page 218

God, my soul both awaits and celebrates your presence. At times I drive you away, replacing your love for me with objects of my own desire. On other days, I welcome you with wild abandon, preparing a feast for all to enjoy. Help me to find the places between, the places where I can be still and know that you are God and that I am not. For in those sacred temples, my soul receives you and my life becomes complete. *Amen.*

John 2:13–22

(Jesus and the money changers)

The Passover of the Jews was near, and Jesus went up to Jerusalem. In the temple he found people selling cattle, sheep, and doves, and the money changers seated at their tables. Making a whip of cords, he drove all of them out of the temple, both the sheep and the cattle. He also poured out the coins of the money changers and overturned their tables. He told those who were selling the doves, "Take these things out of here! Stop making my Father's house a marketplace!" His disciples remembered that it was written, "Zeal for your house will consume me." The Jews then said to him, "What sign can you show us for doing this?" Jesus answered them, "Destroy this temple, and in three days I will raise it up." The Jews then said, "This temple has been under construction for forty-six years, and will you raise it up in three days?" But he was speaking of the temple of his body. After he was raised from the dead, his disciples remembered that he had said this; and they believed the scripture and the word that Jesus had spoken.

CR&O

My grandparents' farm stood in the foothills of the Appalachian Mountains. Several hundred acres, quite large for an up-country farm, it had been in the family since the early 1800s. The original plat, hand drawn with notes in the margins, still hangs in my mother's home. It's sort of a testimony, a reminder of the farm that once had lots of hands, as they called the workers, a place where the blacksmith shop was a local hangout, and my great-great-grandfather doled out justice as the only magistrate in the area. By the time I was born, many of its buildings were only memories. The old barn, built from hand-hewn logs, was seeing its last days. I barely remember climbing into its loft. The large barn was in better shape, and I often climbed into the loft there, unless of course I saw a snake, as was often the case.

The large barn was the one closest to the bottoms, low-lying land irrigated by canals. I loved walking there as a child. The road to the bottoms was magical. The leafy trees were thick and encapsulated the little gravel road, which wound its way over bridges that crossed streams flowing with clean mountain water. I heard stories of the swimming hole that had been there earlier, the water dammed up to provide a fresh, cool retreat in the summer. I often wished that someone would've dammed it up again. Jumping into that clean water looked so very fun.

It was in this place that I grew up. In the summer, I would spend long days there, sometimes without a single thing to do other than walk around, look at the rocks, sticks, and flowers, and bug my grandmother to take me for a hotdog down at the café. Usually, that worked. She loved hot dogs herself. But the chief memory of my childhood is captured in my grandmother's table set for a Sunday meal. I suppose this deep memory is the reason that I'm so into food today. I'm just trying to keep up a grand family tradition. For you see on Sundays, my grandmother would provide a feast of more food than anyone in their right mind would cook for such a small group of people. Having lived with the abundance of a farm, she never stopped filling her table with the bounty of God's creation on the Sabbath day. Two meats, two beans, two starches, two salads, two breads, two desserts was her norm.

Cooking such a meal was my grandmother's way of declaring the holiness of the Sabbath. Her preparations started days in advance. A cake was usually in the plans for Thursday or Friday with a pie following soon thereafter. Saturday morning was reserved for last-minute shopping, unless she had to go into town. That meant a whole different schedule and usually a Friday trip, which of course depended upon my grandfather and his schedule, for my grandmother didn't drive. I can still hear her saying, "That's not my job." But I can also still hear her when my grandfather was too busy to take her into town. "I'm thinking of getting my license and buying a new car" would come forth from her mouth, and within minutes, I would hear the engine roar in the drive, my grandfather waiting patiently for her.

With butter and fresh milk for mile-high biscuits, fresh beans from the farm, macaroni with locally made cheese, she would descend into the kitchen for hours on Saturday afternoon. I can still see her standing there in a dress with an apron tied around her waist, flour all over the place, smells of ham and chicken wafting through the air. If I was there for Saturday night, she would usually make a sandwich using the ham. It was like getting a foretaste of the heavenly banquet ahead of time, a communion of sorts, a real presence of the meal that was still coming.

Usually, I was at home with my parents on the weekends and we'd head to church Sunday morning. Immediately afterward, in a mad dash, we'd all pile into the car and head off into the countryside. When we arrived at the farm, the smell of the meal would almost knock me down as I got out of the car. Everything prepared the day before was in the massive oven for a final warming, a final touch of God's goodness; the smell permeated every molecule of the air.

In the spring and summer, we'd walk through the kitchen into the dining room and encounter a covered table. She'd set the table Saturday night and then place another tablecloth on top so no dust or bugs would find their way into our meal. I always thought it looked strange, sort of like something had died and the doctors had pulled the sheets up over the corpse. I can still see my grandmother on one side of the table and my mother on the other, just before the meal, reaching down, picking up the cloth, and with great precision folding the tablecloth. It looked holy, like the folding of the flag at the end of a school day. The meal would follow, as would the desserts, and in the summer we often churned homemade ice cream. My arm still hurts from turning the crank.

When my grandfather died, my grandmother moved to town. The meals stopped. She still cooked from time to time, but in all truth, it was never the same. Something happened when we left the farm, when the house that had stood there all those years became empty. I'm not really sure why. We could've had the same meal. We could have eaten upon the same table. All of us would have helped. But it just wasn't the same. Sabbath meals just seemed to die.

I have my own children now. My parents live in another state, hours away. There's no family farm to return to on a weekly basis. No place to center ourselves for the Sabbath. No place to fold the ritual tablecloth. Instead, my Sunday is of course filled with work. As a priest, I disappear from the house before seven each Sunday morning. And, if we're lucky, we have a good sandwich for lunch around 1:00.

Most Sundays we venture to places that weren't open when I was a child. We head to the sporting goods store for our children's shoes or to the department store for household items. Sunday afternoon has become the principle shopping time in our busy lives. Sometimes we go to a soccer game or play tennis. I regularly buy our groceries on Sunday evening with all the young people returning from out-of-town parties. It's quite a happening place, the grocery store, on a Sunday evening. And with great regularity, I do return home with bags full of God's abundance in order to cook the best meal of the week. We dedicate Sunday evenings to each other in our family; it's our time to just be with each other. Sometimes we play cards or watch a movie after a great meal.

But each Sunday around 1:15, my heart goes to a different place. My soul remembers the feeling of gravel underneath the tires of my father's Oldsmobile 98 and I look up for the trees towering above. Sometimes, I even feel myself rolling down the window and leaning out, trying to catch a glimpse of the white house on the hill. I want so very much to see that porch, to hear the screen door bang behind me, and encounter my grandmother standing at the stove, the little apron tied around her waist, the smile of approval creasing her whole face. I want to see the table and to know that it's still there, waiting in great expectation of the Sabbath meal, keeping it holy, undefiled, free from all the moneychangers that make it like any other day. And, perhaps more than anything, I want to watch as the cloth is lifted from the table and folded to reveal the bounty of God's grace.

I wonder if it's time for me to turn over the tables of my life and let the farm be more than a place drawn on a plat hanging on the wall. Is it possible, with just a little effort, to reclaim the temple of my life for the holiness of Sabbath? Is it possible that with my grandmother I too might stop selling my life short, trying to substitute a last-minute sacrifice for a pure Sabbath? I think so, for the memory will not fade and the meal cannot be forgotten.

Therefore, shall we keep the feast?

EXERCISE
CLEANING OUR TEMPLE

A simple word collage can be incorporated into your daily meditations. I use this method more than any other because it can be done anywhere with only a pen and paper. Sometimes, I will even stop work at the office and use this method to discover what is really going on with me in times of stress. By working quickly with the thoughts that flow from our subconscious, we discover what is truly captivating our souls at any given time. This discovery is not only helpful to self-understanding in any situation, but of course makes it possible to be more honest in our prayer. Discovering what is truly bothering us allows us to present more of ourselves to God, and hence experience more of God's grace and mercy. While this exercise draws on the themes of this chapter, the instructions will show how easy it is to adapt this method for daily use.

Materials
- A sheet of paper, preferably 11 x 14 construction paper.
- Two colors of pens, fine-tip markers, or colored pencils.

Method
After preparing your space, preferably with a table or lapboard, read through this entire exercise so that you can do the whole thing without referring back to this book. You might make index cards containing reminders of the questions that follow or other instructions that would be helpful. Feel free to use this same technique at other times throughout the book.

When you're ready, begin with a prayer. Then, if you can, sit in silence with your eyes closed for ten minutes or so. Try to put aside any thoughts and let your stream of consciousness fade into meditation with God. After this time of mediation, ask yourself a question: What interferes with my relationship with God? As words come to mind that answer this question, write them down on the paper, using only one color of pen, marker, or pencil. Write creatively, diagonally, horizontally, and perpendicularly. You might even write words in a circle, starting in the center of the page and spiraling out as you go. Vary the size of the words—some might seem more important than others and you might make those larger. Write the words or phrases quickly, being sure not to reflect or ask yourself why you included any particular one. The quicker you work, the more the right side of your brain will guide your meditation and the more you will learn about what interferes with your relationship.

When you have exhausted your answers, usually when more than fifteen seconds pass between responses, stop, put down your pen, and close your eyes. Take a minute or two to breathe deeply, letting each breath cleanse your thoughts. When you have re-centered, ask yourself a second question: How does Christ respond to my answers? Then, picking up the other color of pen or marker, write the response you hear. You might hear many responses, a different one to each of the things you have written. Sometimes, you might hear one response to all of them, written over and over throughout the page. Write what the Spirit reveals to you and do so creatively. The words of God tend to be more creative than our own!

When the responses cease, stop, close your eyes, and again take several deep breaths. Thank God for the opportunity to be honest and for God's response to you. After a couple of minutes, open your eyes and reflect upon the exercise.

Soul Questions

- Was it easy to list what interferes with your relationship with God? Why or why not?
- What themes emerged in your responses? Was a particular event or person present in what you wrote?
- What surprises did you discover in your responses?
- How did you feel when you entered the second phase of the exercise? Was it easier or harder to respond to your honesty? Did scripture influence your response?
- How can you adjust your life in light of what you have discovered?

Thoughts for the Journey

On future days, use the scripture lesson for the day to form your word collage. Is there a question in the scripture itself? If so, use it to frame your exercise. Or ask yourself a question, such as "Why am I so anxious today?" or "What would help me see God more clearly in a particular relationship or person?" When appropriate, you can add a second mediation, as in this chapter's exercise, by asking "What does God see in my prayer?" or "How would Jesus see this differently?"

WINDOW SIX

Fourth Sunday in Lent

Gracious Father, whose blessed Son Jesus Christ came down from heaven to be the true bread which gives life to the world: Evermore give us this bread, that he may live in us, and we in him; who lives and reigns with you and the Holy Spirit, one God, now and for ever. Amen. —*The Book of Common Prayer,* page 219

You are always welcoming me back to the feast, God, no matter how far I stray, no matter what I do, or what I say. Let me see that you have always loved me and that you are always welcoming me home with a feast of new life. *Amen.*

JOHN 6:4–15
(The feeding of the five thousand)

Now the Passover, the festival of the Jews, was near. When he looked up and saw a large crowd coming toward him, Jesus said to Philip, "Where are we to buy bread for these people to eat?" He said this to test him, for he himself knew what he was going to do. Philip answered him, "Six months' wages would not buy enough bread for each of them to get a little." One of his disciples, Andrew, Simon Peter's brother, said to him, "There is a boy here who has five barley loaves and two fish. But what are they among so many people?" Jesus said, "Make the people sit down." Now there was a great deal of grass in the place; so they sat down, about five thousand in all. Then Jesus took the loaves, and when he had given thanks, he distributed them to those who were seated; so also the fish, as much as they wanted. When they were satisfied, he told his disciples, "Gather up the fragments left over, so that nothing may be lost." So they gathered them up, and from the fragments of the five barley loaves, left by those who had eaten, they filled twelve baskets. When the people saw the sign that he had done, they began to say, "This is indeed the prophet who is to come into the world." When Jesus realized that they were about to come and take him by force to make him king, he withdrew again to the mountain by himself.

☙❧

God feeding us is the most basic image we are given in the biblical narrative. Adam and Eve ate from the abundance of the Garden of Eden, living in paradise where the goodness of the earth's bounty was evident in every plant and animal. The Israelites gathered manna, the bread of God's grace and love, as they wandered in the wilderness. God's mercy was showered upon them as they gathered just enough food for the day. And of course, the disciples gathered together for the

Passover, only to be transformed by the love of the Eucharist, God's giving of God's very self to us in the bread and wine. God's food is the very image of God's love to us.

It's no mistake then that God shows up when food is shared in love. And likewise, it's no mistake that God is most evident when food is shared among those we often forget or fail to see.

No one really saw Billy. He was homeless. Suffering from schizophrenia, he'd been on the streets for many years, probably about twenty-five. According to what people who knew him pieced together, Billy had been a normal twenty-something when the first signs of his illness emerged. Within a few months, he started on a roller coaster of ups and downs, in and out of mental facilities, fighting with family and friends over whether anything was wrong with him. Like so many, he couldn't fathom that the people and things in his mind weren't true, so he gave up battling the people who couldn't see his world and withdrew to a place where his world was free to be real. On the streets, he lived completely in his world; there, the people and places no one else could see moved freely. The streets became the easiest place for all of them to live with each other. As cars drove by, he stood on the corner with his friends, waving, talking, and arguing.

Billy lived in about a six-block area. It was well-selected real estate. In the winter, he lived over a grate next to a government building. The warm air from steam generated for heat warmed his lean-to refrigerator box covered with a tarp. On warmer days, he had a little porch with several folding chairs for his guests. They often sat in the late December sun talking and arguing for hours. In the warmer months, the western sunshine was too hot, so Billy moved to his summerhouse down the street. It was in a shaded alleyway with a large open grate from the underground parking garage and skyscraper next door. Since it was so cold in there that the lawyers and accountants wore coats on the hottest August days, the leftover air that escaped out the grate and up from the garage was just right for Billy. The refrigerator box was recycled and an old mattress from the dump just sat on the ground. I'm sure Billy enjoyed the stars in the summer as he fell asleep.

Billy's routines were set in stone. Each morning he arose early, walked over to the state capitol and sat on a bench. Usually, he found a newspaper, just a day or two old, for his morning read. He read the paper from cover to cover. Since he knew most of the people who were featured in the stories, especially those causing international havoc, he wanted to keep up with their latest movements. He often argued with them late in the afternoons, trying to convince them to abandon their foolish ways.

After reading the paper, he would take out food he had saved from the day before. Half a sandwich, a pack of crackers, anything that would provide a nutritious beginning to the day. When he was lucky, he enjoyed an apple. Sometimes the people in the tall building would leave perfectly good food in the trash bin next to the grate. Billy especially enjoyed those days—sometimes finding whole meals from a meeting or a party. One time, he found shrimp. It was great but he had so much trouble breathing afterwards that he had to go to the hospital for a few days. He always hated being in the hospital because they usually gave him things to erase his friends on the street—destroying their lives, as he said.

By midmorning, Billy would move down the street to the Methodist church. Every weekday, good men and women from the city came and made a fresh lunch. In the winter soup and sandwiches were the staple. They cooked a massive pot of soup on Monday and gave it different flavors each day of the week. What started as tomato on Monday was a great stew by Friday. Billy always said that Thursday soup was the best; more flavorful than Monday and not too leftover like Friday. In the summer, the Methodists served salads instead of soup. Billy didn't really like salad.

But Billy's favorite day was Sunday. At the cathedral across the street from the capitol, the people of the parish had been preparing a hot breakfast on Sundays for over twenty years. Scrambled eggs, grits, bacon or sausage, toast, and beans were all served fifty-two Sundays a year, plus Christmas morning. A bag lunch was also given to all two hundred or so of the guests. But Billy was not a guest, of course. Billy was a member and a volunteer who brought many people with him.

He was often first in line so he could proceed to the other more important work he had to do in the cathedral. He'd stand there ready for the doors to open, ready for the hot meal, ready to see people who needed him, his community. He especially liked one member of the cathedral, a lady who had been the chief organizer of the breakfast for many years. She understood Billy, and more importantly, all his guests. She'd talk with them like no other. In addition, she listened to everyone who had a need and she'd find things for them when they told her about missing socks, gloves, or toiletries. An angel in the flesh, she was the image of God to many—a savior, a redeemer, one who took their prayers and really prayed for them.

Billy would finish his breakfast, and without being asked, wash his hands and face in the restroom, and then come back into the grand hall ready to clean. With oil portraits of nineteenth-century clergymen looking on, Billy would wipe down tables, get a broom, and help clean the floors. "This many people make a mess in my Father's house," he'd say as he worked. Sometimes, he'd also talk to the other people he was supervising. There must have been twenty of them some weeks. Calling them each by name, he could see them all working, listening to his every command. Sometimes, a parishioner or two would give money to Billy. One even told him to share it with the other workers.

When his work was finished, Billy selected a chair and sat down to survey all he had done. He'd sit and wait for hours sometimes, and if he could, he liked to stay for Sunday school. He'd sit in the back of the hall listening, sometimes talking softly about what was said. Sometimes, when he had brought lots of people with him, he was preoccupied with their behavior. "They often have poor manners in church," he'd say.

One Sunday, Billy didn't show up for breakfast. And neither did he the next week. Or the next. Asked about him, no one said a thing at first. Information on the street is often hard to come by if you live in a building, because you are viewed with suspicion. Eventually, a man I'd never heard speak said that Billy had been knifed really bad. He thought I needed to know. Pressing for more information, I heard that another man living over the grate by the skyscraper wanted Billy's mattress and Billy didn't want to give it to him. So, the man cut Billy and left him there to die. The next morning, an officer on patrol who knew Billy and checked on him regularly found him there in the alleyway. The man who cut Billy had already disappeared into another dark corner of the city, probably getting on a train by sundown. News of crime among the homeless spreads quickly and their own police force is responsive.

By the time I arrived, Billy had been in the hospital for several weeks. Not only had the doctors performed several surgeries to repair all the damage, the psychiatrists had also been giving Billy lots of medication to quiet all the people who had come with him to the hospital. It had worked. The guests had left the hospital for about five days when I saw him. When I walked into the room, I didn't recognize him. Clean, shaven, with his hair recently cut, it was as if I had known his photographic negative before and now I was encountering the full-color image of him. Instead of dark, hollow eyes, he had lively, warm, glowing eyes that spilled light into the room. His hands, which had always seemed larger than my head, now appeared smaller, the dirt and grime washed from them. Still a large man, he'd lost lots of weight; his thinner frame looking strangely familiar and alien all at the same time.

"Good morning, Billy," I said, walking into the room. "Good morning," came his reply in a deep yet lively voice. Thirty minutes later, I had learned more about this man than I had ever thought possible. Stories about his childhood, his parents, how he missed his family and friends, and his remarkable desire to get a job. He talked openly about extensive drug use and how his brain really didn't work well anymore, as he put it. And near the end of our conversation, he told me he'd stay on his medication this time, how he wanted the voices to go away, and how he planned to make life right this time around. As I left the room, he prayed for me and thanked "all those good people at the church" for all they did to bring hope to his life. "Lord," he prayed, "give 'em lots of food for the souls lost out in that mean, cold world."

I went back a couple of days later only to find his bed empty. Billy had checked out as soon as the confinement order had expired. The nurse just looked at me, sadness overtaking her face. I suppose she saw lots of people from her ward check out too soon.

That Sunday, Billy was back at church, eating breakfast, sweeping the floors, overseeing all the workers he had brought with him. And as I caught his eye, he stopped sweeping, looked squarely at me, and stared intensely. I could almost see him thinking, reflecting, and wondering all at once. And then, he smiled. A massive smile from ear to ear. "I'm back," he yelled. "Welcome back, Billy," I replied.

And at the table next to him, one no one else could see, even I heard their cheerful reply, "Welcome back, Billy. Welcome back."

EXERCISE
IMAGES OF FOOD

For most of us, food is no longer tied to hunger. Out of the prosperity of our lives, we see food more as a commodity or product than as the goodness of God's earth. Because of Billy's life, he experienced the breakfast at the cathedral as a nourishing meal of abundance amid the harshness of his life. Because of that, even in his darkness, he was also able to bring hope to others as he embraced the breakfast as his home, a place to welcome others and do his part in making the whole experience enjoyable for those he served.

Materials
- Numerous magazines, including food periodicals if possible (available from friends and sometimes the local library). The magazines should be disposable.
- Small poster board, approximately 12 x 12.
- Scissors.
- Rubber cement or glue stick.

Method
This exercise is a simple collage.

First, prepare your work area. Assemble your magazines in stacks on your worktable and prepare your poster board and other materials. When you have prepared the area, prayed for God's guidance during your exercise, and centered yourself, take the magazines and begin to look through them quickly. Without reflection or study, tear any food image from them that appeals to you. As you go, also note any images of people that appeal to you and tear those out as well. The quicker you work and the less reflection you have, the more authentic your response to this exercise will be. You might consider using your nondominant hand as mentioned in the Introduction.

As you look, also consider any images of those society often forgets. Are there any homeless or disadvantaged people in the magazines? Are images of suffering or despair available? If so, tear any out that speak to you and place them with the images of other people and the foods that you find as you work.

Continue to tear images from the pages for several minutes. Then, without reflection, begin to cut the images and place them on the poster board. Don't stop to glue them but just arrange them as it comes to you. It remains crucial at this stage that you work quickly and without reflection. If you start wondering why you chose an image, move on. There will be ample time for such considerations when you are finished.

As you arrange the images, allow them to overlap. If you can, create a collage in which the images flow from one to another and the background paper is completely covered. If you can do this, the collage will be a powerful composition of relationships. Again, don't worry about meaning. Just work as quickly as you can.

When you are happy with the arrangement, begin to use the rubber cement to glue everything into place. Don't be surprised if some of the items change as you glue them. Often, you'll discover new relationships that you like. Go with the flow and allow the creative process to guide you. And if an inner critic emerges, move on and continue to work.

When you have completed the project, sit with the composition for a few minutes. Reflection and consideration can now emerge as a guide to your understanding and the Spirit's revelation to you. Use the Soul Questions to guide your mediation.

Soul Questions
- What types of food did you include in the composition? Are they your favorites?
- Are any of the foods you included tied to memories?
- Did you include any items you don't like? Why?
- What people did you include? Why did these images appeal to you? What might their inclusion be saying to you about your own life at this time?
- If you found images of the homeless or people often forgotten, how did you relate them to the food in the composition? What do you believe that your soul was discovering in the way that you arranged these people with the food items?
- How do you fit within this collage? Is it totally foreign to you? Familiar? Why or why not?

Thoughts for the Journey
- Have you known people such as Billy? Do you see them when you're driving in your car or do you fail to see them? How might you see others as they are as you travel your road with God?
- Have you ever had a relationship with a homeless person? If so, what drew you to them? Pity? Respect? Family relationship? If you haven't known such a person, why not? Are you afraid of homeless people?
- Is there a soup kitchen, church program, or social service agency where you might be able to meet a person like Billy and help provide food to those often unseen in our culture?

WINDOW SEVEN

Fifth Sunday in Lent

Almighty God, you alone can bring into order the unruly wills and affections of sinners: Grant your people grace to love what you command and desire what you promise; that, among the swift and varied changes of the world, our hearts may surely there be fixed where true joys are to be found; through Jesus Christ our Lord, who lives and reigns with you and the Holy Spirit, one God, now and for ever. *Amen.* —*The Book of Common Prayer,* page 219

At times, God, I feel lost and abandoned, not really knowing where to turn or how to seek you. When the darkness of life seems too great to bear, enfold me in your arms and let me feel your love surround me, that where you are, there I will be also. *Amen.*

JOHN 12:20–33
(Those who lose their lives will save them)

Now among those who went up to worship at the festival were some Greeks. They came to Philip, who was from Bethsaida in Galilee, and said to him, "Sir, we wish to see Jesus." Philip went and told Andrew; then Andrew and Philip went and told Jesus. Jesus answered them, "The hour has come for the Son of Man to be glorified. Very truly, I tell you, unless a grain of wheat falls into the earth and dies, it remains just a single grain; but if it dies, it bears much fruit. Those who love their life lose it, and those who hate their life in this world will keep it for eternal life. Whoever serves me must follow me, and where I am, there will my servant be also. Whoever serves me, the Father will honor. "Now my soul is troubled. And what should I say—'Father, save me from this hour'? No, it is for this reason that I have come to this hour. Father, glorify your name." Then a voice came from heaven, "I have glorified it, and I will glorify it again." The crowd standing there heard it and said that it was thunder. Others said, "An angel has spoken to him." Jesus answered, "This voice has come for your sake, not for mine. Now is the judgment of this world; now the ruler of this world will be driven out. And I, when I am lifted up from the earth, will draw all people to myself." He said this to indicate the kind of death he was to die.

CRPO

The after-school enrichment program at the inner city middle school brought many of us together week after week. Lawyers who came to teach drama. Doctors who left the office early to come teach tennis. The retired teacher who helped students get that extra push for English or science. We all came together on Thursdays with anywhere from 70 to 120 students, and for an hour and half, dozens of people from the best addresses in town became the friends of those whose addresses only knew police and locked doors after sunset amid drug deals.

The sixth- through eight-graders were really quite amazing. Many of them had younger brothers and sisters who depended upon them for supper, the nightly bath, and bedtime stories. Faced with all the demands of such a life, study was next to impossible when all the daily chores were completed. Our tutoring on Thursdays was a huge help to those who came, and because of the relationships that emerged, I sometimes wondered whether we were going to help them or learn from them. Luckily, both often happened.

Many of these young men and women lived in the reality of a one-parent home—just like the rest of middle America. But instead of living in a picture-perfect neighborhood where neighbors watched out for neighbors, they lived in an inner city area that was beset with many problems. Unlike the stereotypical scenarios we hear, the great majority of people just wanted a good life, a good future, and a community supporting them all the way. But because of a handful people who were responsible for much of the violence, drugs, and gangs, the dreams of the families were often thwarted by the nightmares imposed upon them by those with power. It always seemed that the nightmare came out of nowhere in this neighborhood. Week after week the students told us of gunshots, drug deals, prostitution—the darkness of life seemed to live on every street corner. No wonder most of the children went inside at dark, locking the doors and windows behind them. It was just a way of life.

I'm not certain when I met Trudy. Perhaps it was during a cooking demonstration or an art class I was teaching for one of the enrichment activities. Or during math tutoring— fractions, decimals, and percents. That was always a major topic after school. But the first image I recall of her was in the math tutoring session. I remember thinking she was amazing. Trudy had not only finished doing her math homework, she had moved on to helping everyone around her. I must have heard her explain fractions at least three different ways as she adjusted her words to fit each person's understanding. She understood the problems so well that she was able to move from her own comprehension to the learning pattern of another. She was on top of her game and pushing herself hard. After talking with me for several minutes, she giggled as she told me that she was going to make all As on her report card for the year, a huge smile crossing her face. She wasn't really looking to me for approval, instead announcing her goal as a matter of fact. I remember wondering what within pushed her so, made her so desire to do well. From my own world, I had no idea how she felt living in her world. It seemed so foreign that I thought I'd probably do nothing if I were she. I had always been motivated by the prosperity around me; she had a deeper desire, something within her. I planned to keep up with her for years to come.

The very next week, I missed the tutoring program for a meeting at the parish. As I walked into my office around 4:30, the phone rang. A teacher was on the other end of the line that connected our two worlds. I immediately heard the hesitation in her voice, the pain in her soul not wanting to sound forth into the world. And then, in three short words, the pain hit me in the chest. "Trudy is dead," she said. A gang member had mistaken her brother for another young man in the neighborhood, and while Trudy and her brother studied on the front porch of their home, basking in the afternoon sun, preparing for all As, college, medical school, a good life, Trudy's life ended. A life of promise was cut short when she jumped up and the shot intended for her brother killed her instantly.

Days later, this white, privileged minister walked into an African-American Baptist church, was given a seat of honor, and was asked to read a lesson. I stood there, in the church filled beyond capacity, and the words of Christ began to roll off my tongue with new meaning, new power. "Very truly, I tell you, unless a grain of wheat falls into the earth and dies, it remains just a single grain; but if it dies, it bears much fruit. Those who love their life lose it, and those who hate their life in this world will keep it for eternal life." A huge part of me, a huge part of every person in that room was thinking, "If it dies it bears much fruit?" You must be kidding. This little girl with so much promise, this little girl with so much life, this little girl gone because a gang member didn't care about human life. You must be kidding.

But then it struck me. With each word read, the congregation responded. A "yes, Lord," or another's "Help us, Jesus" rang forth as the scripture became a living vessel of the community's grief. A woman in the choir wearing all white with a large, beautiful hat began to hum early in the reading, and before long, the choir was also responding to the words of Jesus. The organ chimed in. I continued reading. The whole community of the faithful was giving voice, the whole community letting God know the pain, the anguish, and the disappointment.

But likewise the hope. A little girl was no longer with us. A life had ended. But the single grain of wheat was sprouting forth before our eyes. The community was not letting this single grain fall upon arid soil. This community was making sure that Trudy's life would spring forth in newness, in resurrected light. This community was not letting darkness overcome it. And in the darkest hour, they proclaimed a light like no other. Eternal light sprang forth.

EXERCISE
LOSING AND FINDING LIFE

Trudy was just beginning to live her beautiful life when it was taken in a single gunshot. But the community found new life in the midst of her death when it became willing to hear the Good News proclaimed in the midst of their deep hurt. This exercise helps us find the words of Christ in our own lives and looks for the light possibly missed among the darkness.

Materials
- Photographs selected from the Preparing for the Journey exercise.
- Poster board, preferably about 12 x 12 inches.
- Rubber cement or glue stick.
- Scissors.
- A computer and printer.

Method
What Bible verses speak to your life? Is there a favorite story or a verse that has helped you through dark days in the past? Select one or more short passages or verses, type them on the computer, and then print them on cardstock or other paper. If you like, use decorative papers and fonts to make the words appear more creative. You can either trim the verses in preparation for the exercise or wait to trim them as a part of the meditation itself.

If you don't have a favorite story or selection of scripture, take the time to find some that appeal to you. If you are new to the faith or just exploring what the Bible means in your life, consider asking a friend to help you find passages that address where you are in life.

Suggestions for possible reading and selection might include Psalms 23, 90, or 121, or perhaps John 1:1–5. Any of these passages might contain possibilities as they address the theme of light and darkness in our lives.

When you have selected some verses, place all the materials in your workspace and prepare for the exercise in quiet and prayer. You might use the verse or story selected as a way to form your prayer for several minutes before you begin working.

Our method is collage, and by now, you're practically a professional at it. Your task in this exercise is to arrange images of your life with the verse or story that you've selected. You're attempting to see how life relates directly to the biblical narrative that has meant so very much to you. Just like the congregation at Trudy's funeral, you are looking for the deep and abiding presence of God's voice speaking into the darkness of your life. Let the photos tell the real story of your life, the very essence of who you are, and allow the scripture to speak directly to your inner self. As you place scripture among the photos, paste the entire story in the middle of the pictures or weave individual verses, phrases, or words among them, using the previously cut selections or customizing as you go. By seeing how your life relates to the verses, you tie yourself back to the ancient narrative of God's love and the light of Christ can begin to shine anew with you.

Soul Questions

- If you selected scripture that has been important in your spiritual journey thus far, do you recall when it emerged in your path? Why did it speak to you then? How does it speak to you now?
- If you selected a new verse or narrative, why do you believe it spoke to you today?
- What characters in scripture do you identify with from time to time? Do you know the biblical narratives well enough to refer back to them with regularity? Can you find your life within the story of God's love throughout history?

- What is it like to see images of your life directly related to scripture? How did seeing the words of sacred story with you affect your understanding of the texts?

Thoughts for the Journey

- Do you read the Bible daily? Have you ever considered Daily Office readings (from resources such as the Book of Common Prayer) or a study Bible?
- How do you react to the Bible? Is it a comforting part of your journey? Or are there aspects of its study that you don't like?
- Many people no longer understand the basic biblical narratives. Take the time to read and study the charter narratives of our faith, such as Genesis chapters 1–11. Notice the themes of God's faithfulness and redemption despite humanity's mistakes. Reflect upon God's love and mercy in your own life.

WINDOW EIGHT

Passion or Palm Sunday

Almighty and ever living God, in your tender love for the human race you sent your Son our Savior Jesus Christ to take upon him our nature, and to suffer death upon the cross, giving us the example of his great humility: Mercifully grant that we may walk in the way of his suffering, and also share in his resurrection; through Jesus Christ our Lord, who lives and reigns with you and the Holy Spirit, one God, for ever and ever. *Amen.* —*The Book of Common Prayer,* page 219

We travel through life unaware of the twists and turns that will come our way. Places of celebration and parade become places of difficulty in a moment, and plans for the future are sometimes shattered quickly. But you are always with us, God, providing a pathway back to light and life. If we get stuck along the journey, move us along. Push us and show us a new way when we have lost our direction. *Amen.*

MARK 11:1–11

(Jesus arrives in Jerusalem)

When they were approaching Jerusalem, at Bethphage and Bethany, near the Mount of Olives, Jesus sent two of his disciples and said to them, "Go into the village ahead of you, and immediately as you enter it, you will find tied there a colt that has never been ridden; untie it and bring it. If anyone says to you, 'Why are you doing this?' just say this, 'The Lord needs it and will send it back here immediately.'" They went away and found a colt tied near a door, outside in the street. As they were untying it, some of the bystanders said to them, "What are you doing, untying the colt?" They told them what Jesus had said; and they allowed them to take it. Then they brought the colt to Jesus and threw their cloaks on it; and he sat on it. Many people spread their cloaks on the road, and others spread leafy branches that they had cut in the fields. Then those who went ahead and those who followed were shouting, "Hosanna! Blessed is the one who comes in the name of the Lord! Blessed is the coming kingdom of our ancestor David! Hosanna in the highest heaven!" Then he entered Jerusalem and went into the temple.

C33&50

Several years ago I took a group on pilgrimage to Ireland. We were ready to spend a week together walking and exploring early Celtic sites along the southwestern coast. The Rings of Kerry and Dingle were to provide the canvas for our souls' exploration of this ancient land of changing landscapes, standing stones, ring forts, oratories, and amazing people. We'd prepared for the pilgrimage with prayer and study, meeting several times to celebrate, get to know each other, and talk about why this pilgrimage was so central to our faith's journey.

So when we set out, we were incredibly excited. Even the seasoned travelers who had literally touched every continent knew that this trip would be different. It was to be a pilgrimage in the best sense of the word—an adventure into our souls' delight and into God's love for us. We said our prayers, passed out the journals, and embarked upon the first leg of the journey. Just one short flight would take us to our gateway city of Baltimore and we'd be off to the Land of IRE, full of promise.

But as soon as we set out, the journey changed. We departed on the short flight to our gateway, and then about twenty minutes before we were to land, the pilot informed us of a storm ahead. "Ladies and gentlemen: We're encountering turbulence and we'll have to circle a few minutes before we're clear to land," was his first remark. But of course circling didn't do it, and in just a few more minutes, the pilot informed us we'd been advised by the control tower to land at Richmond's airport and wait out the storm there. Apparently, the storm appeared to be gaining strength, possibly containing a tornado. When we landed in a city we hadn't planned to visit, I realized we had a good two hours until our next flight so I didn't worry too much. But the short minutes became longer periods of time, and by the time the storm cleared, we were all worried. We'd be able to land at our gateway, but would all eighteen of us make the flight to Ireland?

As soon as we landed, we faced the unbelievable answer: no way. Because it was an international flight, we hadn't arrived in time to board; no ifs, ands, or buts. We'd missed the flight to Ireland and the airline wasn't budging.

The eighteen of us just looked at each other, and all at once, I knew that I had a major job before me. A group of pilgrims on the way to a holy isle was depending upon me. They could sense this formative time they'd anticipated for months slipping away as each minute ticked upon the clock. As their leader, I just had to get them there no matter what the obstacle. I remember standing in the airport thinking that what had started as a grand and glorious parade had all of a sudden become a tragedy. What had started as a loud "Hosanna" was more like a cross to bear.

Thus began hours of working with the airline travel desk. Hours. No one wanted to deal with eighteen stranded travelers at ten o'clock at night. No other flights to Ireland were available until the next day and seats on those planes were looking very slim. Overbooked even. I recall thinking we wouldn't make it. We'd just be flying back home. And then, out of nowhere, a man from the airline walked up to the desk, took over the situation, and began looking at all the options. We couldn't fly out of Baltimore like we'd planned. But what about Washington? New York? Other possibilities? He worked furiously, looking up each flight. Somehow, we all remained patient and just let him do his job. After almost three hours, he filled out vouchers for a hotel, called taxis, and told us that the next day we'd be traveling by car all the way to Philadelphia to catch a flight there. I was stunned. Amazed. We would make it after all.

Many times the grand parade turns into a horrible traffic jam. Something that starts so wonderfully takes a wrong turn, and before we know it, we seem stranded in the midst of a barren desert. It can happen in a relationship, job, marriage, vacation, or anything else in life. Something that has so much promise can at once become total disaster with all its disappointment.

When Jesus rode into Jerusalem, all was well. "Blessed is he who comes in the name of the Lord! Hosanna in the highest!" was all that he could hear. Can you see it? The palm branches swaying in people's hands, the fronds thrown at his feet, almost like a Macy's Thanksgiving Day Parade for our Lord's arrival in the Holy City. And then, out of nowhere, the cheers fall silent, the crowd disperses, and people of judgment appear on the scene.

And yet, Christ continues upon the journey, never looking back, and never asking why him—why not another parade, another party, another celebration. With patience, endurance, and devotion, Jesus the Christ walks forward even in the darkest hour, and in so doing, provides the icon we all need to see more often in our own lives. Jesus teaches us that the journey changes.

Our pilgrimage group ended up going to three cities we hadn't originally planned to visit. We stopped en route, we departed from a different gateway, and we even landed at a different destination—still in Ireland, but a different place. We lost a whole day in the land of green. When we arrived, we were tired, hungry, and dazed. And yet we had made it, we realized, as we stood on the southwest coast looking out at the Three Sisters, a peninsula of three peaks rising from the sea. With the setting sun gently warming our faces, it struck us all: we were indeed pilgrims. Not on vacation. Not just traveling. But seeking and discovering the light in midst of darkness.

And as we stood there, looking out over the ocean, the broken Hosanna sang forth from our lips.

EXERCISE
FINDING HOPE IN DISAPPOINTMENT

Disappointment can thwart what we think is our journey. Just when the parade has begun, something upsets the whole plan and what we had looked forward to comes crashing down around us in an instant. Sometimes, we don't pause to discover the true journey before us. We get so wrapped up in the disappointment, we fail to see that God has already cast light on a new pathway, a new place, a new promise. In this simple word collage, we find new hope in a disappointment from our past.

Materials
- A sheet of paper, preferably card stock or construction paper, 11 x 17 inches.
- Two markers of different colors.

Method

This exercise is similar to the one in Window Five, Cleaning Our Temple, but requires more preparation. Before you begin the actual exercise, you'll need to identify a major disappointment in your life. A failed marriage, the loss of a job, a miscarriage, a soured friendship, or some other unresolved time when the great Hosanna turned into a cross to bear should be your aim. If you have trouble singling out just one, the exercise can be repeated again and again with each disappointment you identify. Whether you focus upon one or select several, take time to journal or reflect upon each event. Consider who was involved and why you were so disappointed. Be sure to identify the feelings you have today about what happened and see if those feelings differ from the time when it occurred. Once you've considered the who, what, when, where, and why of the situation, you're ready to begin.

Start by saying a prayer of thanksgiving for the time that God has given you and claim the time by removing all distractions from your workspace. Because this exercise is so simple, you could do it outside or in a sacred space such as church or chapel. When working with disappointments, sacred spaces can sometimes liberate our feelings and allow for more expression. If you think that might be the case for you, seek out a favorite holy spot—anything from a rock by a stream to a side chapel in a great cathedral.

The exercise itself is straightforward and builds upon the Cleaning Our Temple technique from Window Five. Take one color of marker and begin writing words and phrases that relate to the disappointment haphazardly all over the page. Work as quickly as possible, allowing all the preparation to come out in a stream-of-consciousness approach. Don't write paragraphs or even sentences. Work with one word at a time, if possible, and try to limit the number of phrases. The aim of working so quickly is to let the subconscious take control. If you've done your work beforehand, the real issues of the disappointment will emerge as you work quickly. Once the answers stop coming, say when you haven't written anything for ten to fifteen seconds, stop, put down the marker, and close your eyes. Breathe deeply three times, pausing for a couple of seconds between your inhalation and your exhalation.

After you've cleared your mind, open your eyes and take the other pen. Using this different color marker, answer each word or phrase with something that would bring transformation to each part of the disappointment. What would transform the brokenness from cross to Hosanna? What would redeem the qualities that still bring sadness, anger, or frustration? How might God bring light into a place of darkness? As answers come, write them. And again, don't pause to reflect. Look at what you have written previously and write the first response that comes to you. It's fine if the response is silly. Laughter and comedy often contain redemption. Just work quickly and let the transformation take place in the words on the page.

Soul Questions

- What feelings did you have when you identified the disappointment in your life?
- Did reflecting upon the event in advance of the exercise help you as compared with earlier collage exercises that didn't include preparation? Why or why not?
- Did the exercise reveal the need for more soul-searching in order to find transformation?

Thoughts for the Journey

- If you can, work on other disappointments with this same exercise. Are there common themes in what you feel no matter what the actual disappointment? Are there common responses? What could you learn for the future from what you have discovered? Is there a way to find redemption more readily in other disappointments because of what you've discovered?
- Did you learn how to cope with disappointment as a child? Who taught you how to approach the feelings that come with failure? Was this person a good role model? If he or she is still alive, could you talk with him or her about what you've learned?
- What sacred stories capture disappointment? How might these stories inform your understanding of your own failures?

WINDOW NINE

Maundy Thursday

Almighty Father, whose dear Son, on the night before he suffered, instituted the Sacrament of his Body and Blood: Mercifully grant that we may receive it thankfully in remembrance of Jesus Christ our Lord, who in these holy mysteries gives us a pledge of eternal life; and who now lives and reigns with you and the Holy Spirit, one God, for ever and ever. *Amen.* —*The Book of Common Prayer*, page 221

Christ, you gently reach down and cleanse us, as a mother washes a child's hands coated with dirt from the playground. But many times, we turn and run away, seeking not your face nor you love in those around us. Help us to see our place with all your children, and knowing your grace, to gather together in feast and famine, in joy and sadness, in hope and despair. *Amen.*

JOHN 13:1–9
(Washing the disciples' feet)

Now before the festival of the Passover, Jesus knew that his hour had come to depart from this world and go to the Father. Having loved his own who were in the world, he loved them to the end. The devil had already put it into the heart of Judas son of Simon Iscariot to betray him. And during supper Jesus, knowing that the Father had given all things into his hands, and that he had come from God and was going to God, got up from the table, took off his outer robe, and tied a towel around himself. Then he poured water into a basin and began to wash the disciples' feet and to wipe them with the towel that was tied around him. He came to Simon Peter, who said to him, "Lord, are you going to wash my feet?" Jesus answered, "You do not know now what I am doing, but later you will understand." Peter said to him, "You will never wash my feet." Jesus answered, "Unless I wash you, you have no share with me." Simon Peter said to him, "Lord, not my feet only but also my hands and my head!"

CR℘

When I was in the first grade, segregation had just ended. As a six-year-old attending public schools in South Carolina, I was on the front lines of social change. But because my parents always taught me to respect everyone no matter the color of their skin, I was more than naïve about what was happening around me.

I was so naïve that I had no clue that being in the class of a black woman was progressive. To me, Mrs. Brown was just a great teacher. She was older, seemed loving, wise, and quite good to me. I was oblivious to those who disagreed. I watched Sesame Street every morning as a kindergartener and wouldn't have believed that people on my street couldn't watch it because of its "progressive social agenda," let alone think that someone might have been transferred out of Mrs. Brown's class because of how God made her. But several kids did leave our class-room and more than one transferred in. But one little boy forever placed an indelible mark on my life when he walked into the room one day to replace a little girl, who in retrospect needed a "different teacher."

Sam was that boy. He had a funny walk, his feet seemed to move at a different pace than the rest of his body. And his voice—well, it seemed like it too moved at a different pace, as if the words got ahead of the meaning. He would say things like, "Mrs. Brown, may restroom go," or "Chocolate milk me today," at which we wanted to laugh, but didn't. We'd just wrinkle our brows as if the creases would somehow complete the words of his sentences. I remember one day when Mary said that since his head was smaller than those of the rest of the class, a part of his brain was missing, the part that put words together. She said her grandmother had told her that some children's heads were smashed when they were born and that the brain was squeezed out and didn't work as well. It sounded true, but our discussion on the merry-go-round never yielded a positive analysis of how anyone's head could be smashed in the hospital.

The thing that I remember the most about Sam was the smell. Just like his walk and just like his talk, it seemed out of step with the rest of his body. The only problem was that the smell had a quicker pace than he did; it arrived before he came into the room. Now, six-year-olds in that day knew not to make fun of his walk or his voice—at least not in front of him. But there is nothing in social norms or manners that can prevent a six-year-old from exclaiming, "What's that smell?" each and every time Sam walked into the room. Mrs. Brown would try to stop us, but we noticed her expression too. You couldn't mistake her eyelids twitching and brows lifting for an expression of loveliness; no, Mrs. Brown couldn't stand it either, and we all knew it.

One day, Mary climbed to the top of the jungle gym and began to lecture us all on the meaning of Sam's life and why he smelled so very bad. After recalling the smashed head routine once again, she said she knew another truth from her grandmother and that all of us needed to hear it, too. I'll never forget it. On a cool October day with the sun high in the sky, Mary opened up a chapter of life that I had no idea existed. The naïveté of my Sesame Street life was getting ready to end.

Mary started with the rule that "cleanliness is next to godliness," something I vaguely remembered as a saying my mom would impart on Saturday mornings when I had to clean my room. But the next line, another truth from Mary's grandmother, changed me forever. Sam wasn't clean, said Mary, because he was black. She went on to say that Sam was dirty because he had the mark of Cain upon him. She said it was in the Bible and that her grandmother told her it was true. Cain had killed his brother Able, and because of it, God put a mark on Cain and his race forever to show that Cain had sinned. God had made Cain black because he had killed, and according to Mary, blacks would suffer through the ages. In her world, Sam was dirty because he had the mark of Cain, and he smelled because someone in his family had done something really, really bad.

I was no theologian. But this was too much for me. Several of us told Mary she was crazy, that Sam was just like us, he just didn't have the money for clean clothes and soap for a bath. But the more we resisted, the more Mary argued. Sam was dirty with the mark of Cain. Sam was dirty because he was black. In desperation, we all stopped arguing with Mary. I stopped playing on the monkey bars that day; the swings and merry-go-round became my new hangout.

A few days later, Sam didn't come to school. Mrs. Brown said nothing. Days went by and we began to wonder if Sam would ever come back. So one day, just as recess began, a group of us from the swings ventured over to Mrs. Brown to ask, "Where's Sam?" Mrs. Brown looked at once sad and happy, something I had only seen a couple of times before in my life, like when my Dad didn't get a new job in another state. Mom said she didn't want to move but that the money would have been nice.

Mrs. Brown said that she couldn't tell us much. The only thing she revealed was that he had gone to live with his grandparents now, and that in a few days, Sam might come back to school. I remember thinking that she knew a whole lot more, but that what she knew had to be scary, a secret she didn't want to let out and hurt us with. It was like she could see something in her eyes as she told us these few words, as if she had lived them herself. As she talked, I remember thinking that she had the most beautiful and loving eyes I'd ever seen, the kind of eyes you're just happy knowing you yourself appear in from time to time. And I remember thinking that there was no way any mark of Cain was upon her, Sam, or anyone else. Mary's grandmother had to be wrong. I just knew it.

A few weeks later, a new boy came to school. He walked in, sat down at the desk next to me, and looked a little scared. Mrs. Brown walked him to the desk as she announced, "Boys and girls, let's welcome Sam back today!" Sam! Sam who? This boy with the neat clothes, the sparkling skin, the closely-shaved head? This boy with the new shoes, the new notebook, the straight walk, and the smell of Ivory soap? All of us gasped in disbelief.

I don't remember when I learned the rest of the story, of how Sam's parents had left him alone with his brothers and sisters just before the beginning of school that summer in the 1960s, never to return. Of how his older sister, just thirteen years old, had tried to care for them all so they could stay together and not be turned over to social services. No, I don't remember when I found out the rest of their story. All I really remember was that Mary and her grandmother were wrong; Sesame Street was real after all.

Now, when I look back on the first grade, I don't remember anything that I learned from books, worksheets, or bulletin boards. But what I learned from Mrs. Brown is written in my heart. I know that she was the one who helped Sam, helped his brothers and sisters, and got them to the people that they needed to be loved and cherished. That was the look in her eyes that day. And in the end, I suppose that's enough to learn in the first grade. Enough to know for a lifetime.

EXERCISE
WASHING AWAY THE GRIME

There are places within each of us that we're unwilling to acknowledge. Places where we put others down, pushing them into a corner
and barring all light from shining. But when we close others off from
the possibility of new life and light in their lives, we also close ourselves off from God's grace. By identifying these places in our journey,
and asking forgiveness, we too are liberated. Since we've done word
collages several times, you should be comfortable with this technique,
and because of that, you're likely to go deeper in this exercise.

Materials

- A sheet of paper, preferably card stock or construction paper,
  11 x 17 inches.
- Two markers of different colors.

Method

This exercise is similar to other word collages thus far. We begin
in our workspace and take time to center ourselves, letting go of all
the daily events and challenges that preoccupy our minds. If meditation would be helpful as you begin, take ample time. Pray for God's
faithfulness and safety to surround you as you venture into a new area
of the journey.

Ask yourself a simple question: Whom have I hurt in my life?
What forgiveness should I seek? As you consider these questions, begin to write quickly, as in past exercises. Write the person's name and
why you need forgiveness, and as before, use single words and short
phrases. Work quickly and continue to work as long as people come

to mind. Also be sure to write creatively, let the word collage become more of an art form than a paragraph.

When you are no longer writing, stop and take time to reflect on what you've written. When you're ready, take a different color pen and begin to write quickly how you might respond. What would bring forgiveness to each situation? A phone call? A note? A face-to-face visit or confession? Write what would bring wholeness to each situation and see if you can identity the way to bring forgiveness and reconciliation.

When you've finished, reflect on the exercise, noting any similarities, themes, or other commonalities. Use the Soul Questions as a guide.

Soul Questions
- Was it easy to identify the people you've hurt? Were you surprised by anyone that you listed or was it pretty much what you expected?
- What were the common themes among the relationships? Were there any similarities in how you hurt others? Do you believe that similarities say more about you or those you hurt?
- Is it easy for you to forgive others? Yourself? Why or why not?
- How can you accomplish the steps you outlined in the exercise? Can you set a schedule to contact those you have hurt and seek reconciliation?

Thoughts for the Journey
- How can you be more honest in your relationships? How could finding that honesty help prevent future hurts among relationships?
- How could identifying common themes in past hurts help you transform your life for the future?
- Could you include an inventory of relationships in your spiritual discipline? How might regularly considering your life and how it intersects with others' lives bring wholeness to you?

WINDOW TEN

Good Friday

Almighty God, we pray you graciously to behold this your family, for whom our Lord Jesus Christ was willing to be betrayed, and given into the hands of sinners, and to suffer death upon the cross; who now lives and reigns with you and the Holy Spirit, one God, for ever and ever. *Amen.* —*The Book of Common Prayer*, page 221

Today, God, I go with you as we carry the cross. Help me to let you take my life as we walk the journey toward Golgotha, and trusting in you, let me plumb the depths of your light and love in my life. *Amen.*

JOHN 19:1–37
(*The crucifixion*)

Then Pilate took Jesus and had him flogged. And the soldiers wove a crown of thorns and put it on his head, and they dressed him in a purple robe. They kept coming up to him, saying, "Hail, King of the Jews!" and striking him on the face. Pilate went out again and said to them, "Look, I am bringing him out to you to let you know that I find no case against him." So Jesus came out, wearing the crown of thorns and the purple robe. Pilate said to them, "Here is the man!" When the chief priests and the police saw him, they shouted, "Crucify him! Crucify him!" Pilate said to them, "Take him yourselves and crucify him; I find no case against him." The Jews answered him, "We have a law, and according to that law he ought to die because he has claimed to be the Son of God." Now when Pilate heard this, he was more afraid than ever. He entered his headquarters again and asked Jesus, "Where are you from?" But Jesus gave him no answer. Pilate therefore said to him, "Do you refuse to speak to me? Do you not know that I have power to release you, and power to crucify you?" Jesus answered him, "You would have no power over me unless it had been given you from above; therefore the one who handed me over to you is guilty of a greater sin." From then on Pilate tried to release him, but the Jews cried out, "If you release this man, you are no friend of the emperor. Everyone who claims to be a king sets himself against the emperor." When Pilate heard these words, he brought Jesus outside and sat on the judge's bench at a place called The Stone Pavement, or in Hebrew Gabbatha. Now it was the day of Preparation for the Passover; and it was about noon. He said to the Jews, "Here is your King!" They cried out, "Away with him! Away with him! Crucify him!" Pilate asked them, "Shall I crucify your King?" The chief priests answered, "We have no king but the emperor." Then he handed him over to them to be crucified.

So they took Jesus; and carrying the cross by himself, he went out to what is called The Place of the Skull, which in Hebrew is called

Golgotha. There they crucified him, and with him two others, one on either side, with Jesus between them. Pilate also had an inscription written and put on the cross. It read, "Jesus of Nazareth, the King of the Jews." Many of the Jews read this inscription, because the place where Jesus was crucified was near the city; and it was written in Hebrew, in Latin, and in Greek. Then the chief priests of the Jews said to Pilate, "Do not write, 'The King of the Jews,' but, 'This man said, I am King of the Jews.'" Pilate answered, "What I have written I have written." When the soldiers had crucified Jesus, they took his clothes and divided them into four parts, one for each soldier. They also took his tunic; now the tunic was seamless, woven in one piece from the top. So they said to one another, "Let us not tear it, but cast lots for it to see who will get it." This was to fulfill what the scripture says, "They divided my clothes among themselves, and for my clothing they cast lots." And that is what the soldiers did. Meanwhile, standing near the cross of Jesus were his mother, and his mother's sister, Mary the wife of Clopas, and Mary Magdalene. When Jesus saw his mother and the disciple whom he loved standing beside her, he said to his mother, "Woman, here is your son." Then he said to the disciple, "Here is your mother." And from that hour the disciple took her into his own home. After this, when Jesus knew that all was now finished, he said (in order to fulfill the scripture), "I am thirsty." A jar full of sour wine was standing there. So they put a sponge full of the wine on a branch of hyssop and held it to his mouth. When Jesus had received the wine, he said, "It is finished." Then he bowed his head and gave up his spirit.

Since it was the day of Preparation, the Jews did not want the bodies left on the cross during the sabbath, especially because that sabbath was a day of great solemnity. So they asked Pilate to have the legs of the crucified men broken and the bodies removed. Then the soldiers came and broke the legs of the first and of the other who had been crucified with him. But when they came to Jesus and saw that he was already dead, they did not break his legs. Instead, one of the soldiers pierced his side with a spear, and at once blood and water came out. (He who saw this has testified so that you also may believe. His testimony is true, and he knows that he tells the truth.) These things occurred so that the scripture might be fulfilled, "None of his bones shall be broken." And again another passage of scripture says, "They will look on the one whom they have pierced."

CRSO

Every Sunday, I do the same thing just before services: I take all the bulletins and papers out of my Prayer Book so that they don't fall onto the floor as we pray. Episcopalians like tidiness in liturgy; it's one of our hallmarks. Inevitably, there's more paper than I recall putting there. A bulletin or two, a joke someone printed for me, and pretty often an editorial cartoon that someone clipped out of the paper. Some people realize priests need a good laugh from time to time.

But one week not long ago I realized I was throwing away four funeral bulletins. In a simple weekly ritual, a mere fling of the wrist, four people were falling down into the trash with all the tissues, cough drop wrappers, and everything else. Sometimes I would throw away one or two such bulletins, but four at once? It had been a long time since that had happened. I was stunned as I looked at the trash can: a beloved lady in her nineties, a card player extraordinaire who loved her family with all her might for close to a century; a bishop who had been on our staff and who had restored a sense of love and charity to a parish that desperately needed to need each other; a twenty-two-year-old man, a golfer with great promise who died in a tragic accident no one could have prevented; and a young man who could make anyone laugh and whose life ended far too early just after his twentieth birthday. The deaths of all these people had so numbed me into my priestly stupor that I had merely reached into my Book of Common Prayer as if I were tossing away another Family Circus cartoon. I was grieving so deeply on the inside, and yet on the outside, I was so very pastoral that I couldn't see my little ritual of book cleaning for what it really was: denial.

Denying our cross is something we don't often realize we are doing. We think we take it up and "follow him" with great regularity. But usually, we're so busy following our own self-devised way, truth, and life that we miss the opportunity to walk with Jesus toward the real crosses of life. The chance to be Simon of Cyrene, the man who bent down and picked up Jesus' cross, passes us by. Instead, we fashion our own sacred story at a comfortable distance. In our narrative, Jesus surely bears his cross and suffers, but he does so on stage with us comfortably seated in our cushioned chairs. Our plot is so full of denial, we watch as spectators, thinking we're in charge. We perpetuate the myth that we can do the right thing, alleviate our pain and suffering, by watching the great drama, and after a great performance, reap our miraculous reward. In our denial of the true crucifixion we share with Jesus, we direct a new drama where our own power allows us to get the miracle, to get what we want, to be the way, truth, and life.

Being in charge and reaching for the golden miracle is a mentality that pervades our souls. You'd think that those walking the way of the cross would be immune to such worldly pursuits, but instead, it seems that this pathway may be the most tempting place to try your hand at denial and usher in your own kingdom. When we face the death of a loved one, loss of a job, end of a marriage, or any other loss, the grief can be overwhelming. In the first stages, we enter into a deep denial and begin thinking that the difficulty will go away if we just have more faith, reach for the stars, and find the golden ring. We think that faith is a commodity, something that we acquire by hard work. For me, a fierce competitor, the idea of trusting in God's faithfulness to me instead of my faith in God—that's way out of control. Too vulnerable. Too dangerous. Too scary. Becoming vulnerable, actually letting the difficulty of the cross come my way and embracing it for what it truly is, no way. Every molecule within me just knows that I can lick the pain, the frustration, the very real and present danger. Sort of like running in a race, I think that I can push through the wall of pain and find a new breath on the other side all on my own—something I do, by myself, in my way, truth, and life.

Most of the time, it seems to work. I can handle a death here and there. I can handle a little darkness. That stuff just comes with life and we learn early on how to let the Jesus drama take some of our pain. We sit, watch, listen, and think about how much more Jesus suffered, and knowing that, well, it seems to take our pain away. And when others face darkness, sure, I can help them reach for the brass ring. But when we face one loss after another, such as four funeral bulletins in the trashcan, the cracks in our way, truth, and life are exposed. When we face something like four people dying in just a few days, the bulletins in the trash can are a wake-up call. Burying a dear and lovely lady who lived a long and graceful life is something any of us can do; despite the difficulty of the death, we know deep within that the life was good, long, fulfilling and that the next life is there waiting. Even when a community's past pastor dies after a long illness, we face the reality. Losing the pastor and friend is remarkably difficult, but the loss is not overwhelming to most of us. We've all said it: "He's better off," or "She's suffering no more." At some level these statements are still a type of denial, a way of coping with death, keeping Jesus as a character on the stage.

But when a string of deaths comes or two young men in their twenties die or any massive loss comes our personal way, the cross comes off the stage and lands directly at our feet. The work we do, reaching for the next brass ring, the next rung of faith, seems more intolerable than hopeful. Lives ended in their twenties, or the death of a parent, or the loss of a best friend. Crucifixion, agony, despair, torture all come to mind. Deaths out of nowhere, so unexpected, so unreal, so unbelievable, expose our denial and reveal the fallacy of our Jesus on stage. If we've been clinging to our own way, truth, and life, the darkness of deaths such as these plunges us onto a journey of the soul we don't want. It's as if we walk into a nightmare in living color. As each day passes, any clarity we had falls away as the nightmare blurs our life, as if someone were moving the lens of our eyes; exhaustion sets in. Before we know it, the colors have bled into each other and shades of gray and black begin to appear. Denial, which had been our close friend and served us well in the past, becomes anger as we realize we are not in control. A deep loss exposes us for what we are: idolaters. We've worshiped our way, our truth, and our life as we watched the drama of our control.

And that is where the miracle occurs. At the moment we lose control, at the moment we give in and let go, Jesus cries forth from the cross, "It is finished." For most of us, it's the first time we really hear Jesus from the cross. It's not that all has ended, that the darkness has become the norm. Instead, Christ's final words on the cross usher in the greatest hope of light. For with the proclamation from him, healing has begun. When we let go of our conjured power and start letting God lead, guide, and direct, the nightmare of whatever we cannot bear is given to God. Death, divorce, despair, depression, a wayward child, a friend no longer talking to us. Whatever brings us to the foot of the cross brings the hope of healing, not of our own fashion but of God's. And the possibility of light piercing our tomb becomes all the more possible.

For when we realize we aren't God, we know God will be faithful. We don't have to climb another rung on the faith ladder. We don't have to prove ourselves before God to get a brass ring. We don't have to make straight As on the heavenly report card. Instead, all we really have to do is realize it's not our way, our truth, our life. And any time that happens, the miracle is possible. God is faithful. Resurrection comes when we let God be God.

EXERCISE
THE CROSS AND SEEMING DARKNESS

When life presents difficulties, we discover our powerlessness. At any time, the boundaries between the light and the dark can become harder to see. The cross we bear can plunge us into a place of darkness where the colors bleed into each other and grays and blacks appear all along the horizons. With this exercise, which is a two-step process also involving the next chapter, we begin to see our lives in the cross of Christ as we attempt to give ourselves over to the way, truth, and life.

Materials
- Black and white copies of all the previous exercises, made on a copy machine or by scanning and printing images on your computer and printer.
- Scissors.
- Rubber cement or glue stick.
- Large poster board, preferably extra-heavy stock, or a large piece of foam core.

Method
With this exercise, we begin to see the expansiveness of our journey. By assembling all your work in one location, copying it, and reflecting upon it, you'll encounter the fullness of the path thus far. Bringing all the exercises together, we go with Jesus to the cross and give ourselves to his love and mercy. If you're able to present all of who you are to the Christ, Good Friday will not be a day of darkness, but the greatest possibility of new life and light in your walk with God.

Assemble all your original work around you. Let it create a sacred space for this exercise, icons into your life and God's. After creating this holy space, arrange the black and white copies of your work on a table before you. Revisit each one, taking time to reflect upon the discoveries of each. Where did you find the dust in your life? How were you able to cleanse your temple? Have you been able to reclaim your life and the people in it as gifts because you have begun to accept the Lenten journey of our lives? Have you identified the crosses you bear and the people you've hurt along the way?

As you reflect, begin to take the black and white copies and cut or tear from them images that really speak to you. Many images will be important, but if you've done the exercises throughout the book, you'll be able to work quickly and readily identify the images most important to your journey. At first, just identify the images and place them before you. Don't worry about arranging them. Once you've found all the images that grab your heart and soul, begin to arrange them rapidly, without thought. Don't glue them onto the board at this point. If you like, you might arrange them in the shape of a cross; you can even cut the poster into the form of a cross if you like. It doesn't have to have neat edges—it could be a torn and battered shape itself. As you work, you might ask yourself which of the images needs Christ's light the most? Which of these parts of my life need to face the darkness of Jesus' final hour, hear the words "It is finished," and then await the coming of Easter light? Play with the arrangement as you ask yourself these questions.

When you feel as if you've exhausted the process, begin to glue the copies, overlapping the images, as you like. Try not to put them in rows or in neat arrangements. Let the chaos be a part of the creation itself and let the images form an expression of what crucifixion looks like in your life.

When you've finished the cross, take time to sit with it and reflect for a while. Imagine that you are able to carry this cross with Jesus to Golgotha. Imagine that everything upon your cross is upon Jesus' cross. Let your life be present with God as the darkness of the after-noon comes and as the final breaths flow from Jesus' body. Hear him say, "It is finished." Let go and let God.

Soul Questions

- What was it like to revisit prior exercises? Did you see the earlier chapters in a new light? Has the journey helped expose more than you knew would come your way when you set out?
- What new things about your life did you discover? Were there common themes among the chapters? Common stories? Common people?
- Have you found yourself responding differently to memories as you've made the journey through this book? Why or why not?
- How have you seen yourself in the scripture readings and various stories on the journey? How has this been different for you?

Thoughts for the Journey

- How might you continue to identify the things you need to take to Jesus upon the cross? What exercises have helped the most? How might you repeat them?
- Are there other spiritual disciplines that you need to make your continued journey with Christ? How might you incorporate them into daily living?
- Are there parts of your life you still cling to, unwilling to take to Christ? If so, why? And what do you have to lose if you open yourself up to God in new ways?
- How has this process allowed you to trust in God more? How have you begun to see the light in your life?

WINDOW ELEVEN

Holy Saturday

O God, Creator of heaven and earth: Grant that, as the crucified body of your dear Son was laid in the tomb and rested on this holy Sabbath, so we may await with him the coming of the third day, and rise with him to newness of life; who now lives and reigns with you and the Holy Spirit, one God, for ever and ever. *Amen.*
—*The Book of Common Prayer*, page 221

God, I don't like to wait on you. Too often, I prefer my own ways to yours and either stay stuck in darkness or afraid to consider new life because I can't fathom turning things over to you. Help me to let go and let you lead and guide, and through my own cross, may I too find my empty tomb. *Amen.*

Matthew 27:55–66
(Sealing the tomb)

Many women were also there, looking on from a distance; they had followed Jesus from Galilee and had provided for him. Among them were Mary Magdalene, and Mary the mother of James and Joseph, and the mother of the sons of Zebedee. When it was evening, there came a rich man from Arimathea, named Joseph, who was also a disciple of Jesus. He went to Pilate and asked for the body of Jesus; then Pilate ordered it to be given to him. So Joseph took the body and wrapped it in a clean linen cloth and laid it in his own new tomb, which he had hewn in the rock. He then rolled a great stone to the door of the tomb and went away. Mary Magdalene and the other Mary were there, sitting opposite the tomb. The next day, that is, after the day of Preparation, the chief priests and the Pharisees gathered before Pilate and said, "Sir, we remember what that impostor said while he was still alive, 'After three days I will rise again.' Therefore command the tomb to be made secure until the third day; otherwise his disciples may go and steal him away, and tell the people, 'He has been raised from the dead,' and the last deception would be worse than the first." Pilate said to them, "You have a guard of soldiers; go, make it as secure as you can." So they went with the guard and made the tomb secure by sealing the stone.

CRᏋᏇ

Dan was an amazing boy. He had one of those mischievous smiles that made you anxious and happy at the same time. You know the type, the one that says, "I love you," and "I'm up to something," all at the same time. In everything he did, he was the incarnation of Dennis the Menace before your eyes, and despite all the craziness, you knew that deep within him was something so holy, so beautiful, that God's very self laughed in each expression upon Dan's face. At the amazing age of eleven, Dan knew himself, and because he was so very in touch with his soul, he had perfected the ability to make everyone around him feel good. He didn't give others an empty happiness, but a full and abundant sense of joy, the kind C. S. Lewis expressed, that emotion of reality that celebrates among the difficulties of life.

Counselors and children alike loved Day. At the camp where I met him, he was a kind of legend. Everyone thought of him as a kind of hero. From the cooks in the kitchen to the maintenance man, every person in the camp loved Dan. He was a part of their lives and each person would have done anything in the world for him. You couldn't help but feel that way about Dan. New campers were introduced to him, and amazingly, he never forgot a name. From the six-year-olds to the teenagers, Dan knew them all. And in his laughter, his constant smile, his frequent pranks that never devalued another, everyone knew him. He was the camp itself for many people, I believe. They came to see him, not to do the crafts and swim. No, they came because Dan cared and helped each laugh at him- or herself. Yes, Dan was an amazing boy.

And he couldn't walk.

Dan had been born with a genetic disorder that affected the muscles in his legs. Because the nerves from his brain could not send signals to his legs, he had absolutely no movement in them. Dan had never walked, run, or even crawled. His whole life had been spent coping with the undeniable reality of weakness below the waist, and compensating with an unbelievably strong upper body. At the age of eleven, Dan sat, never setting foot upon the earth under his wheelchair. But never once, never throughout the long and hot summer camp, did the wheelchair or lack of leg muscles stop him. He played sports, maneuvering his chair down the court and shooting from three-point range. And he strapped on a life vest and got in the water, swimming to his heart's desire. His amazing upper body strength could propel him through the water or enable him to wheel up and down a court. Some days he even had counselors place him upon the blob, a huge inflatable balloon-type thing in the middle of the lake. Sitting there, eagerly awaiting a counselor jumping onto the other end, Dan looked like the happiest human being in the world. And when the counselor hit the blob and propelled Dan into the air, a smile appeared on Dan's face, a smile so wide all could see. In seeing their hero thrust high into the air, the whole camp would light up, smiles all over. Sometimes, even the cooks would come out to see.

But we all wondered what Dan would do the day his cabin went on the high ropes course. This particular summer, Dan was now old enough to go with his cabin for the high ropes. In previous years, counselors had figured out ways to incorporate Dan into low ropes and the exercises they entailed. Everyone always talked about how Dan did so well, and how his perseverance helped them to build a true community along the course. But the high ropes were a different matter. Counselors were ready to help, but most of us couldn't figure out how Dan would accomplish some of the elements. We knew he would be disappointed, not able to join the others, just sitting in his chair watching. Dan never liked the sidelines nor accepted them easily. He was fighter and always seemed to come out on top.

So we were amazed when he announced he was ready at the zip line. Several people tried to talk him out of it, but Dan wasn't listening. Helmet upon his head, harness around his waist, the rope of the belay ready to go; we suspected that the counselors would have to hoist him up the pole. He was belayed and could have easily been pulled up the stripped tree. Instead, Dan took each of the spikes nailed into the tree, and pulled himself mightily, his biceps and back muscles doing an incredible amount of work as we watched in disbelief. Dan ascended, going higher and higher, making it to the platform some forty feet above us. This amazing child of God, who had never walked, had pulled himself up the tree and was ready to fly on the zip line.

And at once, just as we all expected him to zip forth in new life, he froze. Dan had had no difficulty climbing the pole; he had faced the hardship head on, and he had amazed every one of us. He had accepted his Good Friday. He had borne his cross, the cross of his whole life, and reaching the pinnacle, the opportunity to take flight, he stopped. He was now sitting on the cusp of something new, something incredible, and all he wanted to do was wait. Wait. To sit and wait.

We all thought he had made it and now didn't know what to do. And so the cheering started almost immediately. "Come on down, Dan!" some people were shouting. "You can do it; we know you can," another cried. But Dan did not respond. He just sat there in total silence. He was looking straight ahead, straight down the line. And after thirty minutes or so, some of us started wondering if Dan would ever come down on his own. He had climbed in wild abandon. He had made it to the top, the hardest part, we thought. Little did we know how very much he needed the time to just sit there on top of the world, ready to fly, but waiting.

Dan had always lived on Good Friday. He had borne his cross his whole life, and unlike so many of us, Dan had faced the crucifixion head on. He had not denied the difficulties but had accepted them, living one day at a time with the cross life had dealt. But in retrospect, not a one of us had seen his true suffering. He had merely been a hero to us, someone who had made the most of life and had pushed us to see how lucky we were. But in our shallow pity for Dan, we had failed to see his real life. When we saw him stuck there on the platform, we saw his true soul longing to leave his cross behind, longing to be on the cusp of resurrection, longing to let Holy Saturday be his final part of the journey toward new life and light.

Holy Saturday is not a big day in most churches. In fact, few parishes even have a Holy Saturday liturgy these days. It only lasts about ten minutes. A prayer or two, a short scripture reading, maybe a homily. Why go and mark the day when nothing happened? Why mark the day when Christ was merely in the tomb, stuck between Good Friday and Easter morn?

Because the greatest promise of light comes in the darkest hour. Dan understood that being in the world means some crosses never really go away. Instead, they are borne as a part of life itself. But Dan also showed us how wonderful it can be to sit, stuck between Good Friday and Easter morning. When we see a glimpse of resurrection coming in our own lives, when we see the possibility of the cross being removed, we savor it. We sit in silence. We behold the possibility of all that comes in letting go and letting God.

Too often, even those of us who make our way to the Good Fridays of life skip immediately to the Easter parade, the party with the lamb, the wine, and the chocolates. We want to escape the waiting time because sometimes that means accepting the cross of our lives for what it is and likewise accepting that Easter may not bring what we want. We jump to the happy morn because we don't want to deal with the waiting, the in-between time where so many of us live our lives. We're too scared to move from the tomb and wait on the platform, too scared Easter might not be what we expected. How do we move from a life where there are still unexplained accidents, shootings, diseases, disappointments, and struggles to arrive on the platform, the zip line dangling above our heads?

By letting go. It's really that simple. Deep within each of us we know our own Good Fridays, we know the things that hurt and claim our souls. We know the things that make us pause, and sit, wondering what it will be like to move from a place we know too well. Knowing these things, we must let go and with God patiently wait on the Holy Saturdays of life. It's there in that place where the line becomes clear and the possibility of resurrection hope becomes real. When we skip from the hardness of Good Friday directly to Easter, we miss the waiting time. We miss the letting go.

You can let your heart be free in the silence of Saturday. By just sitting there in the tomb of your life, Christ can begin to move within you. By accepting the stillness, by letting the darkness invade, you allow the darkest hour to become the greatest hope. And in that moment, the broken "Alleluia" sings deep within your soul as you find its truest song.

And with wild abandon, in the midst of the screaming silence, you will reach up and with Dan find the zip line. In letting go and letting God, you will accept the cross, accept the silence, and enter into a new Easter joy. You will encounter the resurrection just before dawn, and with the wind in your hair, the ground blurring under your feet, you will zip into the dawning light of a new day.

EXERCISE
MOVING FROM FRIDAY TO SATURDAY

In the last chapter you created your cross by revisiting all the exercises used in this book. All the things that claim your life and pull you down were placed upon the cross for God to transform. We heard Jesus proclaim, "It is finished," as the sun set on our Good Friday. We now come to the last part of our journey as we wait with God for new life. We let go, let God, and find the ability to glimpse Easter light breaking in upon us in the darkness of the night. on Holy Saturday. We prepare for our resurrection with God.

Materials
- The cross you created in the last exercise.
- Markers, colored pencils, or pastels.

Method

If you've faithfully engaged the exercises, you've embarked upon a time of self-discovery in God that makes your humanity more of a gift than a burden. By giving yourself over to the narrative of God's grace, your cross has begun the transformation of moving from darkness into light. You've found areas in your life where light is shining brightly and the love of God is manifest. You've found what it means to be a human being, created in the image and likeness of God, and in that you've let go of judgment to encounter a new level of consciousness or mindfulness in God. You've also likely found areas that need more love and mercy if you're to let go and trust God enough to plumb their depths. This exercise allows you to claim each of those areas through the gift of color.

You took time in the last chapter to reflect upon the cross you created. Now, you take that reflection deeper. Ask yourself which areas are basking in the light, which are coming toward the light, and which are still stuck in the darkness. Take the plunge and get honest with yourself and God about the work left to do. As you reflect upon these questions, select colors that portray where you think you are on the journey. Are there some areas of golden sun, things that have basked in the fullness of God for a while? Are there things that sit in bright yellow, as if at noonday? Are some just seeing the light, breaking forth at dawn in shades of gold and orange? Are there some just before dawn, purplish-blue? Or some still stuck in midnight colors of black and blue? Try to identify these areas and use the pencils, markers, or pastels to portray where the various areas of your life are. Be creative. If using acrylics, smear the colors along edges to portray how the colors are never pure but instead emerging from each other. Let your creativity come fully to the page as you claim God's light and life in you humanity, the center of your life becoming the heart of God.

Soul Questions

- Which was easier to identify, the areas of brightness or the areas of darkness? Why?
- Do areas that bask in light already surprise you? Are there any that have changed because of this Lenten journey? What were you able to do that allowed the transformation?
- If there are areas of darkness, why do they linger? How might you see more promise in their darkness? Do you believe you are stuck on Good Friday or are you sitting on the promise of a new day as you encounter Holy Saturday?

Thoughts for the Journey

- How can you incorporate the image of light into your everyday life?

- What steps do you need to take to make sure you continue plumbing the depths of who you are in Christ?
- Are there activities that need to be removed from your life if you're to continue along the journey this discipline has brought to you? Are there things you need to add?
- Which exercises do you need to repeat often? Which ones didn't work well for you?
- How can Easter light become a part of all that you do? Of all that you are?

WINDOW TWELVE

Easter: The Day of Resurrection

O God, who made this most holy night to shine with the glory of the Lord's resurrection: Stir up in your Church that Spirit of adoption which is given to us in Baptism, that we, being renewed both in body and mind, may worship you in sincerity and truth; through Jesus Christ our Lord, who lives and reigns with you, in the unity of the Holy Spirit, one God, now and for ever. *Amen.*
—*The Book of Common Prayer,* page 222

God, you promise new birth in the midst of life and you offer light wherever I find my darkness. As you rise forth from the ashes, bring me with you along the pathway to a new hope and show me how to see my journey as an invitation to fullness in all that I encounter. *Amen.*

MATTHEW 28:1–10

(Mary Magdalene and Mary go to the tomb and encounter Jesus)

After the sabbath, as the first day of the week was dawning, Mary Magdalene and the other Mary went to see the tomb. And suddenly there was a great earthquake; for an angel of the Lord, descending from heaven, came and rolled back the stone and sat on it. His appearance was like lightning, and his clothing white as snow. For fear of him the guards shook and became like dead men. But the angel said to the women, "Do not be afraid; I know that you are looking for Jesus who was crucified. He is not here; for he has been raised, as he said. Come, see the place where he lay. Then go quickly and tell his disciples, 'He has been raised from the dead, and indeed he is going ahead of you to Galilee; there you will see him.' This is my message for you." So they left the tomb quickly with fear and great joy, and ran to tell his disciples. Suddenly Jesus met them and said, "Greetings!" And they came to him, took hold of his feet, and worshiped him. Then Jesus said to them, "Do not be afraid; go and tell my brothers to go to Galilee; there they will see me."

CB℃SO

I'll never forget burying Greg. I'd come to know her almost immediately upon accepting the call to serve the parish where she worshipped. A lifelong Episcopalian with family roots as far back as the state of Virginia, she was one of those parishioners who just exuded all things proper about our denomination. She sat upright with perfect posture in the pew. She sang old hymns and even simplified Anglican chant as if that were all she listened to. When she entered a room, others around her lit up like the sun piercing the clouds on a spring day. She attended many classes, contributed much discussion, arranged flowers from her garden for the altar, and did most anything asked of her at the parish.

She was also suffering from cancer. Years before, she had been diagnosed with breast cancer. Chemotherapy, radiation, and surgery had carved out several years of cancer-free life for her. But by the time I arrived, the cancer had reappeared as shadows on her latest scan. As it had metastasized in several areas of her body, the prognosis wasn't good. New treatment, some experimental, could delay the inevitable, but we all knew that Greg wouldn't be with us very long. The cancer would take her from us some day. The real question was when.

As her pastor, I watched Greg and the disease. She amazed me with her never-failing courage and optimism. Unlike some of her friends who kept saying, "God will heal her and take away this disease," Greg kept insisting that God had always been healing her and that cancer, whether it left her body or not, wouldn't prevent God's healing. She once told me, "You know, Michael, God heals us no matter what happens to our bodies." As her priest, I didn't have to remind her that it wasn't her way, truth, and life. No, she already understood God's faithfulness to her and Christ's unrelenting love even in the midst of her cross.

As we all watched the disease progress, little clues along the way began to tell us what was really going on with Greg. She lost weight, had no appetite, and started to look far older than she was. But her attitude toward life and toward God never changed. If she ever doubted God's faithfulness, I never heard it. I'm not sure if it was the fact that she accepted God's faithfulness early in her life or whether she gave it to God through her disease. But whenever she had accepted God's faithfulness in her life, by the time she was facing the last days of cancer she was singing, dancing, and praying the whole way. Cancer claimed a part of her journey, but she trusted that God had redeemed it.

So when I buried her, it was an occasion of grace and mercy for all. But none of us could have imagined what would happen the day we took Greg to her final resting place along the James River. Her family had built a beautiful home along the James in the seventeenth century, and although the house had passed to another owner, the family retained rights to the burial plot there. We arrived after our two-hour journey to the long drive, amidst oaks and poplars, winding its way to the beautiful house, a stately brick Georgian. After stopping there for a brief moment to check on the luncheon to be served after the service, we jumped back into the car and drove through the estate, with huge boxwoods framing our car as we journeyed down a narrow path. And then, as if straight out of a novel, a brick wall protruded from boxwood forming the family burial ground. With magnolias and azaleas all around, we walked into the hallowed space where Greg's family had been buried for several hundred years.

Just to the right, in a well-lit spot, there was an opening in the earth. The resting place for Greg's ashes was duly prepared and waiting. I took her urn to the stand beside the opening, covering it with a silk pall, and we waited for the guests to arrive. One by one on the hot August day, the people walked into the walled yard. And one by one, they came over to the pall to say something, to remember, to give thanks for this life well lived.

After a few people had gathered, a small yellow butterfly appeared. Winding its way through the people, it flitted all over the place, lighting on clothing or even someone's head from time to time. It flew around us, just sort of hovering here and there, a beautiful and constant image of new life to us all.

I had buried many, many people. Many an urn, many a coffin, many a box had passed through my hands into the earth. Well, not exactly. Usually my hands touched the beautiful silk pall we used to cover up whatever we couldn't bear to face. But Greg didn't want it that way. She was the first person to ask me to stoop down to the earth and put the ashes themselves into the ground. No container. Nothing. Just ashes.

And so when all had gathered, we prayed, sang a song, and came to the committal. But this time around there was no acolyte to hold my prayer book. There was no urn or wooden box on a stand. Instead,

I took my book, laid it on the ground, and knelt down to the earth before the hole so carefully dug. Staring directly into the ground, I slid the top of the box open and started to pour, ever so slowly, as the words began: "In sure and certain hope of the resurrection to eternal life through our Lord Jesus Christ, we commend to Almighty God our sister Greg, and we commit her body to the ground; earth to earth, ashes to ashes, dust to dust." The words rang within me. They seemed louder than usual, as if I were shouting to everyone, "Dust to dust. Dust to dust. Dust to dust."

I continued to pour Greg's ashes into the ground. "The Lord bless her and keep her, the Lord make his face to shine upon her and be gracious to her; the Lord lift up his countenance upon her and give her peace." Shine upon her. Shine upon her dust. All of a sudden, staring into the earth, I saw so many people, their faces racing through my mind and soul: the first teenager I buried; William; my grandmother; Michael; so many others; and then, even my own self.

And at once, through the tears streaming down my face, I saw my own son Jack standing in that glorious church on that fateful Ash Wednesday, his little voice shouting, "You've got William on your head. You've got William on your head." It was in that moment that God's light shone brightly and all the windows into my soul opened.

And in my heart, all I could say was Alleluia. Alleluia. Alleluia. Thank God for three-year-old theologians.